The Nicaraguan Catholic Church and the Revolution

Joseph E. Mulligan, S.J.

Sheed & Ward

*To my friends in Nicaragua
struggling for liberation, justice, and peace,
and to my friends in the United States
engaging in the same struggle.*

Sheed & Ward™ is a service of National Catholic Reporter Publishing
Company, Inc.

Library of Congress Catalog Card Number: 90-63486

ISBN: 1-55612-411-2

Published by: Sheed & Ward
                115 E. Armour Blvd. P.O. Box 419492
                Kansas City, MO 64141

To order, call: (800) 333-7373

Contents

Acknowledgements

Grateful acknowledgement is made to the following for permission to reprint previously published material:

Excerpts from *Nicaragua's Mosquito Shore: The Years of British and American Presence,* by Craig L. Dozier, © 1985 The University of Alabama Press, used by permission of The University of Alabama Press.

Excerpts from *Christians in the Nicaraguan Revolution,* by Margaret Randall, © 1983 New Star Books, used by permission of New Star Books.

Excerpts from *People of God,* by Penny Lernoux, Copyright © 1989 by Penny Lernoux. Reprinted by permission of Viking Penguin, a division of Penguin Books USA Inc.

Excerpts from the dissertation, *The Catholic Church and Socio-Political Conflict in Nicaragua, 1968-1979,* by Manzar Foroohar (University of California at Los Angeles, 1984), used by permission of the author.

Excerpts from *Where is Nicaragua?,* by Peter Davis, Copyright © 1987 by Peter Davis, reprinted by permission of Simon & Schuster, Inc.

Excerpts from "The Manipulation of the Religion Issue," in *Reagan versus the Sandinistas,* ed. Thomas W. Walker, © 1987, used by permission of Westview Press.

Excerpts from *Church: Charism & Power: Liberation Theology and the Institutional Church,* by Leonardo Boff, English translation © 1985 by The Crossroad Publishing Company, reprinted by permission of the publisher.

Excerpts from *Guardians of the Dynasty—A History of the U.S.-created National Guard of Nicaragua,* by Richard Millett © 1977, *The True Church of the Poor,* by Jon Sobrino, translated by Matthew J. O'Connell, © 1984, and *The Hidden Motives of Pastoral Action,* by Juan Luís Segundo, © 1978, reprinted with permission from Orbis Books.

Excerpts from *A History of the Church in Latin America,* by Enrique Dussel, translated and revised by Alan Neely, © 1979, used by permission of William B. Eerdmans Publishing Co.

Foreword

When Fr. Joseph Mulligan told me that he was writing a book about Nicaragua, I was very enthusiastic about it. Now that I have read it, I am very pleased to write this foreword for it.

Fr. Mulligan is a priest of the Society of Jesus from the Detroit Province. He has for many years integrated his priestly ministry with a concern for issues of social justice and peace. He has had a particular interest in the struggle for justice in Nicaragua since before the revolution and overthrow of the U.S.-supported Somoza regime. He has lived in Nicaragua since 1986. His ministry there has included historical research and writing for the *Instituto Historico Centroamericano* (Central American Historical Institute) at the University of Central America in Managua. In addition to his scholarly work, he has carried out a very active pastoral ministry, especially among the poor and with the Ecclesial Base Communities. Among the important pastoral activities he has been involved in is a special ministry to families whose sons have been killed in the war. Often he was the only priest available to grieve with them and perform the memorial rites for their children. Obviously, he is well prepared to write about the Church and the revolution in Nicaragua.

I hope that this book is widely read. Those who have generally been supportive of the revolutionary process and sympathetic to the struggle of the poor in Nicaragua will find here a very carefully documented history of the struggle. But the careful documentation is complemented by a personal involvement in the lives of those who participated in the struggle. The result is history that is presented from a close personal understanding of the people involved.

This book will also provide extraordinary insight into the background of the people's struggle for justice and the relationship of the Church to the struggle. This will be especially helpful for the reader who wants to be on the side of the poor and for justice, but who might be confused by the constant negative rhetoric in the United States about the Sandinista party and the government which was established in 1979 after Somoza fled together with so many others of the elite of

Nicaragua. Most of them have consistently opposed the revolutionary process and joined with the U.S. Government in the 10-year effort to undo the revolution.

Fr. Mulligan brings much clarity to the continuing friction between the government and Cardinal Obando y Bravo. The struggle within the Church itself over how to bring the teaching of Medellin and Puebla into some kind of concrete realization begins to be more understandable because of Fr. Mulligan's careful exposition.

One of the most helpful aspects of this book is the background it provides on both the political history and the Church history of Nicaragua. To many U.S. citizens, the long-standing involvement of our government in the internal affairs of this tiny country may come as a surprise and perhaps bring considerable dismay or even anger. The fact that the Church has not always been truly on the side of the poor will not be too much of a surprise, but the considerable effort of so many to bring about significant change will surely be a cause for great hope and rejoicing. It might also be an inspiration for us to work more steadfastly for the continuing conversion of the Church in the United States to the side of the poor.

One of the most appealing aspects of this book is the way Fr. Mulligan has of making the people involved in the recent history of Nicaragua so real. This is true of those on both sides of the struggle. No one is presented as one-dimensional nor are their positions made to appear simplistic. A careful reading of this book will help any reader to have not only better knowledge of the historical facts but also more awareness of how complex human situations almost always are.

As a reader who has visited Nicaragua a number of times and who has been convinced of the rightness of the struggle of the poor in their support of the revolutionary process, I finished the book with renewed hope that justice and peace will finally prevail in Nicaragua. The struggle has brought a new sense of dignity to the poor. This can never be taken from them, and that sense of their dignity is the foundation for optimism for their future.

My hope is that we in the United States will come to respect these extraordinary people and never treat them as a "backyard country" again. This book could help make that happen.

— Thomas J. Gumbleton
Auxiliary Bishop of Detroit

Preface

If the February 1990 electoral defeat of the Sandinistas meant the end of the "Sandinista revolutionary process," then this book would be deprived of much of its meaning for the present and future of Nicaragua. It would be merely a chronicling and analysis of past history.

As the Introduction shows, however, the Frente Sandinista is alive and well, along with the Christian base communities and other groups in the "Church of the Poor"[1] which participate in and support the "revolutionary process." The latter, an expression common in Nicaragua, encompasses more than the Ortega administration which has now come to an end. It refers to the long historical process of struggle for national dignity and for social change which is described in this book. Sandino was killed in 1934; the Frente Sandinista was founded in 1961. It remains the strongest party in the National Assembly, and its mass organizations can mobilize large sectors of the population. Progressive Christian organizations have given "critical support" to the Frente Sandinista without idolizing the organization and without pinning all Christian hope on the Frente's ability to be re-elected. Christian involvement in the revolutionary process, which is the special focus of this book, continues in the new stage, even while conservative Church sectors (whose thinking is analyzed in detail in Part Five) are enjoying the Chamorro victory.

In this book I have tried to offer the reader an introduction to Nicaraguan history (with special focus on U.S. involvement) and to the distinct roles played by various sectors of the Roman Catholic Church in that history. Due to space limitations and my own limited research on Nicaraguan Protestantism, I must reserve discussion of that important and multifaceted part of Nicaraguan Church history for a future work.

---

1. The "Church of the Poor" is a general term including Christian base communities, Christian centers and institutes, and parishes which tend toward a radical interpretation and application of the Church's official "option for the poor" and generally support the revolutionary process.

I wish to give special thanks to three fellow Jesuits—Fathers Alvaro Argüello, Juan Hernández Pico, and Arthur McGovern—for their helpful comments on my manuscript. Errors in fact or interpretation are of course my own responsibility.

The Introduction, which deals with the electoral defeat of the Sandinistas in February 1990, shows that the vote did not express a massive rejection of the goals of the revolutionary process.

Part One presents two aspects of my own personal experience in Nicaragua. Chapter 1 describes my contact with the U.S.-supported war through the Masses I have celebrated for those who have given their lives in the defense of their country and its revolution. Chapter 2 describes my contact with the war (and what I learned about it) through a pastoral journey I made in contra territory.

Part Two presents the political history of Nicaragua and the history of the Roman Catholic Church. Chapter 3 (political history) takes the reader from the first U.S. intervention to the most recent (the U.S. victory at the polls). Chapter 4 deals with the history of the Church from the beginning in the sixteenth century (with special emphasis on its relationship to state power) to the late 1960s, when the breezes of Vatican II began to reach the shores of Nicaragua.

Part Three deals with the Church in the crucial decade of the 1970s. Chapter 5 outlines the history of the Christian base communities in Managua. Chapter 6 introduces Father Gaspar García Laviana, the pastor whose decision to join the Sandinista revolutionary army had a profound impact on the predominantly Catholic population. Chapter 7 presents the posture of Archbishop Miguel Obando y Bravo and the Nicaraguan bishops' conference toward the Somoza dictatorship and toward the revolutionary movement.

Part Four presents two important trends in the 1980s. Chapter 8 follows the development of the Christian base communities in the post-triumph era. Chapter 9 shows the growing opposition between the hierarchical sectors of the Church and the Sandinista government; the chapter is devoted almost entirely to the early years of the decade, when the main lines of the conflict became clear.

Part Five seeks to analyze and explain that conflict, citing five essential factors (Chapter 10) and discussing three underlying theological questions (Chapter 11).

Finally, the *Postscript* deals with political developments since the inauguration of President Violeta Chamorro and with the relationship between the new administration and the Church.

Introduction

The Electoral Defeat of the Sandinistas

At 4 a.m. on February 26, 1990, Father Fernando Cardenal acknowledged that his party had lost the previous day's election. While the Sandinista Minister of Education could not hide his deep disappointment, he expressed his conviction that "the struggle for justice and liberation goes on, and we will continue to work for the cause of the poor."

In the poor barrios where I minister, I encountered surprise, shock, and grief among most of the members of our Christian base communities. One woman whose three sons had served in the Sandinista army went into a deep depression, not eating for several days; after a few hours of hospital treatment, she returned home and gradually recovered from what she called "an attack of nerves."

Progressive Christians had adopted an attitude of "critical support" for the Sandinista revolutionary process, considering it to be in the best interests of the country's impoverished majority. While recognizing mistakes made by the government, these Christians pointed to the relentless U.S. policy of "low-intensity warfare" (supporting the contra war, blocking trade and credit, and using all forms of diplomatic and political pressure to weaken the Sandinistas) as being chiefly responsible for the vote against the incumbents.

During the first days after the elections, revolutionary Christians met in their homes and chapels mainly to support one another by sharing their sense of shock. Some parents whose children had been killed by the National Guard before the Sandinista victory in 1979 or by the contras in recent years likened their experience of this electoral defeat to that of their own personal loss. Many observers felt that this was indeed the cruelest blow of U.S. aggression: to hit the Sandinistas and their supporters in the heart, confronting them with rejection at the polls by a majority of voters.

Indeed, that had been the objective of U.S. policy over the years: to make the revolution appear to be disintegrating from within (thus eliminating it as an example) rather than to destroy it by an invasion. President Ortega compared the majority vote to torturing a prisoner into betraying his friends. Others, describing the coercive process as "starving out the revolution," saw the result as representing not so much a rejection of the Sandinista program for change as an exasperated effort to gain release from the economic vise and the war.

Many people were partially consoled by President Daniel Ortega's statesmanlike speech delivered to the nation at 6 a.m. Daniel and his cabinet ministers looked very tired after a sleepless night following an intense campaign, and he was clearly downcast. He took the occasion, however, to recount the achievements of the Sandinistas: spearheading the liberation of the country from under the Somoza dictatorship, initiating land reform, improving social services for the poor, encouraging the people to develop a sense of their own dignity, and struggling for years against the contras and other instruments of U.S. intervention.

The president went on to note that the U.S. government had employed all possible means short of invasion to defeat the Sandinistas. He noted that the majority of voters had opted for what they thought was a path to peace and to economic recovery. While he considered the majority mistaken in their political judgment, Daniel expressed understanding rather than animosity toward them. He concluded by stating clearly that the Sandinistas recognized the victory of the opposition coalition called UNO and that his administration would turn over the reins of government on the appointed date, April 25.

Gradually people began to look to the continuance of life and struggle, to speak of the good example being given by the Sandinistas at this moment as before, and to count their strengths now as an opposition movement. On February 27 thousands demonstrated in the Plaza of the Revolution to show themselves and the world that they are not only alive and well but strongly committed to defend the social gains of the revolution and to grow as a party, looking toward new elections in six years.

Why the Surprising Result?

Two main factors—the ailing, almost crippled economy and the ravaging war—are constantly mentioned as being responsible for the election result. Both were intended effects of the U.S. strategy of "low-intensity warfare." Ronald Reagan declared war on the Sandinistas during his 1980 campaign, and from his very first year in office took measures to topple their young government. The U.S.-financed contra war took a total of 30,000 Nicaraguan lives (on both sides), with many thousands more permanently disabled or orphaned, and resulted in the destruction of cooperatives, schools, health centers, and key economic installations. Economic damage was estimated in the billions. In addition to the material destruction, much land was taken out of production due to contra aggression, and a considerable part of the labor force went into military defense. Gradually over 50 percent of the government budget was going into defense, thus making it impossible for the government to keep up the subsidies in health, education, and other services. Exports fell to about one third of what they had been at the start of the decade, and the average wage dropped by about 90 percent between 1980 and 1989.

In a bold show of political extortion, President Bush announced explicitly that the damaging trade embargo and credit blockade would be lifted as soon as Violeta Chamorro would win. At the same time, his administration was giving mixed signals as to whether a Sandinista victory would be recognized and whether the contra war would be called off.

Although the pre-election polls proved to be wrong in predicting a solid if not overwhelming Sandinista victory, they were not based on a false assumption that people were doing well. President Ortega had begun his speech at the huge rally closing his campaign with a politically unusual acknowledgment of the fact that the economy was going badly for most Nicaraguans. When he asked, however, whether that would lead most people to reject the Sandinistas, the crowd yelled back, "no." That was the mistake. He, and many Christian supporters of the revolutionary process, thought that the Nicaraguan people as a whole could have enough "revolutionary heroism," as some have put it, to rise above the daily misery and anxiety.

Although the Sandinistas did not challenge the election results, serious questions could still be raised. Throughout the campaign the contras, identifying with UNO, kept up their intimidation of the peasant population by killing or kidnapping some Sandinistas and Sandinista sympathizers. The message was clear: if you vote for the Sandinistas, we will know it, and we will take serious reprisals. Perhaps the contras would not have been able to discover how an individual voted, but they would have seen the public results showing how each little polling district went. In the case of individuals or 'groups known to be pro-Sandinista, the message was: stay home.

Reports also abounded of UNO activists buying votes with some of the dollars provided by U.S. government campaign contributions. Some claim that UNO gave people a few dollars in advance and promised more if the results turned out in their favor; others say that voters who had sold their vote somehow had to give UNO poll watchers a glimpse of their ballot. Be that as it may, UNO certainly was able to pay their campaign workers rather handsomely, especially by Nicaraguan standards.

Many analysts recognize that these factors—contra violence and intimidation and UNO payoffs—were present but believe that they did not affect a significant percentage of the turnout. In general the election was honest in a technical sense (secret vote, fair count), but the contest was hardly a fair one. The result was a victory for the power and violence of a relentless superpower against a very small and poor nation. Perhaps, given the economic conditions which U.S. policy had created and the ongoing war which showed no clear signs of stopping in the event of a Sandinista win, it would have been a minor miracle had the incumbents been re-elected.

Sandinista Self-Criticism

While Sandinistas point to these powerful factors as responsible for their defeat, they do not absolve themselves of all blame. In fact, over the years Sandinista leaders have admitted many mistakes and have tried to correct them. For instance, the land reform at first concentrated on the large state farms, then on cooperatives; only in later years did the government respond to the peasants' demands for individual parcels.

In 1988, when Omar Cabezas became national coordinator of the Sandinista neighborhood committees, he denounced their ineffectiveness, unrepresentativeness, "verticalist" or top-down structure of decision-making, and even in some cases corruption.

Sandinistas recognize that in some instances power corrupts and in many instances removes the office-holder from real contact with the people. Indeed, some voters were reacting to unresponsive treatment they had received from certain bureaucrats. All of this means that Sandinistas are mortal and fallible like the rest of humanity.

Moreover, many were without training and administrative experience when they found themselves with a ravaged country to manage after they swept out the old system in 1979. Swept it out partially, that is—some of the old Somoza cronies remained on the job, and some younger people with the "values" of the Somoza system worked themselves into positions which ideally required dedicated Sandinista revolutionaries.

These normal faults and failings of Sandinistas and other government workers—especially at the lower end of the power structure—were exacerbated by the security concerns related to U.S. hostility and by the lack of material and human resources to meet constituents' demands. Some bureaucrats under criticism too facilely labeled their critics "contras," and some security agents picked up some innocent people for questioning; but then again they were facing a multi-faceted strategy by the United States to discredit the government and overthrow it.

Medical personnel and clerks in clinics, school administrators, and other civil servants with very limited resources found it increasingly difficult to serve a demanding public. Frustration led some to adopt an uncaring attitude or an unresponsive posture, which naturally did not win or solidify political support.[1]

Taking Stock

On the rebound, Sandinistas began to speak with pride of the example of democracy their government had given by holding free and fair elections and abiding by the results. They also pointed to the solid 40 percent of the electorate who stayed with them in spite of all the pressures of U.S. "low-intensity warfare." Since the UNO coalition consists of 14 parties which have already shown signs of serious divisions, the

---

1.   One of the most critical articles to appear in the early months after the change of government was "We Erred to Win" by René Mendoza (*Envío*, English edition, October, 1990; Spanish edition of September 1990, entitled "Los Costos del Verticalismo"). Based on his research in the rural areas of Arenal and Wiwilí, the author criticizes some middle-level Sandinista leaders for their top-down approach, their failure to listen to the people, their catering to the bourgeois sectors in an effort to have "national unity," and generally for devoting too much attention to the national and international agenda and not enough to specific local problems. Mendoza shows how some Sandinista leaders in Wiwilí took significant steps to correct their ways. While the article itself can be critiqued in some respects, it is a challenging aid to discussion.

In his *Thanks to God and the Revolution* (Columbia University Press, 1988), Roger N. Lancaster had observed that all was not well, especially in the moribund Sandinista Defense Committees (neighborhood organizations), but like many of us did not seem to foresee the serious impact this would have on the 1990 elections. See Lancaster, Ch. 5.

Sandinistas are by far the strongest single party. They have retained control of some municipalities, and they occupy 39 of the 92 seats in the National Assembly, thus making it impossible for the opposition on its own to amend the constitution.

The constitution, which went into effect in 1987, has special importance now, since it protects many of the social, political, and economic gains of the revolution—such as land reform and the role of the public sector. A popular weekly paper among the Christian base communities devoted a special issue to the constitution.

Moreover, the Sandinista People's Army is the constitutionally established army of Nicaragua; this is seen as protection against any intentions the new government may have of dismantling the army and replacing it with contras or former National Guardsmen.

Sandinistas see the new period as a time to clean up their ranks, weeding out the opportunists, the lazy, and the corrupt, many of whom became sudden converts to the revolution only after the 1979 triumph. Calling the election results a "setback" rather than a defeat, the Sandinistas also plan to get back in closer touch with the people, overcoming the barriers and distance which power inevitably entails.

Progressive Christians Look to Future

Although a sense of shock and depression lingered, the prevailing spirit in the Christian base communities soon became one of renewed dedication. Their basic commitment continues as before: to shape a political and economic system which would approximate as closely as possible the contours of the Kingdom of God. Most members of the communities will be looking carefully at the Sandinistas' proposals and actions as an opposition force, expecting to maintain their attitude of "critical support" for the Frente Sandinista, now struggling "from below" for basic social change.

Progressive Christians remain loyal to the Church's "option for the poor" and commitment to liberation, knowing that the struggle is worldwide and centuries-old and that their own struggle in Nicaragua goes back to Sandino's anti-imperialist and pro-poor fight in the twenties and early thirties.

The assassination of Sandino and the annihilation of his movement in 1934 seemed an unredeemable crucifixion, but the Frente Sandinista (FSLN) emerged in 1961 and after a long struggle with many ups and downs defeated the overpowering Somoza dictatorship. The Frente has been voted out of office, but the struggle goes on. Bishop Pedro Casaldáliga of São Felix, Brazil, on a visit to see how his friends were holding up in Nicaragua, told a group at the Jesuits' Central American University that "Sandinismo did not begin with the Frente's arrival in power in 1979 and certainly does not end with President Ortega's departure from office."

In 1990, the tenth anniversary of the killing of Archbishop Romero of El Salvador lifted spirits and brought new hope and energy to the revolutionary Christians of Nicaragua. On March 24 hundreds participated in an ecumenical procession and celebration, which included the dedication of a monument to the slain martyr. "If they kill me, I will rise again in the Salvadoran people," Romero had said. That rising is seen not yet in victory but in the hope, courage, and love of the Salvadorans as they continue the struggle; and Nicaraguans hope to be similarly faithful.

In April members of the Christian base communities joined U.S. citizens in a demonstration outside the U.S. embassy, demanding the demobilization of the contras. Protestants and Catholics throughout the country also fasted and prayed for five days for the same purpose.

Part One

Personal History

1

Requiems for the Young Soldiers

Arrival in Nicaragua

After many years of working in solidarity with Latin American struggles and visiting the Dominican Republic, Colombia, Chile, and other countries, I came to work in Nicaragua with the Jesuits' Instituto Historico Centroamericano (Central American Historical Institute)[1] in early 1986. I wanted to understand the revolutionary process and, through writing and speaking, share my understanding of that process with people in the United States. And as a priest I hoped to find some way to accompany the poor of Nicaragua in their struggle for a better life.

Coming into Managua from the airport, I looked in vain for evidence of the "state of emergency" which had been put into effect because of U.S. hostility. There was no curfew. Troops and police did not stand menacingly, with heavy weapons at the ready, on every street corner. In fact, the Nicaraguan security forces did not have the same role as they do in other Latin American countries—that of terrorizing and intimidating the poor masses into accepting their subhuman lot. Here, the poor and those of modest means felt that the government, for all its problems and limitations, was *their* government.

Shortly after my arrival I met nine Jesuit seminarians who had just returned to Managua after two months of social service. Several of the young Jesuits had worked as orderlies in a hospital which mainly treated soldiers wounded in the war. The foreigners in the seminary were not subject to the draft, and the Nicaraguans were exempt as seminarians, but they considered their service in this hospital as an appropriate way to

---

1. The Institute publishes the monthly journal of political and economic analysis, *Envío*, available in English from the Central American Historical Institute; Georgetown University; Washington, D.C. 20057

3

contribute to Nicaragua's self-defense and to show solidarity with their peers in military service. At the same time, their pastoral presence as Jesuits was a source of comfort and strength to the wounded.

Several other seminarians joined in the efforts to bring in the coffee crop, an important export product and source of revenue for the country. Others lent their services in one of the *asentamientos* (settlements for those who have had to move out of the war zones).

Confiteor

I soon found myself in a somewhat ironic but profoundly meaningful situation: celebrating a memorial Mass on the anniversary of the death of a Nicaraguan soldier killed by forces armed and trained by the U.S. government.

The Mass was held in the open, outside a small chapel. A table adorned with flowers had been set up just in front of the tomb of the fallen soldier. The site, on a bluff overlooking a lake near Masaya (about 20 miles from Managua), provided a magnificent view of the splendor of nature enveloping and perhaps slightly softening the tragedies and injustices of history.

The peasants told me that José Angel Ruiz had been an outstanding young man and that he had signed up for a second hitch in the service, believing that the defense of his country and its revolution was a just cause. I welcomed the people, about 200 in number, to the celebration of José Angel's life, love, and courage, and I suggested that we the living pray for renewed hope and strength to continue steadfastly in the construction of a new society and in the struggle to defend it.

The words of the "confiteor" had special meaning for me on this occasion, as I confessed to my brothers and sisters that I have sinned "in what I have done and in what I have failed to do." I said that I had been involved in solidarity work in the States, but I had to recognize that all American citizens share in the responsibility for U.S. policy. But the Nicaraguan people—and their government—consistently made the distinction between the American people and the American government, and they readily accepted American citizens who came to help and to learn.

For the gospel reading I had selected the Last Judgment scene in Matthew 25. I emphasized that the criterion for eternal life in this passage is the *practical service of the needy*, in whom we encounter the Lord himself.

I mentioned, however, that today this practical service has taken on a structural and political dimension as a logical and necessary outgrowth of its inner dynamism toward effectiveness. That is, it is not sufficient to give a piece of bread to the beggar at the door. Such an individual response may be called for at the time, but the giver (and the beggar) should ask: Why can't the poor afford to buy their daily bread?

That question has been raised in the Christian base communities throughout Latin America for many years, and in Nicaragua the question led many Christians to join in the struggle against Somoza and in the revolutionary process since 1979. The Sandinista government sought to feed the hungry and shelter the homeless by making the necessary structural changes in society. José Angel gave his life in defense of that process.

"Christ Is the People"

Another young soldier, Pedro Mayorga, also brought the war home to me in a personal way. When I was in Nicaragua for a visit in 1984, I interviewed Pedro, who had spoken during a Mass in his parish church while on a brief home leave. Father Uriel Molina, then pastor of the church in the Riguero neighborhood of Managua, had invited Pedro and others to share in the homily. In the interview Pedro said: "On my next journey to the mountains I may be killed, as many of my companions have given the best they have, their blood. But beforehand I say to the youth and the Christian communities of the United States that I am ready to give my life, since I am aware of my role as a Christian."[2]

The young soldier shared his spirituality: "I have learned to see God with the eyes of faith, in sharing the suffering, the sorrow, the joy, and food and water with my *compañeros*. There in the mountains I have seen God who is present, who energizes and helps us in the most difficult moments. So if I give my life, I will give it generously."

---

2. Interview published in the December 1984 newsletter of the Detroit-based Michigan Inter-faith Committee on Central American Human Rights.

Pedro gave his life five months later. From time to time I had thought about Pedro but did not know what had become of him until I returned to Nicaragua. An article in *Barricada*, the national daily newspaper published by the Sandinistas, told how Maria del Carmen, a member of the parish, keeps the memory of Pedro alive: "In her house she keeps a tape recording of his talk in the church, and in a prominent place in the living room she keeps a large picture of the martyr with a crucifix on his chest so that he continues to strengthen the struggle of his Christian brothers and sisters."

On visiting the home, I was deeply moved to recognize Pedro's voice in the recording. When the violence sponsored by the U.S. government takes the life of someone you have gotten to know, the reality becomes very personal and concrete.

In 1984 Pedro had told me why he was fighting: "We are willing to sacrifice ourselves so that the revolution may go forward, so that the children may grow and have more schools and health centers, so that we may be free and independent." He felt that he was helping to carry Christ's cross by suffering in the defense of his country and in defense of a government which was doing everything possible to meet the needs of the poor. Only by being willing to risk our lives, he said, "will we begin to form the new community, which is the community of Christ, and the new person who follows the way of Christ, which some people want us to forget."

I asked Pedro if he had a message for the American people. He said: "At present we are enduring a crisis caused by the war, caused by the aggression planned and financed by the Reagan administration. The only thing this brings to my people is more poverty, misery, and sadness.

"I want to tell you," he continued, "that we want and hope for your support in solidarity with us and with our cause, which is a just and honest cause, the cause of the poor, the cause which Christ took up many centuries ago and which is under attack by the Reagan administration, financing the mercenaries, trying to crucify Christ once again. And Christ is the people."

Jesuit Alumnus Killed in War

On April 21, 1986, Alvaro Avilez Cevasco, the son of a nutritionist and a physician in Managua, was killed in combat by the contras. In two more months he would have finished his stint in the army and returned to his studies at the Jesuit high school.

Alvaro was well-liked by his peers and by his teachers, and by the Jesuits who got to know him when he would visit the Jesuit community where his favorite teacher lives. One week after Alvaro was killed, his family and friends came to Mass at our Jesuit house. The shared homily was filled with expressions of shock and grief, but amidst the tears there were also expressions of admiration and pride for the boy's love in laying down his life for his friends. His father said that the family found consolation in the meaning of Alvaro's death.

One of the concelebrating priests said that the Holy Spirit was at work in an unusual way in Nicaragua, touching the hearts and homes of the upper classes and asking them to sacrifice even their own flesh and blood "in defense of the cause of the poor."[3]

In most Latin American countries, parents of students attending private Catholic schools need not worry very much about a military draft affecting their sons. They are usually urban dwellers of the middle or upper class, whereas it is the sons of the poor peasants in the countryside who are rounded up (often as crudely as that expression suggests) and taken into the military.

But in Nicaragua under the Sandinista government there was greater "equality before the law" in this regard. Thus, 17-year-old students from the Jesuit high school in Managua went off to military service, with the anxious but real support and prayers of their Jesuit teachers, who believed that the Nicaraguan revolution and national sovereignty were worth defending and that their students had a responsibility to defend their country against U.S.-sponsored aggression.

Benjamin Linder Anniversary

In April 1988, on the first anniversary of the death of Benjamin Linder, the young American engineer killed by the contras, Mass was celebrated in the church in the Riguero barrio. Ben's parents, other family members, and many friends participated in the celebration of Ben's life

---

3. The above reflections on Pedro and Alvaro were published as an article, "First-Hand Look at Results of Contra War," in *National Jesuit News*, December 1986.

and commitment to the revolution. In the homily I spoke of Pedro and quoted some of his reflections. Ben and Pedro had found strength in Father Uriel Molina's parish, and their example of love and courage continues to nourish hope and commitment in Nicaragua.

2

In Contra Territory

For two weeks in late 1988, I traveled on muleback to eight chapels in a rugged mountainous region of central Nicaragua, accompanied by a sister who had made the pastoral journey several times before. In all my 45 years I had never ridden a mule, or even a horse; nor had I gone camping since my brief experience with the Boy Scouts in New York City. Sympathetic friends in the U.S. had helped me get fitted out with extra-strength insect repellent, boots (which turned out to be too big for the stirrups), raincoat, water purifying tablets, pills to fight diarrhea, and other paraphernalia.

The venture was a huge success in that I didn't fall off the mule even once; it fell once, or sort of sank in the deep mud, but I held on at the advice of our guide and the magnificent beast picked itself up and moved on. Thanks to the muddy and incredibly steep terrain in most places, plus my own reluctance to use the spurs, we usually traveled at a modest pace which was kind to my anatomy. I grew in admiration of the strength, sure-footedness, and generally cooperative attitude of the mule.

During the two-week journey we saw no vehicles of any kind, or even a road fit for vehicles. We made our way mainly through narrow mountain paths; sometimes our guide led the way where there was no path at all.

In that region you can ride for a half-hour or more between farm houses. It became clear to me that a lonely peasant family simply could not say no to a well-armed group of contras.

A guide escorted us on the three or four-hour ride from one chapel to the next. Sister and I were making the trip in response to a request from the Catholic pastor; baptisms, confirmations, first communions, and weddings would be duly inscribed in the parish records.

9

The pastor and others had told us very clearly that our itinerary would take us through the very "nest" of the contra troops. A couple of years ago, when the pastor and sister were making a similar journey, the contras stopped them and relieved them of everything they were carrying, including hosts and wine for Mass, and forbade them to continue. Faithful to their mission, they continued without further incident. On another occasion the contras prohibited the pastor from conducting the mission at one particular chapel.

The priest, like many others in Nicaragua, has an attitude of critical support for the revolutionary process. The contras, however, accuse him of being a Sandinista priest and have gone so far as to threaten his life. He and others had told us not to provoke the contras or their civilian sympathizers by speaking about the revolution, the Sandinistas, U.S. imperialism, or other sensitive issues. We could and should talk about the need for peace, he said, and in our homilies and discussions we would try to help people to understand the biblical basis for liberation, justice, community, and the Christian option for the poor. In some instances I was moved to preach about the rules of war which are binding on all sides: no violence against innocent civilians, no torture. I also spoke about the futility and un-Christian nature of acts taken out of a spirit of sheer vengeance.

Armed contra troops, in groups of ten to forty, were present at each of the eight chapels we visited. In some cases they arrived during the mission, with gunfire in the distance announcing their imminent appearance; in other cases they were already at the chapel, appearing to be well ensconced and rather at home. One contra soldier told me that religious missions were important in the fight against communism; another young contra soldier sported a "Vietnam Veteran" cap. (He fully appeared to be a Nicaraguan; I presume he got the cap from his U.S. trainers in Honduras.)

With a government cease-fire in effect since March 1988, Sandinista troops were not conducting offensive actions against the contras; indeed, they were nowhere to be seen during our journey, nor were any other government workers. Some grade schools exist in that part of the country, but none was functioning. No medical or nursing care was available; seriously sick persons had to make a two or three-day journey by mule to the nearest town. We were told that the contras discouraged people from going to town and that some people were afraid to leave the mountain "sanctuary" because they have reason to believe they would be arrested as contra collaborators. Teachers and health personnel had been assassinated by the contras over the years. In fact, anyone sympathetic to the revolution (including Delegates of the Word in charge of the chapels) had been killed or driven into nearby towns.

One evening someone threw a rather heavy stick at me as I was sitting in the door of one of the chapels, hitting me in the neck, knocking off my glasses, and causing me to wonder if it might be a prelude of things to come. Perhaps it was just a mischievous child, but that didn't seem an adequate explanation.

Although that was the only physical act of hostility I experienced, a series of feelings and intuitions led me to believe that our lives were in danger. Turning to scripture for strength and inspiration, I was struck by how frequently and how profoundly the Bible deals with the theme of conquering fear. The reality of fear is clearly recognized, and from Moses to Pentecost people experience the presence of the Lord in their struggle against fear. One of the positive aspects of my journey was to share something of this experience.

A fundamental political and historical question had to be confronted. Why is there a social base for the contras in that region? (It is true that many contra officers were former National Guard members; but the contras were able to recruit thousands of young peasants into their ranks.) First of all, as I have mentioned, pro-Sandinista people (residents as well as visiting teachers and health workers) were killed by the contras or driven into the nearby towns for protection. The contras destroyed health posts, cooperatives, and other signs of the revolution's capacity to improve the quality of life.

Secondly, that capacity was very limited in the central mountains of the country because of the geographical remoteness as well as because of contra terrorism. Since travel is on foot or by mule, possibilities are very slim for transporting construction materials, medical equipment, medicines, and books. Furthermore, the government did not have the resources even to try to bring the programs of the revolution to all parts of Nicaragua at once. And as the war escalated the government had to devote more than half its resources to defense, thus depriving important social programs of funding.

Thirdly, due to these limitations, the draft which was initiated in late 1983 was the first real contact many peasants had with the revolutionary state. Mandatory military service is never a popular program, and it was very unpopular in regions where the people had not yet experienced the positive benefits of the revolution. Problems were compounded when draft resisters began to be apprehended by the authorities.

Fourthly, the revolution never really took place in certain parts of the country. People in some parts of the eastern half of Nicaragua and in some central mountain areas did not experience the repression of the Somoza regime as intensely as did those in the Pacific side and did not have the experience of joining the Sandinistas or participating as collaborators with them in the struggle. Thus when the Sandinistas emerged as the leading force in the new government and began to exercise their authority throughout the country, people in some areas viewed them as a new group of outsiders.

Fifthly, owners of medium-sized and large farms and cattle ranches naturally were not enthralled by the prospect of state farms and cooperatives which constituted important elements of the socialism the Sandinistas wanted to develop. Thanks to the paternalism of traditional society, these big farmers and ranchers had considerable ideological as well as economic influence over the small peasants. And many of the small peasants themselves manifested the classic individualism which is often found in peasant societies. Since it took the government a number of years to recognize and respond to the peasants' demands for private parcels of land, the contras were able to gain some recruits in the meantime. The government's control of the market system was also an unpopular feature of the revolution for many peasants.

Sixthly, contra propaganda, orchestrated by the CIA, was able to convince some peasants that the new government was anti-religious. In addition, some foreign teachers and some lower-ranking Sandinistas spoke negatively of religion as a magical or reactionary illusion. This, combined with the growing hostility of some religious officials toward the government, led some peasants to believe they were fighting a holy war against godless communism.

Along with these indigenous factors contributing to peasant support for the contras, U.S. backing played an essential role in turning resentment and protest into open warfare. Without U.S. training and financing, which began in 1981, dissident groups would never have mounted a significant military movement against the government. Washington's intervention, building upon the remnants of Somoza's National Guard left in the country, also made it much more difficult for the government to work toward solving domestic disputes and problems.

Finally, the war itself inevitably created more enemies for the revolution. For military reasons the Sandinistas moved thousands of peasants off their land into protected settlements, in order to be able to fight the contras without endangering the civilian population. People did not always understand or appreciate the reasons for the transfer.

Some families remaining in combat zones suffered from ill-targetted Sandinista artillery shells, army requisitioning of goods, and arrest for suspected or proven collaboration with the enemy. These aspects of the reality of war further exacerbated hostilities.[1]

As a result of my pastoral journey I came to a fuller understanding of the complex reality of the war. Viewing the destruction of the countryside and the dread in people's eyes, my overall reaction was one of sadness and outrage over the immoral policy of the U.S. government. True, the Nicaraguan government made mistakes, giving some sectors of society reason to complain and protest. But Washington took advantage of these problems to mount a multi-faceted campaign to destroy a popular revolutionary government which represented hope for the poor of Nicaragua.

Army Abuses

In an October 1989 report on human rights violations ("The Killings in Northern Nicaragua") Americas Watch (AW) stated: "From 1987 through the early part of 1989, Nicaraguan military and security forces engaged in a pattern of killings of contra supporters and contra collaborators in remote communities of northern Nicaragua . . . ." AW said that it documented 74 murders, 14 disappearances and two severe beatings.[2]

In 1988 and 1989 AW published reports on these violations and noted that "in 1989, especially during the period since April when the U.S.

---

1. For further discussion of these and other motives for the contras' struggle, see "We Erred to Win" by René Mendoza, *Envío*, October 1990.

2. The material in the rest of this chapter was presented in my article on human rights in the December 1989 issue of *Envío*.

media gave our findings prominent attention, the Nicaraguan government has responded vigorously, launching a substantial number of investigations."

AW described the results of those investigations as "mixed," pointing out that "some prosecutions have been launched, convictions have been obtained and appropriate punishments have been imposed; in some cases, culprits have been identified but have reportedly absconded; in some cases, culprits have been prosecuted and convicted but have not been appropriately punished; in other cases, the Nicaraguan government has absolved its agents of wrongdoing."

While regretting that the Nicaraguan government did not respond more speedily, AW was "pleased that a major effort has been underway in the last several months and that . . . some prosecutions, convictions and punishments have resulted." Although disagreeing with some of the decisions to absolve state agents, AW noted "with satisfaction that the prosecutional response that has now taken place has reduced sharply the number of new abuses that have been reported to Americas Watch." AW added: "It is not yet clear to us, however, whether the pattern has stopped," explaining that "it takes time to hear reports of abuses and to get to the remote places where they occur to try to verify those reports."

What are the alleged crimes reported by AW to the government? In general, the pattern "indicates that certain regional authorities of the DGSE [state security] or of the EPS [army] have engaged in selective kidnappings and assassinations of persons they suspected of being couriers for, or collaborators with, the contras." In many cases the corpses "showed signs of brutal torture."

"Couriers," AW explained, is a term that came to signify "a job that not only includes transmitting messages but also collecting military intelligence (spying) on Sandinista troop movements, providing food and shelter to passing contras and storing military hardware such as mines. In some cases *correos* [couriers] assist in laying mines and other military tasks."

This explanation, especially the last sentence, needs to be kept in mind in trying to reconstruct the scene of certain alleged crimes, according to a member of the National Commission for the Promotion and Protection of Human Rights (CNPPDH). "Many contra collaborators alternate between being mere couriers and being full-time contra soldiers," the member said.

AW recognized that these crimes took place in "an area where the war has created profound and lasting wounds in the social fabric. For that reason, many of these crimes could be attributed to personal *vendettas,* or settling of accounts." Nevertheless, AW insisted that the fact that "the culprits have been entrusted with the authority and apparatus of the state . . . converts these crimes into human rights violations."

The organization noted that "certain regional authorities" are responsible for these crimes. "As far as we can tell from the documentation provided by the government, no complicity by higher-ups in the command structure has yet been established. For our part, we lack evidence of such complicity." AW noted, however, that the government took action to prosecute "only after the matter had become a major national and international embarrassment after publication of the cases." Dr. Vilma Nuñez de Escorcia, then president of the CNPPDH, said that in many cases prosecution was initiated as soon as the information was received; in some instances that may have coincided with international publicity.

The exercise of leniency in punishing some human rights violators was of concern to AW. Nevertheless, AW recognized "that, to a degree not matched by other governments in the region, the Nicaraguan government investigates, prosecutes and punishes those responsible for gross abuses. Obviously, this is not a high standard against which to measure the Nicaraguan government's performance. Yet the prosecutions . . . have had the effect of putting a stop to those practices when patterns have emerged."

Father César Jerez, S.J., former provincial superior of the Jesuits in Central America and currently president of the Central American University and board member of the CNPPDH, pointed out that "in Central American countries, with the exception of Nicaragua, it is practically unheard of that military or security personnel are prosecuted for human rights violations."

(For details of charges and the Sandinista government response to them, see *Envío,* December 1989, or the AW report itself.)

Contra Abuses

In letters of April 30 and June 15, 1989, addressed to Adolfo Calero of the Nicaraguan Resistance, AW presented 22 cases of klllings and 39 cases of abduction and forced recruitment attributed to contra forces. In some cases victims' throats had been slit and they had been otherwise mutilated with machetes.

In addition, the April 30 letter reported that in October 1988 contras "ambushed an ambulance (wounding the driver) and attacked a settlement of displaced persons of war." Three civilian passengers were wounded two days earlier when contras "attacked a clearly marked (white with the Red Cross emblem and white flag) ambulance of the Nicaraguan Red Cross." Later the same month, contras ambushed a truck belonging to a coffee plantation carrying 14 passengers, almost all civilians. "Nine persons were killed and at least four were wounded," AW reported. "Once they stopped shooting, the contras . . . stole the belongings of the dead and wounded and proceeded to mutilate [a] lieutenant's corpse with their bayonets." Another incident involved contra looting of a town: "they also stole the medicine from the town health clinic and afterward burned it down."

AW asked Calero for information on "investigations that have been initiated to clarify these violations and to sanction those found responsible for breaking the laws of armed conflict." However, "none of our letters of inquiry to the Resistance has been answered," AW noted in its October report, in which it presented new cases involving four killings, two woundings and two kidnappings. (The organization explained that it was not presenting cases in which the person killed reportedly by contras was armed.)

The report noted that AW was familiar with "many more cases" of contra violations reported by Witness for Peace (WFP). "We have not been able to confirm each of the WFP cases," AW noted, "but in those cases where we have spot-checked WFP information, our research confirms their findings."

On November 2, Witness for Peace stated that "the level of contra activity in October was roughly double that of the previous month, as contras increased their attacks against both civilian and military targets. In the Congressional Bipartisan Accord signed last April," WFP continued, "contras received nearly $50 million in 'non-lethal' aid, and the State Department promised that the contras would not engage in offensive military operations or commit human rights abuses. Since April WFP has documented 59 contra attacks."

WFP cited the October 30 contra attack on a cooperative in which four men were killed and seven other people wounded. The contras told the wounded "to vote for the United Nicaraguan Opposition (UNO)," WFP reported. Earlier in the month contras had killed 18 soldiers and wounded eight when they ambushed two military vehicles taking the soldiers home so they could register to vote. The father of a reservist kidnapped and killed by the contras told WFP: "It's one thing to talk about politics; it's another to terrorize people at gunpoint."

The contras had entered the electoral campaign, WFP noted, "but they're not playing by the fair rules of a democratic election. While contras tell rural residents to register to vote for the UNO coalition, contras continue to commit gross human rights violations as a method of political persuasion." In addition to the millions approved by Congress for UNO's campaign, the previous $50 million for the contras was "sustaining a pro-UNO campaign in the countryside."

Citing numerous examples, WFP said that contras "are still kidnapping, torturing and killing civilians thought to be Sandinista supporters. The message to rural voters is clear: the contras want you to vote for UNO, but if they suspect you support the Sandinistas, you may be tortured and killed." Another aspect of the contra message was explained to WFP by civilians who spoke to the contras and by contras who deserted: If the opposition wins, the war will end, but if the Sandinistas win, the war will continue.

WFP noted: "Ironically, the Bush administration insisted that aid to the contras was necessary to force the Nicaraguan government to conduct a clean election. However, it is the contras who are committing the most violent electoral abuses and who are using terror as an instrument of political persuasion."

The Nicaraguan government reported that between the start of the unilateral cease-fire in March 1988 and October 1989 the contras had been responsible for over 730 killings, for the wounding of over 1,000 persons, and for the kidnapping or disappearance of over 1,400 Nicaraguans.

Americas Watch called attention to a case in which "a contra commander and five other contras were found guilty of murder, rape and torture by a contra disciplinary court and expelled from the Resistance, but that decision was reversed in an appellate proceeding. The contra commander was reinstated and has been appointed Chief of Intelligence of the general staff."

AW expressed regret that Congressman Robert Dornan and publications such as *The Washington Times* and *The New Republic* had used AW's reports on violations by Nicaraguan government forces to support their arguments for aid to the contras. "It appears that the killings in Region 6 have become an argument for repudiating the Tela accord of the Central American presidents for the demobilization of the contra forces," AW noted. "We regret this, above all because those making this argument and seeking further funding for the contras neglect to point out that the contras have continued to kill civilians or prisoners placed *hors de combat*, and that their leadership has ignored our inquiries about killings by their forces."

Labeling contra abuses as "endemic to their method of waging war," AW said it favored "the demobilization of the contras because of their own record of gross abuses of human rights."

A Personal Evaluation

Since I am not sure that the foregoing statistics and reports convey the full truth about the contras, the widespread reputation they have as terrorists, and the feeling of horror which Nicaraguans have toward them, I wish to conclude this chapter with a personal word. As many organizations dedicated to human rights have shown, contra tactics are terroristic—designed precisely to instill dread in the people. It is axiomatic in Nicaragua that the contras have engaged on a broad scale in sadistic torture, the slaughter of civilian men, women, and children (with very frequent throat-slitting), and mutilation of corpses as well as the rampant destruction of farm cooperatives, medical centers, schools, and other parts of the infrastructure which sustain life in society. Perhaps the term "satanic" is necessary for an adequate description of this grip of evil over human persons.

These methods, plus the fact that many contra officers were in Somoza's National Guard, lie behind the people's use of the term "Guardia" in reference to the contras. The people are determined not to allow the contras and their civilian supporters to institute a reign of terror under the Chamorro government.

Part Two

Historical Background

3

19th and 20th Century Political History

The long revolutionary process in Nicaragua has included these fundamental elements: the struggle against imperialism, the insurrection against the Somoza dictatorship, and the efforts to build a new, more just society while defending the country against the U.S.-sponsored contras. With the electoral defeat of the Sandinistas in February 1990, the revolutionary process entered into a new phase: the Sandinistas and their supporters and allies are struggling "from below" to protect the gains of their decade in power and to strengthen the base of support for revolutionary change. This chapter seeks to present an overview of Nicaraguan political history, with special attention to the history of U.S. involvement, as background for understanding the role of the Church.

Nicaragua: Route for Gold Rush and Potential Canal Site

Nicaragua and the rest of Central America became independent from Spain on September 15, 1821, but on the following January 5 the region was annexed to Mexico. This arrangement lasted until July 1, 1823, when the region gained its total independence.[1]

After breaking from Mexico, the region held together in a loose federation known as the United Provinces of Central America until 1838.

---

1. Ralph Lee Woodward, Jr., *Central America: A Nation Divided*, 2nd Edition (New York: Oxford University Press, 1985), pp. 89-91.

"Plagued from the outset by political and economic difficulties," Woodward noted, "the United Provinces never achieved nationhood. The seeds of their disunity were already present in the provincial jealousies and ideological differences of the late colonial period."[2]

In 1848 an event occurred in California which would have profound consequences for Nicaragua in relation to the prospects for a canal: the discovery of gold. What stands out from a quick glance at the map of Nicaragua is the size of Lake Nicaragua, and closer inspection reveals the San Juan River connecting the lake with the Atlantic. From the western side of the lake to the Pacific is only a 13-mile strip of land. In 1849 Cornelius Vanderbilt set up a combined stagecoach and boat transportation system, the Accessory Transit Company, to help bring the gold rushers from New York to California through Nicaragua. One of the most famous travelers on this route was Mark Twain, who made the journey in 1866.[3]

In 1850 England and the United States signed the Clayton-Bulwer Treaty, agreeing that neither nation would exercise exclusive control of any isthmian canal which might be built.[4]

U.S. Warship Shells San Juan del Norte

The San Juan River connects with the Atlantic at the town of San Juan del Norte, also known as Greytown under the British protectorate which then covered the east coast of Nicaragua. As Vanderbilt's Accessory Transit Company got into full swing, Greytown began to grow, becoming more and more Americanized. Conflict soon developed between the city authorities and the transit company.[5]

The company housed its workers on a narrow, sandy spit across the bay from the town. When the company made this spit (Punta Arenas)

---

2. Ibid., p. 93.

3. *Travels with Mr. Brown*, as cited in *La Prensa Literaria*, August 18, 1990.

4. Walter LaFeber, *Inevitable Revolutions: The United States in Central America* (New York: Norton, 1984), p. 30. The author added: "In 1901 the United States forced the British to terminate the Clayton-Bulwer Treaty so Washington could fully control the building and defense of an isthmian canal" (p. 34).

5. Craig L. Dozier, *Nicaragua's Mosquito Shore* (University of Alabama Press, 1985), pp. 83-84.

more and more self-sufficient and passengers did not have to pass through Greytown at all, the town's businesses went into a nosedive, thus worsening relations between the town and the company.

"By spring of 1854," Dozier explained, "there had been many incidents of animosity, including theft of company property and destruction of some of its buildings, after an ultimatum from Greytown authorities for removal of Punta Arenas installations went unheeded. No agreement was ever reached for relocating the company's facilities at Greytown."[6]

The U.S. minister to Nicaragua, Solon Borland, arrived in Greytown at the height of tension. He offered protection to an American river-steamer captain when a Greytown "law-enforcement squad" tried to arrest the captain for the murder of a native, insisting they had no authority to do so. "This infuriated a mob which followed Borland to the U.S. consul's home with the intent of arresting him for interfering in the execution of justice."[7]

Borland's reminder about his diplomatic immunity meant nothing to the people and the police, and he suffered a slight wound from a broken bottle hurled at him. Borland reported the "bad character" of Greytown's populace and administrators, most of whom were Jamaicans, to his superiors. "For this 'insult' to its minister and for the theft and destruction of property at Punta Arenas, the official reaction of the United States was that the people of Greytown, and especially the authorities there, should be held accountable. The transit company was delighted when the warship *Cyane* was dispatched to force reparations and apologies and made no secret of the fact that it hoped the outcome would be company control of Greytown."[8]

When the warship arrived on July 11, the U.S. consul presented the demands of his government to the city council, which found them unacceptable. The next day Commander Hollins issued a proclamation to the people of Greytown, citing "certain gross outrages . . . perpetrated by the 'authorities' (so called) and people of San Juan del Norte upon the persons and property of American citizens." He also said that "a serious insult and indignity has been offered to the United States in the conduct of the said 'authorities' and people towards Mr. Borland."

---

6. Ibid., p. 87.

7. Ibid., p. 88.

8. Ibid.

Therefore, he threatened, "I, George A. Hollins, Commander of the United States ship of war Cyane, and by virtue of my instructions from the U.S. Government at Washington do hereby solemnly proclaim and declare that if the demand for satisfaction . . . is not forthwith complied with I shall at 9 a.m. tomorrow proceed to bombard the town. . . ."

When a favorable reply was not forthcoming, Hollins allowed for the evacuation of some British subjects and a few Americans, mostly women and children, and others headed for the forest. "Intermittent bombardment of the town followed, and finally, with the remaining buildings set ablaze, it was totally destroyed," Dozier noted. "Disapproval of this act came from all quarters: the residents of Greytown, including the Americans; the U.S. Congress; the American public and press; the British. It hurt Americans who lived and worked and had businesses in Greytown as much as any others, and it was seen as unnecessary."[9]

According to Dozier, the real lesson of the bombardment was not meant for Greytown but for the British government. "Achieved at a heavy cost for Greytown, it was a price the Monroe Doctrine-adhering Pierce administration was willing to pay" to emphasize its policy.[10] Although this incident would pale in comparison with later U.S. interventions, it remains alive in the people's memory (e.g., see "Cañonazos por la Ruta del Canal," by Francisco Hernández Segura, in the Nicaraguan daily *El Nuevo Diario*, March 21, 1989).

Civil War and William Walker

Thanks to the contract he had negotiated with the Nicaraguan government, Vanderbilt managed to accumulate a quick fortune with his transit company; but, while he was on a visit to Europe, his partners Garrison and Morgan took over the company. What followed, noted Sergio Ramírez (Vice-president in the Sandinista administration), was an "all-out war" between the Commodore and his former partners for control of the routes to California.[11]

---

9. Ibid., p. 89.

10. Ibid., p. 90.

11. Sergio Ramírez, *El Muchacho de Niquinohomo* (Managua: Vanguardia, 1988), pp. 5-6. Throughout this book, where the title of a work is in Spanish, the material presented is my translation unless otherwise indicated.

In 1854 the large landowners and merchants of Granada, under the banner of the Conservative or "legitimist" party, entered into civil war against the oligarchy of León represented by the Liberal or "democratic" party. The Liberals had refused to recognize the Conservative government of Frutos Chamorro of Granada. Once war broke out, the Liberals decided to hire some North American mercenaries to help overthrow Chamorro.[12]

Thus the American adventurer, William Walker, entered the fray on the side of the Liberals. (In September 1988, on the 132nd anniversary of the Battle of San Jacinto in which Walker suffered a defeat, President Daniel Ortega said of the Walker episode: "It was not the Nicaraguan people who invited the yankees, who invited Walker and named him president; it was rather the representatives of those economic interests which little by little were taking shape, developing and consolidating their power from 1821 to July 19, 1979.")[13]

Walker was financed by Vanderbilt's rivals, Garrison and Morgan, who were "interested in insuring for themselves the transit concession through Nicaragua."[14] After being proclaimed president of the country in 1856, Walker decreed that English would be the official language and that slavery would be reestablished. The United States recognized his government and began diplomatic relations.

Even before becoming president, Walker had declared null and void the concession which had been given to Vanderbilt and had granted a new concession to Morgan and Garrison. Vanderbilt reacted by helping to arm and equip a joint army of the Central American governments, which saw themselves threatened by Walker's expansionist ambitions.[15]

In 1857 Walker was defeated and left Nicaragua. He subsequently made several attempts to gain a foothold in Central America but was

---

12. Ibid., p. 6.

13. *Barricada*, September 14, 1988.

14. Ramírez, op. cit., p. 7.

15. Ibid., pp. 7-8. See also LaFeber, op. cit., pp. 30-31: "Walker made the crucial mistake of trying to destroy Vanderbilt's steamship line. . . . Unlike the Washington officials, Vanderbilt refused to recognize Walker. Instead he crushed him financially and then militarily. . . . Just as Walker had been financed by North American capitalists who had set their sights on Central America, so the greatest of the Yankee capitalists destroyed him."

finally caught and executed in Honduras in 1860, identifying himself to his captors as "the president of Nicaragua."[16]

After the ouster of Walker, the disputing factions "entered into a long truce, letting the Conservative families of Granada govern the country."[17]

Nicaraguan Canal and U.S. Control of the Continent

Washington's need to control and dominate the hemisphere was clearly shaping its foreign policy. Maryknoll Father Miguel D'Escoto, Nicaragua's Foreign Minister in the 1980s, in his introduction to Richard Millett's *Guardians of the Dynasty—A History of the U.S.-created National Guard of Nicaragua*,[18] cited this 1890 statement by William L. Merry, American Minister to Nicaragua: "The construction of the Nicaragua canal will secure the domination of the U.S. over the American Continent, politically as well as commercially. . . . The nation that with the Nicaraguan Government, on a joint agreement, controls Lake Nicaragua will then control the destiny of the Western Hemisphere."

Perhaps with an eye toward agribusiness possibilities, Merry added: "One great advantage possessed by the Nicaragua canal over any other project of the kind is the fertility and resources of the territory through which it passes. . . . Nicaragua is one of the garden spots of the world."[19]

General Augusto César Sandino, the leader of the struggle against the U.S. occupation forces from 1927 to 1933, wrote: "This region of the earth, because of its natural privileges, has been coveted by foreign powers ever since the discovery of America. The Spaniards were always looking for the narrowest point of the continent to go from the Atlantic to

---

16. Woodward summarizes the Walker episode succinctly: op. cit., pp. 136-145. See also Gregorio Selser, *Sandino: General of the Free* (New York: Monthly Review Press, 1981), pp. 15-20.

17. Ramírez, op. cit., p. 9.

18. Maryknoll, N.Y.: Orbis, 1977.

19. Ibid., p. 5.

the Pacific, and since then people have thought about a canal through Nicaragua."[20]

General José Santos Zelaya

A Liberal coup had brought General José Santos Zelaya to power in 1893. His rule until 1909 was characterized by a vigorous defense of national interests and, according to his critics, dictatorial and fraudulent domestic policies as well as adventurism beyond Nicaragua's borders. Sergio Ramírez noted that in 1907 Zelaya's forces invaded Honduras and declared war on El Salvador.[21]

It was his strong nationalism, however, which was the basis for U.S. hostility and eventual intervention. "The construction of a canal was always part of Zelaya's plans," wrote Ramírez. "The canal would be the source of wealth and transformation of the country."[22]

Zelaya's "uppity" nationalistic attitude came through in negotiations with the United States in 1901 about a canal, when he refused to give the United States extra-territorial rights such as having American courts in the canal zone. Sandino later observed: "The United States was convinced that the highly patriotic president would never sacrifice the national autonomy of Nicaragua."[23]

According to Woodward, "the Nicaraguan government made clear demands regarding its sovereignty rights and control over any inter-oceanic canal that the United States might build there, making the Panama route still more attractive to United States interests."[24]

Once Zelaya's independent, nationalistic attitude became clear, the United States decided to build the canal through Panama, suddenly coming to the rescue of an "independence" movement which split that territory off from Colombia. A Nicaraguan canal, however, remained a possi-

---

20. "Manifesto to the People of the Earth and in Particular to the People of Nicaragua," 1933, in *El Sandinismo: Documentos Basicos*, Instituto de Estudio del Sandinismo (Managua, 1985), p. 111.

21. Op. cit., p. 70.

22. Ibid., p. 11.

23. *El Sandinismo*, p. 112.

24. Op. cit., pp. 188-189.

tory off from Colombia. A Nicaraguan canal, however, remained a possibility for someone. The U.S. government's hostility toward Zelaya grew when he began to look to other nations, including Japan and Great Britain, to have a canal built through his country.[25] (Years earlier Zelaya, with U.S. help, had put an end to British political and economic control of Nicaragua's Atlantic region, and the doors were opened for an influx of U.S. investment.)

Other Economic Interests

The canal question was not the only reason for U.S. opposition to Zelaya. He had also cancelled some concessions which had been given previously to American corporations. In one such company, Secretary of State Philander Knox had direct financial interests, and Adolfo Díaz (who would be one of the leaders of the anti-Zelaya revolt) was a secretary. In a *New York Times* interview (Sept. 10, 1912), the leader of the movement against Zelaya, General Juan Estrada, said that his forces had gotten about $1 million from some American companies.

The investment paid off: post-Zelaya regimes gave the United States the power to collect customs revenue, proper assurances were given to U.S. business interests, and Nicaragua became indebted to American rather than British banks.[26]

Nicaragua's credit dependency was another issue in U.S. opposition to Zelaya. On the theory that Nicaraguan independence could be enhanced by diversifying its creditors, the nationalistic president signed a loan agreement for several million dollars with the Ethelburg Syndicate of London. A recent article in *El Nuevo Diario* gave this interpretation: "Imperialism dictated that in the early 20th century the countries of this continent should not ask for loans from Europe. Rather, they were only free to get dollars in exchange for their sovereignty, and this is the main reason for Yankee intervention against Zelaya."

---

25. Millett, op. cit.,p. 23. Ramírez gave a similar explanation of U.S. hostility, attributing the fall of Zelaya at least in part to his canal negotiations with other foreign powers (op. cit., p. 11).

26. See Ramírez, op. cit., pp. 12-14.

The United States Backs a "Revolution"

In 1909 the U.S. government decided to help the Conservative forces in their rebellion against the Liberal president. (It should be kept in mind that generally in Latin America Conservatives and Liberals simply represent two different factions of the exploitative upper class.) The Conservative uprising against Zelaya began in October 1909 in Bluefields on Nicaragua's Atlantic Coast, led by two generals and Adolfo Díaz. When Zelaya sent several thousand troops to put down the revolt, the rebels asked for American intervention. Four hundred Marines under Major Smedley Butler arrived, "ostensibly to protect the lives and property of American and other citizens."[27] The Marines protected the rebel force in Bluefields.

Major Butler is known to students of Latin American history for his amazingly frank account of his achievements and for his recognition of the interests and purposes involved: "I spent 33 years and four months in active service as a member of our country's most agile military force— the Marine Corps. And during that period I spent most of my time being a high-class muscle man for Big Business, for Wall Street, and for the bankers. In short, I was a racketeer for capitalism. . . . I helped purify Nicaragua for the international banking house of Brown Brothers in 1909-1912. I brought light to the Dominican Republic for American sugar interests in 1916. I helped make Honduras 'right' for American fruit companies in 1903."[28] To "purify" Nicaragua, Butler helped to overthrow General Zelaya and to defend the subsequent Conservative government against a Liberal revolt.

The State Department stepped up its pressure on Zelaya after his forces had captured and executed Lee Roy Cannon and Leonard Groce, two American citizens who had been hired by the Conservative insurgent forces to set mines and blow up the government's troop ships in a military campaign to overthrow the Zelaya government. In a public statement to the people of his country, the Nicaraguan president declared: "Those individuals were foreign mercenaries at the service of an internal revolution, hired to destroy and to kill."

---

27. Millett, op. cit., p. 24.

28. Address to American Legion convention in Connecticut, August 21, 1931, as cited by Leslie Cockburn, *Out of Control* (New York: Atlantic Monthly Press, 1987), p. 254.

The execution of the two Americans "gave the United States the excuse it wanted to break openly with the Zelaya regime," Millett noted.[29] On December 1, Secretary of State Knox issued a strong statement condemning the Zelaya regime and breaking diplomatic relations.

In this statement addressed to the Nicaraguan government, Knox said that under the Zelaya regime republican institutions had vanished from the scene, except in name only, and that public opinion and the press had been "strangled." While it is true that Zelaya was a dictator, one of many in Latin American history, the weight to be attached to Knox's concern for democracy must be determined in relation to the other U.S. interests involved in the formulation of U.S. policy. Perhaps the famous statement by Franklin Delano Roosevelt about Somoza, the chief heir of the U.S. military presence in Nicaragua from 1912 to 1933, puts U.S. concern for democracy in its truest light: "He's an s.o.b., but he's ours."

Knox went on to declare that, as far as Washington was concerned, the revolt against Zelaya represented the ideals and will of the majority of Nicaraguans more faithfully than did the Zelaya government. Most analysts of Nicaraguan politics agree that neither the Liberals nor the Conservatives ever represented the majority of the people. FSLN founder Carlos Fonseca once quoted a popular slogan, "five conservative oligarchs plus five liberal oligarchs add up to ten bandits."[30] In any event, Knox's judgment about Nicaragua's internal political life is one of the most arrogant statements in a long litany.

In December Zelaya resigned, explaining that he hoped to stop U.S. intervention by removing the "pretext" for it. Another Liberal replaced Zelaya but was unacceptable to the U.S. government, which continued to support the rebels. In 1910 Zelaya's successor resigned, and the rebels took office. "All threats to American concessions were ended," Millett noted, "perhaps in return for the reported $1 million which American businessmen had contributed to help finance the revolution."[31] After a short period of turmoil, Adolfo Díaz became president and was promptly recognized by the United States.

In 1986 Stephen Kinzer of *The New York Times* drew the following parallels with the 1909 situation: "The United States now is supporting

---

29. Op. cit., p. 25.

30. *El Sandinismo: Documentos Basicos*, p. 264.

31. Op. cit., p. 27.

Nicaraguan rebels, as it did then. Bluefields, the first target of the anti-Zelaya rebels, is nearly as isolated now as it was in 1909, and today's rebels consider it a tempting target. The underwater mines used in 1909 were not the last that Americans helped to plant in Nicaraguan waters. In 1984 the Central Intelligence Agency was involved in mining several Nicaraguan ports. In 1909, 400 United States marines . . . protected the Bluefields plotters. Today's rebels, known as contras, are not under American military protection, but their squad and platoon leaders are being trained by United States Army advisers."[32]

Large-Scale Intervention

The Liberals, however, would not keep still, and so in 1912 Major Smedley Butler had a chance to purify Nicaragua again. When Liberal forces under General Benjamin Zeledón attacked government troops, President Díaz asked for American intervention. On August 14 Butler landed at the Pacific port of Corinto with a Marine battalion, and soon another force occupied Bluefields. This intervention was condemned by the Central American Court, which had been created with U.S. support in 1907, but the United States simply ignored the ruling (as it would the World Court ruling in 1986).[33]

General Zeledón's forces retreated from Managua to Masaya. The American force increased to over 2,700 men, and Butler led some of these troops against Zeledón, who was informed that only unconditional surrender would be accepted. The U.S. Marines attacked on October 4 and soon routed the poorly equipped rebel forces.

Zeledón tried to get away but was captured by Nicaraguan government troops, who asked the Americans what should be done with the Liberal leader. Major Butler telegraphed Admiral Southerland, the overall commander of American forces, saying: "If you direct I can have Zeledón back here under guard or protected by my men in Masaya," but added

---

32. *The New York Times*, Nov. 30, 1986.

33. LaFeber, op. cit., p. 48. The author also pointed out that "Knox justified his policies in Honduras and Nicaragua by announcing in 1911: 'We are in the eyes of the world, and because of the Monroe Doctrine, held responsible for the order of Central America, and its proximity to the Canal makes the preservation of peace in that neighborhood particularly necessary.'"

that he "personally would suggest that through some inaction on our part someone might hang him." Millett observed that the admiral's reply to this message "had apparently been destroyed, but the final result is quite clear. The next day the Díaz regime announced that Zeledón had been killed during the battle. Peace, enforced by American bayonets, had returned to Nicaragua."[34] The kind of "peace" had been predicted by Zeledón himself in 1910 when he said: "An imperialist government, loyal to no principles other than the force of its cannons and its own interests, is trying to turn our people into a market, and in order to do that it is taking away our sovereignty and independence, seeking to enslave us" (Museum of the Revolution, Managua).

Characterizing Butler as "an efficient officer who never let his sense of duty interfere with a realistic appreciation of the situation," author Leslie Cockburn noted that the Marine commander wrote to his wife, decrying "a victory gained by us for them at the cost of good American lives, all because Brown Brothers, bankers, have some money invested in this country."[35]

The Politics of Occupation

The Conservative regimes which the United States subsequently kept in power helped the Americans to gain greater political and economic control over Nicaragua. This was important in view of growing United States interests in the entire Central American region which, as LaFeber noted, "climbed rapidly from $21 million in 1897 to $41 million in 1908, and then to $93 million by the eve of World War I."[36]

In 1916 the Bryan-Chamorro treaty gave the U.S. government the right to a naval base and the exclusive option to build a canal through Nicaragua in return for an American payment of $3 million. Calling the treaty the "sale of a nation's sovereignty," Sergio Ramírez noted that the United States had just completed the Panama Canal, and so the treaty was not a concession for the building of a canal but insurance for the United States that no one else would build one through Nicaragua. "Díaz and Cham-

---

34. Op. cit., pp. 32-33.

35. *The Plot to Seize the White House*, by Jules Archer (New York: Hawthorn Books, 1973), p. 118, as cited by Cockburn, *op. cit.*, p. 254.

36. Op. cit., p. 35.

orro were there to insure that exclusivity, and the Marines to insure them," according to Ramírez.[37]   (In 1972 the treaty was terminated by President Richard Nixon in an act of gratitude to the Somoza dictatorship for its many years of faithful subservience.)[38]

In 1917 the Lansing Plan created a High Commission, consisting of Nicaragua's finance minister, a resident American commissioner, and a third member appointed by the Secretary of State, to control all Nicaraguan revenues in excess of $96,000 a month and to use these funds to pay off foreign creditors. Visitors to Managua's Museum of the Revolution find this explanation as a caption among the exhibits: "From 1911 to 1924, Adolfo Díaz, Emiliano Chamorro, and Diego Manuel Chamorro worked together to give Yankee finance capital the control and ownership of the customs services, the financial system, and the Nicaraguan railroad as collateral on the investments which the New York bankers were making in our country for the supposed purpose of 'rehabilitating' us financially.

"The real objective, of course," the museum caption continues, "was something else: to tie us up financially with their dollars in order thus to justify intervention in our political affairs. This financial control and political subjection were part of a broader plan: the strategic need to exercise absolute dominion over the potential canal route through Nicaragua."

"A Legitimate Sphere of Influence for the U.S."

United States troops left Nicaragua in 1925, but when the Liberals rebelled against the Conservative government the next year, United States troops returned to rescue the regime. In January 1927 the Chilean daily *El Mercurio* carried a UP dispatch reporting that "the State Department declares that any revolution or anarchy in Nicaragua constitutes a threat to U.S. rights to the building of a canal and of a United States naval base as well as a threat to United States commercial interests. However, the State Department does not specifically accuse the Liberal forces of threatening United States rights to the canal, but it says that their actions could lead to such a result."

---

37. Op. cit., p. 15.

38. See LaFeber, op. cit., p. 226.

On January 2, 1927 Under Secretary of State Robert Olds, in a confidential memorandum, had summarized American policy goals in Nicaragua: "The Central American area down to and including the isthmus of Panama constitutes a legitimate sphere of influence for the United States, if we are to have due regard for our own safety and protection. . . . We do control the destinies of Central America and we do so for the simple reason that the national interest absolutely dictates such a course. There is no room for outside influence other than ours in the region. We could not tolerate such a thing without incurring grave risks."[39]

The "outside influence" at that time was Mexico, which was helping the Liberals in their struggle against the Conservative regime which had usurped power. In his memorandum Olds explained: "At this moment a deliberate attempt to undermine our position and set aside our special relationship in Central America is being made. The action of Mexico in the Nicaraguan crisis is a direct challenge to the United States. If this Mexican maneuver succeeds it will take many years to recover the ground we shall have lost. . . . Nicaragua has become a test case."[40]

The State Department felt that Mexico's presence in the Nicaraguan affair would bring "Bolshevik" influence along with it. LaFeber has explained: "Mexico was going through a revolution considered much too radical by State Department officials, and its appearance in Nicaragua occurred as relations were nearly at a breaking point over Mexico's policy of squeezing North American oil companies."[41]

In James Chace's opinion, Olds's attitude "reflected an unwillingness to recognize . . . the nature of the Mexican revolution itself and the nature of the Nicaraguan movement headed by Sacasa. As to the first of these, the socialist rhetoric employed by Mexican leaders was just that, rhetoric, used by those in power to maintain the allegiance of an oppressed population. More important," Chace continued, "there was no genuine threat to the United States of any sort of 'internationalism' from Mexico—but again, the United States was ready to act on a *supposed* threat."[42]

---

39. Millett, op. cit.,p. 52.

40. Ibid.

41. Op. cit., p. 65.

42. *Endless War* (New York: Vintage, 1984), p. 45.

As for Sacasa's movement, "it was, if anything, more conservative than the government of Mexico. Sacasa and his military co-leader, General José María Moncada, were revolutionaries only insofar as they were using the rhetoric of revolution to regain power."[43]

On January 6, 1927, four days after Olds wrote his memorandum, a landing party from the USS Galveston arrived in Managua and "were welcomed by the Nicaraguan government as deliverers from the threat of a Liberal victory."[44] By the middle of March over 2,000 sailors and Marines were on duty in Nicaragua, one of whom said: "It was obvious that had we not arrived to declare the various towns neutral, the Liberals would have swept the Conservatives out of control in short order."[45] A heavy diplomatic campaign, backed up by U.S. military force, resulted in a settlement involving a general amnesty, the disarming of both sides by U.S. forces, and an American commitment to train a national police force and to supervise elections in 1928.

Sandino

Augusto César Sandino, a Liberal general, refused to go along with what he considered a Liberal-Conservative sell-out of Nicaragua's sovereignty and led a guerrilla struggle against the Nicaraguan figureheads and the American forces.[46]

Sergio Ramírez explained that Sandino "had not returned to fight for a party, but for a country." What was important to him was not who would be the presidential candidate in some upcoming elections "which the Marines would carry out to their liking, but that the United States had no right to invade and humiliate a small country."[47]

---

43. Ibid.

44. Millett, op. cit., p. 52.

45. Ibid., p. 53.

46. See Woodward, op. cit., pp. 199-200, and Selser, op. cit. For an analysis of Sandino's thought in relation to Marxism and to Christianity, see Giulio Girardi, *Sandinismo, Marxismo, Cristianismo: La Confluencia* (Managua, Centro Ecuménico Antonio Valdivieso, 1987). English translation, *Faith and Revolution in Nicaragua: Convergence and Contradictions* (Maryknoll, N.Y.: Orbis, 1989).

47. Op. cit., p. 30.

After working for a while in Guatemala for the United Fruit Company and in Mexico for the South Pennsylvania Oil Company, Sandino had returned to his native Nicaragua in 1926 to join in the Liberal struggle. His nationalism was different from that of Zelaya in that Sandino was fighting for a society in which workers and peasants would obtain justice. Both nationalisms, however, by threatening U.S. foreign economic interests, were unacceptable to the northern colossus and provoked violent intervention.

The War Against Sandino

The guerrilla tactics of Sandino's Army in Defense of the National Sovereignty of Nicaragua (ambushes followed by quick retreats) took a considerable toll on the "well-trained Yankee soldiers with their elegant uniforms."[48] As the Marines kept dying in the Nicaraguan jungles, "the lists of the victims came out every day in the U.S. papers, and public opinion became troubled."[49]

Nicaraguans were victimized by U.S. aerial bombing and by atrocities which seem to have set a precedent for the behavior of the U.S.-supported contras in the 1980s. Stanley Atha, a Marine lieutenant in the campaign against Sandino, told writer Peter Davis that he never burned a village, but "it happened." Atha went on to describe the exploits of a Lieutenant Pennington, who was in charge of the garrison at Matagalpa. "He cut off the heads of six bandits and held the heads to be photographed with them. I have one of the pictures," he exclaimed to Davis, "see, there, he holds them by the hair." Atha went on to note that "no Marine officer in his right mind is going to do that," adding that the Marines yanked Pennington out of Matagalpa.[50]

Katherine H. González, who lived for many years in Nicaragua, included an interesting piece of oral history in her master's essay on Sandino: "My cook, from a peasant family in rural Matagalpa, told me the story her father told of how the Marines had thrown babies of famil-

---

48. Ibid., p. 35.

49. Ibid., p. 43.

50. Peter Davis, *Where Is Nicaragua?* (New York: Simon and Schuster, 1987), p. 65.

ies suspected of being Sandinista supporters into the air and caught them on their bayonets, running them through."[51]

Bishop Pedro Casaldáliga of São Felix, Brazil, in a poem addressed to Sandino, referred to his visit to the northern war zones where the contras had been especially active: "I have come from your Segovias, and I have felt the aggression, slitting the throats even of children, and the aggressor was the same, the same aggressor from the North, the same yesterday and today!"[52]

González noted that Sandino himself said that both sides committed atrocities. "Who began to commit atrocities?" asked Sandino in a conversation with José Roman. "That is not important. What is certain is that the Marines are more culpable . . . because they were the intruders. . . . Each side tried to annihilate the other. The principal difference was that they did it to enslave us and we in order to liberate ourselves. They attacked the rural population indiscriminately, including old people, women and children who were totally uninvolved in the fighting. Meanwhile, we only attacked the invading army. . . ."[53]

Atha and others customarily referred to Sandino's people as "bandits." In 1928 Sandino told Carleton Beals of *The Nation* that "we are no more bandits than was Washington. If the American people had not become calloused to justice and to the elemental rights of mankind," he continued, "it would not so easily forget its own past when a handful of ragged soldiers marched through the snow leaving blood tracks behind them to win liberty and independence.

"If their consciences had not become dulled by their scramble for wealth," in Sandino's analysis, "Americans would not so easily forget the lesson that, sooner or later, every nation, however weak, achieves freedom, and that every abuse of power hastens the destruction of the one who wields it. We march to the clear light of the sun or to death. But if we die, the *patria* lives on, indestructible. Others will succeed us."[54]

---

51. "Race and Class Analysis in the Thought of Augusto C. Sandino," master's essay in political science, Wayne State University, Detroit, Michigan, 1988, p. 18.

52. *El Vuelo del Quetzal—Espiritualidad en Centroamérica* (Panama: Maiz Nuestro, 1988), p. 149.

53. José Roman, *Maldito Pais*, pp. 162-163, trans. KHG, as cited by González, op. cit.

54. Cited by Davis, op. cit., p. 74.

In 1928 the Senate Foreign Relations Committee summoned the Secretary of the Navy to explain the Nicaraguan operations, and a resolution was adopted questioning the president's authority to keep occupation troops there. In New York, Los Angeles, Chicago, and Detroit, committees of solidarity with the anti-imperialist struggle began to spring up in support of Sandino, "holding fund-raising meetings which led to government charges."[55]

That same year the Marines "took their first step back," Ramírez noted: they would no longer commit their troops to direct military action but would use them only as "technical advisors." From then on, the chief responsibility would be on the shoulders of a local army, created and trained by the Marines: the National Guard, founded in 1927 by a contract between the U.S. and Nicaraguan governments.[56] Ramírez observed that the continuing loss of Marines' lives shows that their retreat from combat was only partial.

The election which had been agreed upon in 1927, to be supervised by the United States, was won in 1928 by the Liberal José María Moncada, who kept the Marines on the scene and stepped up the fight against Sandino. The latter's enemy now was not one party but rather the "oligarchy supported by the intervention."[57]

Sandino's Plan for Latin American Unity

Sandino had a broad view of the need for Latin American solidarity in the struggle against imperialism. In 1929 he wrote his "Plan for Achieving Bolívar's Great Dream," a proposal to form an alliance among the 21 Latin American nations. In the preamble he explained: "We are deeply convinced that U.S. capitalism has come to the last stage of its development, thus becoming imperialism, and that it does not pay any attention now to theories of law or justice and has no respect for the solid principles of independence of the individual parts of the Latin American Nationality.

---

55. Ramirez, op. cit., p. 43.
56. Ibid., p. 44.
57. Ibid., p. 46.

"Thus we consider it indispensable," he continued, "that the alliance of our Latin American States be formed without delay to preserve that independence unscathed in the face of the pretensions of U.S. imperialism or of any other power which would try to subject us to its interests."[58]

One of the key elements in Sandino's plan was the notion that any Central American canal would be a joint project under the auspices of the Latin American alliance rather than under the exclusive power of one country. In a letter to the president of Argentina suggesting an international conference to discuss the plan, Sandino said that if such a conference decided to give the United States the privilege of building a Nicaraguan canal, it should require the United States to end its intervention in Latin America. Furthermore, with remarkable foresight especially in relation to his own country, Sandino proposed that the conference demand from the United States a commitment "not to foment rebellions against Latin American governments which do not want to become handmaidens of the U.S. government."[59]

Sandino's Goals

Sandino was a nationalist who struggled to free his country from the U.S. military occupation. He thought that the phrase, "America for the Americans," which for many characterized the Monroe Doctrine, was "well put. All of us born in the Americas are Americans. The mistake has been that of the imperialists who have interpreted the Monroe Doctrine as saying 'America for the Yankees.'"[60]

In order to achieve his goal of national liberation, he relied primarily on the poor workers and peasants, but his theory (like that of contemporary Sandinistas) did not exclude others from joining the struggle. He saw, however, that the middle and upper classes had always been allies of imperialism and of its occupying forces, since their basic interests coincided.

---

58. *El Sandinismo: Documentos Basicos*, p. 85.

59. Ibid., p. 63.

60. Sandino, *Pensamiento Vivo*, p. 140, trans. KHG, as cited by Katherine H. González, op. cit., p. 49.

What was Sandino's social and political vision for Nicaragua? He was not a communist. Perhaps the most dramatic expression of this fact was given during his visit to Mexico (1929-1930) when he split with Farabundo Martí, the Salvadoran communist who had joined with Sandino in the Nicaraguan struggle and was killed in the 1932 slaughter in El Salvador.[61]

According to Giulio Girardi, Sandino's project for society "does not radically question the capitalist system but rather seeks to reform it; his method of social analysis is neither structural nor materialistic; his strategy is based more on a broad nationalist and anti-imperialist alliance than on class struggle; his confidence in the triumph of the oppressed is based more on the force of moral ideals than on the determinism of objective processes."[62]

Other scholars emphasize the radical nature of Sandino's social vision but explain that he was keenly aware of the necessary stages in the struggle. He had a "very clear idea of how U.S. imperialism retarded resolution of social and political problems," argued Katherine H. González, "and he knew perfectly well that withdrawal of the Marines was only a first step toward the solution of Nicaragua's social problems." He felt that this work with the peasants and Indians in northern Nicaragua, along with the maintenance of a small army, "would give progressive forces in his country a base for proceeding with the next stage which was a revolt by workers and peasants."[63]

González cited Sandino's statement in a 1933 interview: "There should be work and activity for everyone. I am in favor . . . that the land should belong to the state." Sandino added: "I am inclined toward a system of cooperatives, but this we will have to study further."[64]

Former Minister of Defense Humberto Ortega has noted: "These reforms entered structurally in contradiction with the social relations of production that were predominant. In no way was the bourgeoisie going to permit that the land belong to the state; they were already particularly worried about the colonization projects and the cooperatives. Sooner or

---

61. See Selser, op. cit., pp. 129-134.

62. Op. cit., p. 66. See Girardi's chapter (pp. 55-86) on this entire question of Sandino's relation to Marxism.

63. Op. cit., pp. 22-23.

64. Sandino, *Pensamiento Vivo*, p. 292, trans. KHG, as cited by González, op. cit., p. 23.

later these projects would lead to a frontal clash between the Sandinista movement and the dominant classes."[65] In summary, noted González, "Sandino was more than 'merely' a nationalist and anti-imperialist, but he felt that his social agenda had to be postponed until the correlation of forces was appropriate for a social struggle to have any chance of success."

The founders and present leaders of the FSLN have not tried to claim that Sandino was a Marxist. They have simply pointed to some revolutionary elements of Sandino's thought (e.g., focus on social justice for workers and peasants and on their key role in the national liberation struggle against imperialism), and they believe that their struggle for socialism is an organic development of Sandino's struggle.

Sandino's Last Years

In 1931 Sandino launched a broad offensive against the United Fruit Company plantations in the Puerto Cabezas region and succeeded in razing some of them. The same year, after an earthquake completely destroyed Managua, the Marine commandant became the real chief of state.[66]

With Sandino's army broadening the theater of conflict throughout the country, Nicaragua prepared for elections in 1932. At that point the U.S. ambassador told the two traditional parties that his government would withdraw its occupation forces in January of the following year, but the United States and the parties would have to agree on the naming of the first Nicaraguan head of the National Guard. After the election of the Liberal Juan Bautista Sacasa, the U.S. ambassador chose his candidate to head up the National Guard: Anastasio Somoza García.[67]

In January 1933 the American troops were withdrawn, largely because of their failure to put down the revolt and because of growing anti-interventionist sentiment in the United States. To protect their interests, the Americans left the well-trained National Guard. (In March 1989, when 1,894 members of the National Guard defeated in 1979 were released

---

65. Humberto Ortega, *50 Años*, p. 97, trans. KHG, as cited by González, op. cit., p. 24.

66. Ramírez, op. cit., p. 51.

67. Ibid., p. 53.

from prison, Juan Wong, a former Guard commander who owns a restaurant in Florida, told a reporter that the U.S. government has an obligation to the Guardsmen. "We were created by the U.S. Marines. We are the bastard children of the U.S. Congress," Wong said. "The least they could do is get a little conscience and relocate some of these people.")[68]

In February Sandino signed a peace treaty with Sacasa, and his army put down its weapons. The general kept 100 of his soldiers with him as his personal guard, in accord with the peace agreement, and went to work forming peasant cooperatives in the Wiwili region of northern Nicaragua.

Throughout 1933 the National Guard, which Sandino considered an army of occupation, harassed Sandino and his group with occasional jailings and attacks on the new cooperatives. Sandino made several trips to Managua to discuss these problems with Sacasa, but the weak president could not control the Guard. Sandino told the press that he considered the Guard "an army created on the margin of the national constitution, the result of an illegal act by an intervening power."[69]

A 1933 statement by Sandino to an interviewer had an eery currency to it in 1989 as the Bush administration began to emphasize a political strategy which ultimately led to the electoral defeat of the Sandinistas. "The expulsion of the Marines from Nicaragua does not mean that the nation's problems are at an end," he warned. "There are many dangers, from without and within. Although the United States is clever enough to turn defeat into advantage by recognizing its error and withdrawing its troops, it still doesn't have the freedom of spirit to overcome its economic ambitions and will not stop its intrigues and manipulations aimed at replacing armed intervention with another kind of intervention, so subtle that it can't be fought with arms, but only with the dignity and honesty of our statesmen, a quality that barely exists at this moment."[70]

On February 20, 1934 Sacasa named a Sandinista general as presidential military delegate with jurisdiction in the northern Segovias, thereby trying to buttress his own authority in relation to Somoza's and "assuring Sandino tranquility in his cooperatives. But Somoza, seeing that as a mortal blow against his ambitions for power, quickly called a meeting on February 21 of his most trusted officers and told them of the need to get

68. *Miami Herald*, March 24, 1989.

69. Ramírez, op. cit., p. 57.

70. José Román, *Maldito País* (Ediciones El Pez y la Serpiente, 1979), p. 165.

rid of Sandino immediately, for which he counted on the consent of the U.S. ambassador, Arthur Bliss Lane. That voice of the Yankee pro-consul transmitted to the officers by Somoza signified a death sentence, and they hurriedly approved the scheme."[71] Ramírez also pointed out that Somoza and the ambassador met that same day.[72]

On that night of February 21, after supper with President Sacasa, Sandino was detained and murdered by National Guard soldiers. Two of his generals were killed along with him. His father, Gregorio, who later went into exile, had been taken prisoner. When he heard some shots in the distance, he said: "Now they are killing them; he who gets involved in being a redeemer, dies crucified."[73] Those shots came from the Guard attack on the house where Sandino had been staying and took the life of his younger brother, Socrates.

The next day the Guard took Sandino's cooperatives by surprise, massacring over 300 peasants. A few months later, in a speech in Granada, "Somoza admitted that he had killed Sandino, 'for the good of Nicaragua,' with the backing of the U.S. ambassador."[74]

The house in Niquinohomo where Sandino grew up is a modest but nicely appointed museum. Across the street tourists find silent testimony to a later form of U.S.-backed violence in Nicaragua: a plaque in memory of second lieutenant Felipe Pavón L. (1957-83), victim of the contras exactly 50 years after the withdrawal of U.S. forces. Inscribed on the monument are the words of Che Guevara: "Wherever death takes us by surprise, let it be welcome as long as our call to fight has gotten a receptive hearing and thousands of hands reach out to grasp our guns in the liberation struggle."

---

71. Ramírez, op. cit., pp. 58-59.

72. Ibid., pp. 123-124.

73. Ibid., p. 59.

74. Ibid., p. 60.

The Somoza Era

In 1936 Anastasio Somoza García assumed the presidency, inaugurating a corrupt and brutal U.S.-sponsored dynasty which would keep Nicaragua well within the U.S. "sphere of influence" for more than four decades. The U.S. government, as LaFeber observed, "had found in the National Guard the answer to the perplexing problem of how to maintain an orderly, profitable system without having constantly to send in the marines."[75]

Daniel Ortega put the Somoza era in historical context: "The Somocista domination was not the exception but rather the continuation and culmination of a capitalist-style process of domination in which Liberals and Conservatives took turns in government. In this process they could even find themselves in deep conflicts and even at war with one another; but both were defending the same system, the same interests, and the same power: the power to exploit the people, the power to have freedom of expression for themselves—the privileged Liberal or Conservative minorities—while denying that freedom of expression to the majority."[76]

After Somoza's assassination by the poet Rigoberto López Pérez in 1956, his sons enjoyed the same unqualified U.S. support. By 1967 there were 25 U.S. military advisers in Nicaragua. With the Pentagon providing over $1.2 million, or 13 percent of Somoza's annual defense budget, U.S. military relations with Nicaragua were perhaps the closest in the hemisphere. All of Somoza's officers spent one year at the U.S.-run School of the Americas in the Canal Zone (now located at Fort Benning, Georgia). In fact, the School trained more Nicaraguans during the fifties and sixties than officers of any other Latin American nation. (In recent years Salvadorans have had that distinction.) Meanwhile, other forms of U.S. "aid" and private investment flooded into Nicaragua.[77]

A small symbol of that aid, and an ironic indication of the deterioration of U.S. relations with the Sandinista government, stands across the street from the port in San Carlos on the San Juan River. A public fountain bears a large plaque with the inscription: "Drinking water: a symbol

---

75. Op. cit., p. 69. See also Woodward's summary of the Somoza era, op. cit., pp. 219-223 and 259-262.

76. Barricada, September 14, 1988.

77. LaFeber, op. cit., pp. 163-164.

of cooperation and an expression of cordial relations between the United States of America and the Republic of Nicaragua." The undated monument was put up "just for show," according to a local merchant, "to make Somoza look good." No water has flowed from the fountain for many years, and the structure is in a state of total disrepair and abandonment.

Roosevelt's characterization of Somoza, Sr. as "*our* s.o.b." was not just a slip of the tongue, nor was U.S. support for such a tyrant an exception. In 1948 the State Department's George Kennan pointed out that "we have about 50% of the world's wealth, but only 6.3% of its population. . . . In this situation, we cannot fail to be the object of envy and resentment."[78] He defined the "real task" of the United States as devising "a pattern of relationships which will permit us to maintain this position of disparity without positive detriment to our national security."

This would require dispensing with "all sentimentality and day-dreaming" and not "deceiving ourselves that we can afford today the luxury of altruism and world-benefaction . . .," Kennan said. "We should cease to talk about vague and . . . unreal objectives such as human rights, the raising of the living standards and democratization." Forty years later the U.S. government was using "democratization" as a club to indict, judge, and execute the Sandinista government; there is no evidence that Washington is any more sincere in pushing the concept today than it has been throughout the century. "The day is not far off," Kennan predicted, "when we are going to have to deal in straight power concepts. The less we are hampered by idealistic slogans, the better."

In 1950 Kennan had a meeting in Rio de Janeiro with U.S. ambassadors in South America. He described U.S. interests in terms of "the protection of our [sic] raw materials, the prevention of military exploitation of Latin America by the enemy, and the prevention of the psychological mobilization of Latin America against us."

No quarter would be shown to communists. "The final answer might be an unpleasant one, but . . . we should not hesitate before police repression by the local government. This is not shameful since the Communists are essentially traitors. . . . It is better to have a strong regime in power than a liberal government if it is indulgent and relaxed and penetrated by Communists."[79]

---

78. Cited by Jack Nelson-Pallmeyer, *War Against the Poor: Low-Intensity Conflict and Christian Faith* (Maryknoll, N.Y.: Orbis, 1989), p. 5.

Founding of the FSLN

The Sandinista National Liberation Front (FSLN) was born in 1961 in response to a need described by one of its founders, Tomás Borge: "Without a vanguard the revolutionary potential could not become a powerful fist of the people capable of overthrowing the Somoza dictatorship."[80] Borge, who served as Sandinista Minister of the Interior, also noted that the Frente constituted "a people's alternative opposed to the bourgeois reformist alternative" in the struggle against the dictatorship.

Carlos Fonseca, also one of the founders of the FSLN, "rescued Sandino and his revolutionary ideas," according to Borge. Two ideas in particular were Sandino's legacy to the new movement: "Only the workers and peasants are capable of struggling to the end against imperialism and its local political representatives." Visitors to the ruined center of Managua are struck by a large statue of a man in struggle, with the inscription in the words of Sandino: "Only the workers and peasants will go to the end." With this conviction, Borge explained, Sandino saw "the class nature of the revolutionary movement, the class struggle as the motor of history."

Borge went on to the second of Sandino's contributions to revolutionary theory: "In the economic, social, and political conditions of Nicaragua, armed struggle was the only way to the revolutionary transformation of society."[81]

The Frente had a slow and uneven growth during the sixties. The 1972 earthquake which devastated Managua turned out to be a significant factor in the rise of anti-Somoza consciousness, since all sectors of Nicaraguan society as well as international agencies were appalled by Somoza's greed and crudity in profiting from the vast influx of relief assistance.

During the seventies the Sandinistas began to take bolder actions and to reach out more broadly for popular support, particularly in the neighborhoods and in the progressive Christian circles whose members were discovering their social and political responsibility. "The option for the poor, the liberation of the oppressed, those were the commitments which

---

79. Cited by LaFeber, op. cit., p. 107. LaFeber observed that "Kennan's statement summarized why the United States tolerated Somoza. . . ."

80. Tomas Borge, *Apuntes Iniciales Sobre el FSLN* (Managua, 1986), p. 18.

81. Ibid., p. 19.

Christians were drawing from the gospel," Sandinista leader Francisco Rivera Quintero recalled. "And those were also the essential motives of the Sandinista struggle."[82]

Borge has explained the connection between organizing for immediate gains and working toward revolutionary change: "The objective of this work (in the cities) was to organize the neighborhoods to make immediate demands and to struggle for improvements in water, electricity, medical services, etc., but without making these gains the final goal. For us, unlike other groups, the specific demands and organizing campaigns were a means to find the best people and to show them that they should organize to take power."

One of the specific organizing efforts centered around the release of political prisoners. "In this struggle we got in contact with the most sensitive and militant Christian nuclei within the student movement."[83]

Carlos Fonseca was killed by the National Guard in 1976, but in death as in life he was a powerful inspiration to Sandinistas. Hearing the news of Carlos' death, Francisco Rivera Quintero, whose brother Filemón had been killed in battle the previous year, got weak at the knees and was sorely tempted to despair. "But in my nightmare, feeling like an animal cornered in the woods," he later told Sergio Ramírez, "I heard Carlos coming to talk to me as before: 'Remember, *muchachos*, when you feel sad, disheartened, demoralized, wanting to run away and leave everything and cry, remember that no one has forced us into this; think of the thousands of children begging, without shoes and practically naked, think of the misery caused by injustice, recall that the big landowners will not yield of their own accord, that we are the only alternative for the downtrodden and exploited, the only hope they have in this world. And if you remember that, you will pick up strength, I don't know from where, but you will, and you will continue on.'"[84]

Francisco did continue on and led the three uprisings in Estelí. Spearheading an insurrection which involved practically all of Nicaraguan society, the Sandinistas attained their goal of overthrowing the dictatorship and ushering in an era of revolutionary social change on July 19, 1979—

---

82. Francisco Rivera Quintero, as told to Sergio Ramirez, *La Marca del Zorro* (Managua: Nueva Nicaragua, 1989), p. 178.

83. Op. cit., pp. 35-36.

84. Francisco Rivera Quintero, op. cit., p. 126.

in spite of all the efforts of the U.S. government, the Nicaraguan upper classes, and the Church hierarchy to preserve the basic structure of the Somoza system while cleansing it of its discredited head.

Since the Triumph

Since the overthrow of the dictatorship in 1979, which Nicaraguans refer to as "the triumph," the U.S government has continued to try to dictate how the Nicaraguans are to fashion their own internal structures of society. During the final year of the Carter administration, strings attached to U.S. aid dictated that the bulk of it had to be channeled to Nicaraguan private enterprise (which would strengthen that sector against the revolutionary government). Shortly after Reagan took office, the United States halted all aid, demanding that Nicaragua stop assisting the rebels in El Salvador.[85]

Although the U.S. embassy, within a few months, reported that there was no evidence of any ongoing Nicaraguan aid to the Salvadoran FMLN, Reagan continued the ban on aid while starting covert assistance to the contras. American aggression against Nicaragua became more blatant over the years.

A strong condemnation of such intervention was one of the main points in the World Court ruling on June 27, 1986 (just a few days after Congress approved Reagan's request for $100 million for the contras): "Whatever may be the definition of the Nicaraguan regime, adherence by a state to any particular doctrine does not constitute a violation of international law; to hold otherwise would make nonsense of the fundamental principle of state sovereignty, on which the whole of international law rests. . . . The Court cannot contemplate the creation of a new rule that

---

85. In an interview in *National Catholic Reporter* (September 14, 1990), Father Miguel D'Escoto said, in response to a question about Sandinista government support for the Salvadoran guerrillas: "At one point in time, there was even a direct level of support in regard to weapons, also. And when that happened, we acknowledged that. We supported a group that was fighting against a government that was involved up to its ears in the illegal American war against Nicaragua." Citing El Salvador's cooperation with the contras, D'Escoto said: "We were fully justified in doing what we did when we did it. . . ." He vigorously denied that "there was any similarity between any degree of support we gave to a preexisting group (the Salvadoran guerrillas, . . . and what the United States was doing with the contras . . . (who) were conceived, created, trained, equipped, financed, and directed by the United States."

gives one state the right to intervene in another on the basis that the latter has chosen a particular ideology or political system."

President Daniel Ortega, in his July 1986 speech to the UN Security Council, quoted that statement from the World Court verdict, observing: "The most important paragraph of the Court's decision states that the United States' dissatisfaction with Nicaragua's political, social, and economic system does not give it the right to intervene in the internal affairs of Nicaragua."

Before returning to Nicaragua, President Ortega accepted Rev. Jesse Jackson's invitation to address the National Bar Association in Denver. "It is not an east-west conflict," the president said. "It is about the right of peoples to make their own future. But the United States makes and imposes governments, so the great threat, both for you and for us, is the danger of direct troop invasion."

Since the U.S. government had walked out of the World Court proceedings, it was no surprise that Reagan was undeterred by the verdict naming the United States as the aggressor nation against Nicaragua. In August 1986, Reagan said he was hoping that "the contras have the strength to . . . exert leverage on the Sandinista government. Then we could still have a peaceful political settlement. But if Nicaragua still won't see the light, or the Sandinista government won't, then the only alternative is for the freedom fighters to have their way and take over."[86]

In a slightly different style but with an equally imperialistic message, Senator Jim Sasser (D., Tenn.) had made the following contribution to the debate preceding the vote on contra aid: "We can help the Sandinistas to self-destruct by adopting a policy that is acceptable to the nations of the free world. We cannot expect to achieve our aims by attempting to destroy the Sandinistas through an illegal and immoral war."[87] Almost four years later the U.S. government, after wrecking the economy and bleeding the population for years, succeeded in toppling the Sandinistas through elections, making the revolution appear to self-destruct.

---

86. *Detroit Free Press*, Aug. 20, 1986.

87. *Detroit Free Press*, Aug. 20, 1986.

Conclusion

In the early years of this century, long before there was any "east-west conflict," long before the Soviet Union became a superpower—indeed, before the Russian revolution—U.S. officials were imposing and undoing governments in Nicaragua and elsewhere. The excuses and rationales change with the times, but the basic interventionist pattern has continued.

With "Contragate" it became clear that Reagan's arrogance of power characterized not only his dealings with other countries but also his relations with the U.S. Congress. This revelation nourished some hope that an offended Congress and a surprised and increasingly outraged American public might be able to put a stop to the president's adventurism in Nicaragua. That hope received new sustenance on February 3, 1988, when the House of Representatives narrowly defeated the administration's aid package for the contras, and again on March 3 when the House rejected a Democratic package. Although the aid program finally passed by Congress excluded military assistance and came within the context of a provisional cease-fire, it was firmly and justly denounced by the Nicaraguan government as a continued intervention in the internal affairs of the country and an effort to keep the faltering contras in the ring.

In 1989 the Bush administration, while continuing its "non-lethal" aid to the contras, decided to use the electoral process to oust the Sandinistas. With millions of dollars in support for the UNO campaign and its candidate, Violeta Chamorro, and with a commitment to lift the trade embargo in the event of a Chamorro win, the Bush strategy worked. "Low-intensity warfare" had taken its inevitable political toll.

The Sandinistas and the revolutionary process continue, but now "from below," as Daniel Ortega put it shortly after his defeat at the polls.

4

Church History:
1523 to the Late 1960s

Evangelization by Conquest

In the late fifteenth century, the papacy awarded newly discovered lands to Spain and Portugal and along with this the right and responsibility to propagate the faith. "Pope Alexander VI issued the Bull *Inter coetera* in 1493 favoring the Roman Catholic kings of Spain by allowing them to evangelize these lands and bring them under their domain," Enrique Dussel has observed.[1]

"Thus, in the *Recapitulation of Laws of the Indies Kingdoms* (1681), the first law declares that the Lordship of the king of Spain over the new kingdoms is due to the obligation that the king has incurred with the Holy See to indoctrinate the Indians in the Roman Catholic faith," Dussel continued.

"The conquering praxis is thereby justifed by a theoretical basis—the papal bull. The whole juridical structure of the sixteenth century was obviously a type of *ideology*. Behind respectable principles was hidden the real *meaning* of the conquering praxis. The concealed meaning was the reality of the European domination of the Indian who was reduced to the most horrendous slavery. Death, theft, torture (that was the real fruit of the conquering praxis) was concealed by a false ideological interpretation, namely, evangelization."[2]

---

1. *A History of the Church in Latin America*, translated and revised by Alan Neely, (Grand Rapids, Michigan: William B. Eerdmans Publishing Co., 1979), p. 308. Hereafter, *A History*.

2. Ibid., pp. 308-309.

This was the first time in history, Dussel noted, "that the Papacy gave to a nation the twofold authority to colonize and evangelize, that is, temporal and eternal, political and ecclesiastical, economic and evangelistic authority." Thus the Portuguese and Spanish endeavors were "military and imperial theocracies" with a "fundamental ambiguity between colonizing and evangelizing."[3]

Nicaraguan historian Jorge Eduardo Arellano has described these three steps in the conquest: military "pacification"; economic appropriation and exploitation; and the ideological arm—evangelization—or, as it was also called, "indoctrination."[4]

Baptism and Genocide in Nicaragua

On September 12, 1502, Columbus landed on the Caribbean shore of what is now northeast Nicaragua. Serious colonization got under way in 1523 when Captain Gil González Dávila took possession of Lake Nicaragua, and Nicaragua became part of the Spanish domain. Father Diego de Agüero, the first priest to set foot on Nicaragua, arrived in the same boat and immediately set out to baptize as many Indians as possible. J. E. Arellano noted that "the Indians, facing the conquistador's threat of war, were obliged to accept the ideological imposition of baptism."[5]

A popular illustrated history of the Church in Nicaragua prepared by *Tayacán* (the weekly paper written for the Christian base communities) pointed out that "baptism is an important sacrament by which we enter into the community to follow Jesus freely." But at the beginning of the colony "it was used as a tool to dominate the Indians, obliging them to be Christians, converting them into subjects of the king of Spain, and taking away their wealth. In González Dávila's first expedition, which lasted six

---

3. Ibid., p. 38. Dussel added: "Only the Jesuits were able to constitute as *territorium nullius Diocesis* the newly discovered lands under direct protection of the Holy See, and for a long time this Order enjoyed a greater freedom than other churchmen in Latin America."

4. *Breve Historia de la Iglesia en Nicaragua, 1523-1979* (Managua, 1980), p. 9. Hereafter, *Breve Historia*.

5. Ibid., p. 9.

months, 32,264 Indians were baptized. . . . A year and a half after the conquest, there were 400,000 baptized Indians."[6]

González Dávila claimed that the 32,264 people had received baptism *by their own volition,* but this was doubtful since shortly afterward many of them attacked the captain's forces.[7]

In the New World the Spanish landowners (encomenderos) were supposedly responsible for "evangelizing" the Indians who lived and worked on their haciendas. What actually happened was a horrible genocide: five years after the conquest, only 70,000 Indians out of the original 600,000 in Nicaragua remained. Most had been killed, others had been sent to Peru as slaves.[8]

Prophetic Bishops in Nicaragua

In 1527 the king of Spain, Charles V, seeing that the laws which supposedly protected the Indians were not being obeyed, decreed that the Indians would have a protector and defender. This position was created for humanitarian reasons and also in the interests of the king, who wanted to check the power of the governors since it was a threat to his own power. The Church took up the responsibility for the rights of the Indians. This led to conflicts between the Church and the big landowners and within the Church itself, since some priests and bishops defended the Indians and others were accomplices of the conquerors.[9]

The royal decree named Father Diego Alvarez Osorio, who would become the first bishop of Nicaragua a few years later, the first protector of the Indians in Nicaragua. He carried out his duties "with a truly gospel-like attitude. . . ."[10] After becoming bishop he continued to protect the Indians and to make every effort to convert them.

---

6. *Historia de la Iglesia de los Pobres en Nicaragua* (Managua, 1983), p. 6, hereafter *Historia.*

7. J. E. Arellano, op. cit., p. 10.

8. *Historia,* pp. 9-10.

9. Ibid., p. 11.

10. J.E. Arellano, op. cit., pp. 25-27.

Alvarez Osorio had invited the Dominican priest, Bartolomé de las Casas (1474-1566), to take up residence in León. The Dominican had been "converted to the God of the poor and to the true Church of Jesus, and from then on he devoted his life to defending the rights of the Indians through books, letters, sermons, denouncements, and peace plans."[11] In this cause he crossed the Atlantic fourteen times. Between 1532 and 1535, Fray Bartolomé was in Nicaragua on three occasions. The landowners hated him; the Indians loved him. He was finally expelled from Nicaragua by the governor, Rodrigo de Contreras.[12] In 1543 he was named bishop of Chiapas (Mexico).

Antonio de Valdivieso, a Dominican priest, was named to the diocese of Nicaragua in 1544 and was consecrated a bishop by Bartolomé de las Casas a year later in Honduras.[13]

On his return to Nicaragua, Valdivieso soon came into conflict with the colonial authorities "and with those sectors of the clergy which justified the oppression of the Indians."[14] Fray Bartolomé had given this description of the diocese of Nicaragua: "With respect to God and justice, it is one of the lost and shameless dioceses, full of evildoers and tyrants and great disturbances; and the main cause of all this uproar, although there are plenty of bad Christians, is said to be Contreras."[15]

The civil authority of the country was concentrated in Governor Rodrigo de Contreras and his clan, who owned one third of the province.[16] In 1542 the New Laws had been promulgated, partially suppressing the *encomiendas* and prohibiting the enslavement of Indians. The objective, as J. E. Arellano pointed out, was "to change the Indians into vassals of the crown—that is, into taxpayers—since the *conquistadores* prevented the crown from getting the most out of them. In the struggle between the *conquistadores* and the crown, the bishops carried out the

---

11. *Historia*, pp. 12-13.

12. Ibid.

13. Oscar González Gary, *Iglesia Católica y Revolución en Nicaragua* (México: Claves Latinoamericanas, 1986), p. 75.

14. Ibid.

15. Ibid. p. 76.

16. Ibid.

role of demanding compliance with laws which worked against the former and favored the latter."[17]

Contreras wanted to preserve "the slavery-type exploitation of the Indians against the new policy of the crown, while Valdivieso defended that new policy, concerned at the same time as a deeply Christian person with the lamentable situation of the Indians."[18]

In 1547 Valdivieso wrote to the king: "The state of these Indians is such that slavery would be prosperity for them, because slaves are treated like persons while they are treated like animals. Much more respect is shown to animals than to them."[19]

The bishop knew his life was in danger, and on February 26, 1550, he was killed by Contreras' sons, "in complicity with some adventurers," J. E. Arellano noted. "The cause of his death was none other than his struggle for the Indians."[20]

The Christian base communities see the assassination of the bishop as the beginning of their history: "He was killed for the cause of justice. With the blood of his martyrdom, the Church of the Poor is born in Nicaragua."[21]

González Gary summed up the outcome of the struggle between the prophetic bishops and the rapacious *conquistadores:* "The theses of Las Casas and the martyrdom of Valdivieso were soon forgotten, remaining only on paper; the laws were not obeyed and little by little were revoked; and the *encomienda* system continued, although with some modifications. Through their influence with the king, the bishops had a partial share of power, but it was useless; faced with the astonishing corruption of the powerful, to confront it these few men would have needed to be political gangsters."[22]

---

17. *Breve Historia,* p. 29.

18. Ibid., p. 30.

19. *Historia,* p. 14.

20. *Breve Historia,* p. 30.

21. *Historia,* p. 15. See also articles about Valdivieso by Alberto Vivar and Angel Arnaiz in Amanecer (January-February, 1988), the journal of the Antonio Valdivieso Ecumenical Center in Managua.

22. Op. cit., p. 81.

Christendom in Nicaragua

González Gary characterized the period from the 17th to the 19th century in Nicaragua, as in the rest of Central America, as the era of Christendom, which he defined as "a specific way the Church has of inserting itself in society, utilizing the political and social power of the dominant classes as its mediation instead of inserting itself at the margin of society or against the power system."[23]

In Nicaragua the Church has not only legitimized the dominant political power, González Gary continued, "but it has also exercised an especially active role in the constitution and conservation of civil society, which is the ethical and intellectual foundation of that political power. This is the role which the Catholic Church will play in the maintenance of the colonial system. . . . As a beneficiary of colonial domination, the hierarchical Church is at the same time the ideological justifier of the oppression of Indians, crioles, blacks, and mestizos—an institution both colonized and colonizer. It shares in the prosperity of the dominant classes, and in gratitude it conceals, blesses, and legitimates a merciless exploitation of the Indians."[24]

J. E. Arellano noted that a few bishops during this period (until independence in 1821) reported to the king on the abuses committed by the colonial authorities.[25] The most notable critic was Andrés de las Navas y Quevedo, who was named bishop of Nicaragua in 1677 and arrived two years later in León. Within a few days he set out on his first pastoral visit to his diocese, with a view toward sending the king a report.

A Guatemalan historian had this to say about the bishop's reports: "A hurricane or earthquake would have caused less havoc than what Fray Andrés wrought in the hearts of those whose lives had consisted of committing every kind of abuse of authority, robbery, abuse, and harassment."[26]

---

23. Ibid., p. 88. The author also cited Pablo Richard's description: "In Christendom there is a relation of mutual legitimation between the Church and the power of the dominant classes" ("Religiosidad Popular en Centroamerica," en *Religión y Politica en America Central*, DEI, San José, 1981, p. 30).

24. Ibid., pp. 88-89.

25. *Breve Historia*, pp. 32-36.

26. Agustin Estrada Monroy, *Datos para la Historia de la Iglesia en Guatemala* (Guatemala, 1972), p. 345, cited by J. E. Arellano, *Breve Historia*, p. 30.

The Church and Independence

With the opening of the 19th century, the independence movement in Central America began to gain ground, with the Church playing a major role in the drama. "In general there were two groups: the hierarchy, tied in with the royal power, on the side of the established order, maintaining a reactionary position; and the lower clergy carrying out an important role of support for the true *independentistas*."[27]

One of the leading figures in the struggle for independence in Nicaragua was Father Tomás Ruíz, the first Nicaraguan Indian to become a priest and also the first to receive a doctorate (in law). He was professor of philosophy and vice-rector of the seminary.

Tayacán's popular illustrated history of the Church of the Poor in Nicaragua presents Father Ruíz in this way: "As an Indian, he was very sensitive to the injustices which his Indian brothers were suffering. As a man of great learning, he had clearly been influenced by the most advanced ideas of his time (the Enlightenment), and that gave him an internationalist way of thinking. He was also a great preacher.

"He was a humble, pious, and traditional priest who had a close-up knowledge of the suffering and hopes of the poor. Love for justice led him to make a political commitment in the struggle for independence, convinced that it was a Christian and priestly commitment."[28] (This same conviction would later inspire Gaspar García Laviana, Fernando and Ernesto Cardenal, Miguel D'Escoto, and other priests.)

In 1805 in El Viejo, Ruíz, along with the Franciscan José Antonio Moñino, headed up the first Nicaraguan uprising against the crown.[29] In 1811 he took part in the uprising in León, along with two other priests. Two years later he was imprisoned in Guatemala for his involvement in an independentist conspiracy.

The question of independence naturally divided Nicaraguan society. "On the one side were the Spaniards (those born in Spain), who held all

---

27. J. E. Arellano, *Breve Historia*, p. 49. See also Dussel, *A History*, p. 89: "Those bishops who had been named by the Patronato system remained for the most part strong supporters of the Crown rather than of the new revolutionary governments." On the role of the lower clergy in the Latin American independence struggles, see Dussel, pp. 90-91.

28. *Historia*, pp. 28-29.

29. González Gary, op. cit., p. 98.

political power and had a monopoly on commerce. On the other were the Creoles (born in Nicaragua of Spanish parents), who wanted that power. And then the majority—Indians and mestizos—who wanted justice."[30]

González Gary explained an important division within the independence movement: "The Creoles of León and Granada wanted independence without changes, while the upper middle classes of those cities wanted independence in order to implement substantial reforms."[31] The latter group was able to involve the lower classes in the struggle, which they saw as necessarily a violent struggle. Priests like Tomás Ruíz and Benito Miguelena belonged to this sector, which was revolutionary for its day. "But the conservative Creoles controlled almost all the independence movements, and with independence itself their class definitely took power."[32]

A historical analogy with the later struggle against Somoza suggests itself. The lower and middle classes, under the leadership of the Sandinistas and with the involvement of some priests and religious, wanted to change more than the political superstructure; the upper classes in general would have been content to remove the embarrassing, greedy, and cruel dictator. Unlike the bishop of Nicaragua in the early 19th century, Archbishop Obando y Bravo did promote political change. As we will see later, what he did not favor was the revolutionary social and economic change envisioned and later implemented by the Sandinistas.

On December 22, 1811 the people of Granada successfully demanded the resignation of all royal officials. A Creole city government was formed, with Father Benito Soto as a representative of the people. At his motion slavery was abolished in January 1812.[33]

That same year Father José Antonio Chamorro, vicar of Granada, issued a proclamation denouncing the independence movement in the name of God as well as the king: "By disobeying the Spaniards who have come here, the people have disobeyed the kings of Spain and have transgressed all their laws. The people have fired officials without trial. The people think they have more power than God, the Church, and the king.

---

30. *Historia*, p. 32.

31. Op. cit., p. 96.

32. Ibid.

33. J. E. Arellano, *Breve Historia*, p. 50.

From this it can be deduced that the people in rebellion have been and are traitors to God, the king, and the nation."[34]

In *Tayacán's* popular history, the vicar's proclamation is followed by a cartoon of a peasant saying: "But they didn't fool us with their threats; we knew that God is on the side of the poor and is pushing history forward."[35]

On September 15, 1821 the treaty of independence was signed in Guatemala, breaking Central America's colonial relationship with Spain. With independence some of the demands of 1811 and 1813 were met, but it was a victory for the elite. The whole social, economic, and political structure was maintained, with the white Creoles replacing the Spaniards in public offices. There had really been two independence projects: the one promoted by the first uprisings was revolutionary; the other, that of the Creoles, was reformist. The latter gained the victory.[36]

The Church allied itself with the victors. "The Church, which was linked hand in glove with the monarchy during the colonial period, became closely tied to the new Creole and later bourgeois oligarchies of the new Latin American countries."[37]

From 1821 to 1823, the Central American provinces (Guatemala, El Salvador, Honduras, Nicaragua, and Costa Rica) were an annex of Mexico. After severing that tie, they remained united in a federation until 1838, in spite of many crises. According to the treaty of independence: "The Catholic religion which we have professed in centuries past and will profess in those to come is to be kept pure and unalterable." In the new situation the Catholic Church, its priests, and its religious houses were assured of their social and economic privileges. The practice of other religions was forbidden.

But in 1830 Honduran liberal Francisco Morazán, president of the federation, suppressed all the privileges of the Catholic religion and ordered the suppression of the Franciscans, Mercedarians, and Recolección. Members of these orders were given thirty days in which to arrange their secularization.[38] These laws against Church privilege expressed a rejec-

---

34. Ibid. p. 51.
35. *Historia*, p. 33.
36. Ibid., p. 34.
37. Dussel, *A History*, p. 77.

tion of the "anti-independence politics" of the Church hierarchies more than an anti-Christian sentiment.[39]

The experience of the Church in Nicaragua was part of a larger pattern. In general throughout Latin America, Dussel noted, "The Church was deprived of all the economic advantages it enjoyed during the colonial era. . . . In most of Latin America the Church lost virtually all its agricultural properties as well as other lands and buildings. . . . The Church was reduced to real poverty in view of the fact that it depended and now depends in a majority of cases on only the financial contributions of the faithful. Bishops and priests no longer enjoy the income from rentals or salaries from the State in the majority of Latin American countries, but this allows the Church as an institution much greater liberty than it enjoyed during the colonial era."[40] The author also noted that in general from the mid-19th century onward the Church progressively lost its legal and political power and influence, with the Liberal parties opposing the Church and the Conservatives supporting it in its legal and political struggles.

With Morazán's moves against the Church in Nicaragua, most of the clergy were scattered and the Church was in crisis. "However, it was far from losing its traditional influence and power: the priests found support in numerous chaplaincies, and popular Catholicism remained intact."[41]

When Nicaragua became a separate state in 1838, its new constitution established religious freedom for the first time, permitting the public practice of non-Catholic religions. "However, religious freedom lasted only until 1854, when the Conservative president Fruto Chamorro wrote another constitution and returned the old privileges to the Catholic Church."[42]

When war broke out between the Liberals and Conservatives in 1854, the Liberals initiated a pattern of political behavior which would be symptomatic of the Nicaraguan oligarchy's struggles for power: enlisting

---

38. J. E. Arellano, *Breve Historia*, p. 55.

39. *Historia*, p. 35.

40. Op. cit., p. 81.

41. J. E. Arellano, *Breve Historia*, p. 55.

42. Manzar Foroohar, *The Catholic Church and Socio-Political Conflict in Nicaragua, 1968-1979* (University of California dissertation, 1984), pp. 100-101.

U.S. intervention, at first in the internal conflicts within the Nicaraguan ruling class and then, with the Sandinista triumph, in the counterrevolutionary struggle against the poor majority. The U.S. mercenary William Walker came to the assistance of the Liberals in 1855, made himself president the next year, reinstated slavery, and was forced out by a combined Central American army in 1857.[43]

The Church and William Walker

Walker received support from the leading clerics, especially Father Agustín Vijil, who helped Walker with funds from his parish in Granada and later went to Washington as Walker's plenipotentiary minister to the United States. J. E. Arellano exclaimed: "There has never been a greater shame for the Church!"[44]

Another "shameful case," as J. E. Arellano put it, was that of Father José Hilario Herdocia, the vicar of Granada. After congratulating Walker on the conquest, the priest received a letter in which Walker expressed gratitude for the Church's support: "It is very satisfying for me to hear that the authority of the Church will support the existing government. There cannot be a good government without the help of religious sentiments and guides, because the fear of God is the basis of all social and political organization. I place my trust in God for the success of my cause and for understanding of the principles I follow."[45]

There was some clergy opposition against the mercenary-turned-president in the person of Father Rafael Villavicencio and a few other priests.

The Church and the Conservatives

After the ouster of Walker, the Conservatives remained in power for over 30 years, giving special privileges to the Catholic Church and helping in the construction of churches.[46]

---

43. See Chapter 3.
44. Op. cit., p. 57.
45. Ibid.
46. *Historia*, p. 38.

Politically the era may be characterized as "the consolidation in power by the commercial and land-owning bourgeoisie, who rewarded the Nicaraguan bishops for their ideological-political support with juicy dividends and privileges."[47]

In 1862 a concordat signed by the Vatican and the Conservative government of Nicaragua went into effect, providing among other things that: the Catholic religion is the state religion; education will be religious and in accord with Church doctrine; the bishops will have the right of censorship; the government will support the Church economically; the government will be able to present candidates to be bishops; pastors will be named by the president himself; after the divine office in all churches the following prayer will be said: "God save the Republic. God save the President, the Supreme Authority"; the pope will grant exemptions and favors to the armies of the Republic.

J. E. Arellano commented that from 1862 to 1892 the concordat was "one of the ideological aspects of the economic and political consolidation of the Granada ruling class. The swearing-in of presidents was solemnized with the presence of the bishop or with pontifical Masses in the parish of Managua."[48]

What was the Church's mindset in being involved in this kind of relationship? "The Church considered the state as the basic element in carrying out its mission. That is why it always sought the state's recognition and protection. The Church found it practically impossible to conceive of fulfilling its mission without the state."[49]

This Church saw itself as an institution with rights and privileges, "a power within society which should act accordingly." It was against this kind of Church as an institutional worldly power that the Liberal state would struggle.

---

47. González Gary, op. cit., p. 112.

48. Op. cit., p. 59.

49. *Historia General de la Iglesia en America Latina,* Vol. VI, America Central (Salamanca, Spain: Ediciones Sigueme, 1985), p. 282. Hereafter, *Historia General.*

Jesuits Deported

The most serious conflict between Church and State during this period of the concordat was the deportation of the Jesuits in 1881.[50] More than 60 Jesuits had arrived in Nicaragua in 1871 after their expulsion from Guatemala by a Liberal administration; they were granted exile status and soon had many communities and missions. Under pressure from the Guatemalan government to expel the Jesuits, Nicaraguan President Zavala found an occasion in 1881.

Tensions between the Jesuits and the government culminated that year when about 1,000 Indians rose up in rebellion against the exploitation and injustice they were suffering in Matagalpa, where the Jesuits had six priests, six lay brothers, and 27 novices. Jesuit Father Antonio Cáceres began to serve as mediator in the dispute, but the government suddenly surrounded the Jesuit residence in Matagalpa and gave the Jesuits 24 hours to move to Granada. Jaime Wheelock, in his book on Indian resistance in Nicaragua, wrote: "The oligarchical government of Zavala tried to explain the Indian rebellion as the result of instigation by some Jesuit priests who had been expelled from Guatemala."[51]

Nine years of apostolic and cultural work had gained for the Jesuits "a decisive influence in the people and in some sectors of the ruling class."[52] When their supporters in León rose up, shouting "death to the government, long live the Jesuits," their deportation was a certainty. When the order came, some of their friends continued to protect them, but the government responded with troops and the Jesuits were deported from Nicaragua. "In spite of the fact that the Conservatives wanted to have very good relations with the Church, they feared the popularity of the Jesuits and their influence and power."[53]

---

50. J. E. Arellano, op. cit., p. 60.

51. Raíces indígenas de la lucha anticolonialista en Nicaragua (Mexico: Siglo XXI editores, 1974), pp. 107-112.

52. J. E. Arellano, *Breve Historia*, p. 62.

53. *Historia*, p. 39.

Liberal Separation of Church and State

One of the most important aspects of the history of the Church is its alliance with the Conservative state. In Part Five we will ask whether a lingering desire for this kind of symbiotic relationship with government was one of the roots of the hierarchy's hostility toward the lay state administered by the Sandinistas. The Frente respected freedom of religion; it did not genuflect slavishly to the Catholic hierarchy. Thus the reaction of the clergy during the 1980s was similar in some ways to the reaction of many clerics to the secularizing thrust of the Liberals around the turn of the century, who took far more drastic action against Church institutions than did the Sandinistas.

In 1893 General José Santos Zelaya, a Liberal representing the interests of the coffee growers, seized power and held it until 1909. The constitution of 1893 decreed the separation of Church and state and with that the annulment of the 1862 concordat. The constitution also established "the liberal principles of freedom in education and the lay nature of the schools, the secularization of cemeteries, and civil marriage."[54]

In 1899 a new law transferred Church property held in *cofradías* (institutions which held large amounts of Church wealth and which were administered by lay persons) to the municipalities. J. E. Arellano explained: "Since that decree undermined the economic base of the Church, the hierarchy and clergy resisted the measure. . . . So in 1904 Zelaya ordered that members of religious congregations could not enter Nicaragua, worship could not be held outdoors, and the religious habit could not be worn outside churches."[55] When a priest in León was assaulted for wearing the habit, Bishop Simeón Pereira y Castellón responded to all this by excommunicating Zelaya. The government reacted by deporting the bishop and several priests. (Pereira y Castellón had been a Jesuit novice in 1881 when the Jesuits were expelled from Nicaragua; he did not continue as a Jesuit.)[56]

---

54. J. E. Arellano, op. cit., p. 69.

55. Ibid., pp. 69-70.

56. Angel Amaiz, *Historia del Pueblo de Dios en Nicaragua* (Managua: Centro Ecumenico Antonio Valdivieso, 1990), p. 79.

This attitude of the Liberal government had more to do with economics than with ideology, according to J. E. Arellano. "The agro-export coffee sector, which also forced many small peasant farmers off their land, wanted to expand by taking over the *cofradía* lands."[57]

From the beginning Zelaya's moves against the Church evoked resistance. A priest who incited people to disobedience and rebellion was sentenced by the president to spend one year in San Juan del Norte under supervision. Another priest served time in jail for preaching a sermon which the authorities considered subversive.[58]

Conservatives Return

After Zelaya was forced by U.S. pressure to resign in 1909, the Conservatives returned to power under U.S. protection. "That put an end to the crisis for the Church," noted J. E. Arellano, "which began to gain ideological, political, and economic power once again."[59] Relations with the Vatican were re-established, and the country opened its doors again to the religious orders, with the government providing material aid for their educational institutions. The Catholic Church, however, did not regain its privileged legal status as the official religion; the Conservatives tried to grant it that status, but the Liberals in the Congress exerted sufficient pressure that the final constitution of 1911 affirmed religious freedom for all churches. Catholic Action was founded to counteract the growth of Protestantism.[60]

Although the law permitted other churches to function, the Catholic Church "in fact could count on the Conservative governments to support and promote Catholicism."[61] The Church's reliance on governmental support could be seen throughout Latin America. "Well into the twentieth century," according to Michael Dodson and Laura Nuzzi O'Shaughnessy, "the Latin American Catholic church clung to traditional methods of assuring its influence in society. Rather than relying on evangelization, it

---

57. Op. cit., p. 70.

58. Ibid., p. 71.

59. Ibid., p. 72.

60. *Historia*, p. 42.

61. J. E. Arellano, op. cit., p. 77.

sought 'legal bases of privilege and the support of political elites.' The church counted on structural relationships to political authority rather than on its pastoral presence among the people. In this sense its broad religious presence masked its religious weakness and institutional dependence."[62]

In 1923, when relations between the government and the Holy See were fully restored, the new nuncio effusively praised the Christian virtues of the Nicaraguan president. The latter, in his turn, welcomed the new papal representative with a speech in which he congratulated himself for cultivating the Catholic faith and declared that human progress was impossible "unless founded on the indestructible base of Christian morality."[63] This "key idea of Catholicism," J. E. Arellano wrote, "was shared by many cabinet ministers of the era." (This "key idea," and the Sandinistas' attitude toward it, played an important part in the hierarchy-Sandinista conflict, as we will see in Part Five.) One cabinet member ordered the image of the Sacred Heart of Jesus to be displayed in all public offices. And during this period the state donated property to the Church.

One such gift, made by President Emiliano Chamorro to Archbishop José Antonio Lezcano y Ortega in 1920, was the real estate for a new cathedral in Managua. Later that year, as the presidential election drew near, the archbishop saw fit to write a pastoral letter offering the president and his government "our most respectful homage and deepest appreciation." He recognized the government's "beneficent deeds for the Holy Church, to which the government has granted complete freedom and independence," and he mentioned especially the appointment of a permanent delegation to the Holy See and "the generous donation of land for the new cathedral of this archdiocese."[64]

Not surprisingly, then, the hierarchy for the most part kept quiet about the U.S. military occupation which kept the Conservatives in power.[65]

---

62. *Nicaragua's Other Revolution: Religious Faith and Political Struggle* (Chapel Hill: University of North Carolina Press, 1990), p. 68. Internal quote is from Ivan Vallier, *Catholicism, Social Control, and Modernization in Latin America* (Englewood Cliffs, N.J.: Prentice-Hall, 1970), p. 7.

63. J.E. Arellano, op, cit., p. 77.

64. J. E. Arellano, *Historia General*, p. 390.

65. Foroohar, op. cit., pp. 111-112.

An important exception, however, was Bishop Simeón Pereira y Castellón, who wrote to U.S. Cardinal James Gibbons in 1912: "Unfortunate mistakes have placed our country, Nicaragua, in special circumstances which deprive it of much of its autonomy, putting it under foreign influences. My beloved brother, your large country has made our small country feel the brunt of its money and its men; and your strong country with its battleships and its powerful cannons has dominated our weak country; and the bankers of the North have built their fortunes on our depleted treasuries, using extortionate loans, unjust treaties and unfair contracts."

The bishop's concern for his country's sovereignty was coupled with a concern about the influx of Protestant missionaries which he associated with the U.S. occupation: "There are other interests more important than fleeting earthly interests; after the material conquest comes the spiritual conquest. . . . The wave of Protestantism seeks to advance by tossing dollars ahead of it to open a path. . . .

"The interests of the Nicaraguan government are strongly tied in with private interests of your country. This connection is used to extend a hearty welcome to those who come here, whose mission is perhaps more political and financial than doctrinal."

The bishop then took up the argument that the U.S. forces are supposedly kept in Nicaragua to keep the peace. "I can promise that, once Nicaragua gains its freedom from U.S. military supervision, the most absolute peace and the strictest order will reign among its citizens. . . ."

The very word "intervention" was galling to the bishop: "Intervention! You have no idea, your Eminence, how hard that word is. You have not felt the double pain, as a bishop and citizen, of having to listen to the echo of soldiers' boots in our churches. You have not cried in pain at the sight of the conqueror's flag flying from our cathedral towers in place of the banner of Christ. You have never had to look at a foreign flag waving, proud and domineering, above the flag of your native country. . . . You have not had to watch a sanctuary becoming a military quarters, or an altar where the eucharistic bread is shared becoming a table for handing out soldiers' grub."

The bishop made a straightforward plea for political action "by U.S. bishops, the Catholic press, Catholic representatives in Congress, and all the Catholic people" to remedy the unjust situation. He pointed out that the intervention was bringing "grave harm" to Nicaragua and that the

Nicaraguan people had "the right to freedom and autonomy." He called for "an understanding between our country and the United States, but an understanding based always on justice and mutual interests."[66]

The Catholic Church and Sandino

Augusto César Sandino joined the Liberal struggle against the Conservative government in 1926. In 1927 both parties signed a peace pact at the insistence of the U.S. government, but Sandino refused to recognize its legitimacy and continued the struggle against the Managua government and its U.S. military protectors.

While not identifying himself as a Christian, Sandino was a man of faith. In Mexico he had come into contact with theosophy. For him, this was not a form of spiritual escapism; he believed that God was on the side of the poor and oppressed against the Yankee invader. In 1928 he wrote to his wife: "There is no doubt that we will win, since God has not only favored our cause but has become involved in it."[67]

The following year he wrote to President Herbert Hoover: "I am aware of the material resources your country has. You have everything, except God."[68] In this Sandino was harking back to the verses of the great Nicaraguan poet, Rubén Darío (1867-1916), in his "Ode to Roosevelt" (1905): "The United States is powerful and great. When it shivers, the enormous vertebrae of the Andes quake to the core. If you cry out, it is the roar of the lion. . . . You are rich. . . . But watch out! Spanish America lives! There are a thousand cubs of the Spanish Lion on the loose! In order to hold us in your iron claws, Roosevelt, you would have to be, by the power of God himself, the terrible Rifleman and the strong Hunter. And you can count on everything; only one thing is lacking: God!" (During the Sandinista administration, the young recruits were known affectionately as *cachorros*—cubs.)

---

66. Letter cited by González Gary, pp. 127-132. This letter took on new life when it was read by Daniel Ortega to Pope John Paul II on the latter's arrival in Nicaragua in March 1983.

67. *Historia*, p. 45.

68. Ibid.

In 1930 the archbishop of Managua and four other bishops issued a pastoral letter addressed to the people of Las Segovias, an area in the north where Sandino was especially strong. "Let Christ our Lord," they wrote, "extinguish the destructive fire, reconcile the hearts and extend the banner of peace over our dear children of the Segovias. The orphans, the widows, and the disabled ask for clemency. Paternally, we exhort our children to abandon the sterile armed struggle. . . ."[69]

No mention here of the "Yankee marines who were bombing and terrifying the civilian population," Father Angel Arnaiz, O.P., has pointed out in his discussion of the pastoral letter. Nor is there any reference to the rebels' conditions for ending their struggle: "the departure of the Yankee soldiers from Nicaragua and the establishment of a government with dignity which is not sold out to the United States."[70]

A year later Sandino wrote: "The clergy is allied with the Yankee bankers."[71] The hierarchy's attitude can also be seen in the fact that one bishop urged his priests and people to have "cordial relations" with the U.S-created National Guard,[72] while another blessed the weapons which would be used against Sandino's army.[73]

Conor Cruise O'Brien in an important article noted that Sandino refused to call himself a Christian "because the most eminent Nicaraguan 'Christians' of his day—like the bishop of Granada, who blessed the U.S. Marines—were in the service of the enemy. These, however, were not really Christians at all but worshippers of Mammon. Had Sandino lived to see the advent of liberation theology, he would have proclaimed himself a Christian revolutionary. And on that last point I think the Christian Sandinistas are probably right."[74]

Sandino's ties with the Mexican government "were enough to convince the Catholic hierarchy that Sandino was an enemy of the Church," Philip J. Williams has noted. "It was during this time (1926-29) that the

---

69. Cited by Foroohar, op. cit, p. 112.

70. Angel Arnaiz, op. cit., p. 95.

71. González Gary, p. 145.

72. Ibid., p. 148.

73. *Breve Historia,* p. 79.

74. "God and Man in Nicaragua," *Atlantic Monthly* (August 1986).

Cristero Rebellion took place in Mexico, a violent struggle between the Catholic Church and the anti-clerical government of Calles. Churches were burned and clergy expelled, possibly leading the Nicaraguan bishops to fear the same from Sandino."[75]

The Church in Central America

During this period, the Central American Church did not place a priority on the social question. "In fact, some bishops were so afraid of it that they preferred to forget about such complicated issues."[76] Why were they so afraid? "The skirmishes of previous decades were still having repercussions. The Church continued to feel threatened, since it had not recovered all its lost privileges and did not feel confident of the few it had regained. That is why it did everything possible to defend its rewon turf. The Church did not want to take up a radical position on the social question in order not to jeopardize its good relations with the state and the ruling class."[77]

The Central American Church found a solution to the Liberal crisis in "conformity and cooperation with the ruling class. The bishops never tired of offering the Church as an institution which would be useful to the state. . . . The best service the Church could offer society would be to make good citizens by forming good Christians. People would be kept docile and passive in the face of the established order, and *the latter was considered just only when it respected the Church's space in society.* Good Christians were good citizens, a priceless guarantee against revolutions and potential social disorder."[78]

This Church always recognized the constituted authorities as legitimate without questioning how they had come to power, their qualities as rulers, or their conduct as public administrators. The unquestionable authority of the ruler even had a sacred quality about it, "which was officially recognized at the start of every new administration." The Church also played

---

75. Philip J. Williams, *The Catholic Church and Politics in Nicaragua and Costa Rica* (Pittsburgh: University of Pittsburgh Press, 1989), p. 18.

76. *Historia General*, p. 359.

77. Ibid.

78. Ibid., p. 360. Emphasis mine.

an important ideological role, getting the people to internalize and believe the dominant norms and values of society. Of course, when this kind of ideological control failed, the coercive power of the state would step in.

In labor conflicts "the hierarchy presented the Church as a balancing factor between capital and labor, thus seeking to put some rationality into the system. But it definitely never accepted or proposed structural changes. Like the ruling class, it knew how to distinguish very well between changes compatible with the survival of the system and those that were not. It considered any change of a structural kind subversive and, like the liberal economists, accepted the inevitability of economic laws and of human misery."[79]

Thus the Church in Central America was paternalistic and minimally reformist. It never failed to defend the ideology "which acclaimed the oligarchical ruling class as the legitimate representative of the common good. This legitimated the whole dominant system, and institutionalized violence was kept hidden."[80]

In order to fulfill its function within the capitalist system, the Church repressed any discordant voices within its own clergy and thus tried to avoid any incident which might occasion difficulties for the government. In its public discourse the Church presented itself as an apolitical institution, meaning by that collaboration with the coffee-growing oligarchy. The forbidden "involvement in politics" was taken to mean opposition to the dominant class and the state. "In the name of this peculiar notion of what it meant to be apolitical, Church authorities were quick to cooperate with the state. This policy silenced any prophetic voice of denunciation and with that shut up the authentic announcement of the good news."[81]

The Church and the Somoza Dynasty

The Nicaraguan bishops were more concerned about the prerogatives of the Church in Nicaraguan society than about social issues. In their pastoral letter of 1950 the bishops dealt with the troublesome principles of the Liberal constitution: that the state has no official religion, that

---

79. Ibid., pp. 360-361.

80. Ibid., p. 361.

81. Ibid.

education is a secular enterprise, that there is freedom of conscience and of worship.[82] The bishops also expressed their opposition to civil matrimony and divorce, among other things.

With regard to freedom of conscience, freedom of worship, and the principle that the state has no official religion, the bishops declared: "the Church would have no objection to freedom of conscience, of opinion, and of expression, if they were understood in a simple and correct sense and if they were kept confined to their proper limits. In so far as they have good elements in them, they constitute inviolable rights of every man, rights whose mere mention communicates life and vigor to the mind and banishes fear of the tyrant.

"But the fact is that our legislators, in affirming these freedoms, left the sacred rights of God unprotected," the bishops protested. "For instance, there is no punishment at all for blasphemy. The true Religion can be fought against, ridiculed, mocked; and any doctrinal error will be able to acquire the same legal right to exist as the truth. And since doctrinal errors are always accompanied by or followed by moral errors, and principles are translated quite soon into deeds, and ideas change customs, it is thus that the free diffusion of error will necessarily produce corruption and immorality, those disastrous extremes which often go unknown until their terrible consequences are reaped."[83]

In regard to the proposition that the source of civil power is the people, the bishops expressed deep disturbance: "Humanity has never held this doctrine," they asserted. "From the beginning humanity has spoken of the will of God. Or it has referred to the gods, in polytheism, but always to a Being superior to man. This doctrine is so harmful that, besides bearing in itself the seed of rebellion and of anarchy, it degrades human dignity." It bears the seed of rebellion "because, if it is the sovereign People who give Authority, the people as sovereign will also be able to demand at any moment that it be given up, leaving the Rulers at the mercy of political passions." And it is said to degrade human dignity "because obedience to a man who has no investiture (authorization) from a higher source will always be humiliating and debasing."[84]

---

82. J. E. Arellano, *Historia General*, p. 407.

83. Ibid.

84. Ibid., p. 408.

With regard to education the bishops deplored the fact that "in a Catholic Country like ours lay education [i.e., publicly administered and not explicitly religious] is imposed. Catholics cannot experiment with a method of teaching the young which would be separated from the Catholic Faith and from the Authority of the Church and which would look only or primarily to natural science and to the purposes of earthly life. . . . We protest against the injustice which is committed when public funds for education are monopolized and used exclusively for the benefit of state schools. State funds are the contributions of the Nation, and the Nation is Catholic. Therefore, private religious schools cannot, without serious harm to justice, be excluded from the favor and help of the State."[85]

These private religious schools, as Foroohar has noted, "were chiefly supported by the wealthy minority devoted to the preservation of the social structure and reproduction and nourishment of its value system." The Church and the wealthy had a common interest "in fighting against any changes endangering their traditional privileged status."[86]

The bishops' statement on education seemed to express a hankering for the old days of Christendom and the Concordat, when the Catholic Church enjoyed the protection and support of state power for its proselytizing. The same longing may have been one of the factors underlying the bishops' dissatisfaction with the secular (though not anti-religious) Sandinista government.

In their 1950 letter the bishops made it clear that their criticism of the constitution did not imply that they felt the Church was persecuted by the authorities. Indeed, they expressed gratitude for the peace of those years and for the "governing authorities' moderation." The hierarchy also urged obedience to government: "For Catholics it must be a certain and exalted doctrine that all authority comes from God. God is the Author of everything that exists, and from Author comes Authority. And when Catholics obey the governing authority, they do not degrade themselves, but rather are performing an act which basically constitutes respect for God."[87]

Thus the hierarchy served to legitimize the dictatorship. "The Church carried out perfectly its traditional function of strengthening the ideologi-

---

85. Ibid.
86. Op. cit., p. 119.
87. J. E. Arellano, *Breve Historia*, p. 85.

cal apparatus of the State," J. E. Arellano noted. "Furthermore, the hierarchy was totally complicit with the governing structure controlled by Anastasio Somoza García. Representing the 'throne,' Somoza got an alliance with the 'altar,' whose visible heads consistently accepted and consecrated his policies. They were present at every official event with their blessings and prayers."[88]

José Antonio Lezcano y Ortega, the first archbishop of Managua, illustrated the altar-throne alliance in various ways. When he was consecrated bishop in 1914 he had as his sponsors [padrinos] the president and vice-president of Nicaragua, "Conservatives imposed by the United States."[89]

In 1938, at the fiftieth anniversary of Lezcano's priestly ordination, Somoza had a special seat of honor at the solemn pontifical Mass. The dictator had the archbishop "walk under an arch of rifles held aloft by an honor guard of the National Guard, while a plane performed aerial acrobatics above."[90] In the pastoral letter which the prelate wrote for the occasion, he expressed gratitude for the special attention and appreciation shown him "by the Supreme Government of the Republic, to which we constantly offer our sincere and respectful loyalty."[91]

In 1942 in the National Stadium Archbishop Lezcano crowned the Queen of the Army—none other than the dictator's daughter—with the gold crown of the Virgin of Candelaria. When Somoza was assassinated by the poet Rigoberto López Perez in 1956 (four years after the death of Lezcano), the hierarchy not only condemned the deed but buried the victim with honors as a Prince of the Church.[92]

The Nicaraguan hierarchy was by no means unique in supporting Latin American dictatorships. The religious and political anti-communism of the post-World War II era was a generalized phenomenon, and the anti-communist banner was used to crush all movements for serious structural change. "This helps us to understand the fact that on his deathbed Somoza received Pius XII's blessing and that the pope, as well as Cardi-

---

88. Ibid., pp. 89-90.

89. Angel Arnaiz, op. cit., p. 93.

90. Ibid., p. 178.

91. Ibid.

92. J. E. Arellano, *Breve Historia*, p. 90.

nal Spellman of New York, sent his condolences after Somoza expired."[93]

The late Penny Lernoux has noted that a succession of popes in the twentieth century "still looked firmly backward to the integralist ideal of a Christendom united under Rome." While the popes made some "relatively progressive statements on economics, they took the aristocracy's attitude toward the lower classes. A classless society was unnatural, they believed, and class violence was godless communism and satanic." Lernoux observed that "the Vatican not only allied itself with politically reactionary groups but in some countries, such as France and Italy, actively promoted them." American democracy was seen as an "aberration" because of the divorce of Church and state.[94]

In 1951 Nicaraguan author Pablo Antonio Cuadra noted in the Church of the time "a dangerous lack of attention to the worker and peasant social problem." The rural areas of Nicaragua were "painfully abandoned for lack of clergy and religious, even in the most fundamental aspects of their spiritual life, the word of God and the sacraments." Looking beyond the strictly pastoral, Cuadra observed that "the Church, which includes hierarchy and faithful, has not faced the social problem." Thus, he complained, the Church "has not moved ahead of Marxism and Communism and has not given to the social problem the solutions which it possesses as a divine and national entity." The Church should take up as its own, he urged, "the cause of the poor and of the workers."[95]

---

93. Ibid., p. 91.

94. Penny Lernoux, *People of God: The Sruggle for World Catholicism* (New York: Viking, 1989), pp. 19-20.

95. "El Catolicismo Contemporaneo en Hispanoamerica," ed. Richard Pattee (Buenos Aires: Editorial Fides, 1951), p. 342. Cuadra's chapter on Nicaragua contains one of the most uncritical presentations I have ever seen of the Spanish "evangelization" of the Americas and a classic conservative presentation of the ideal relations between government and the Catholic Church. But Cuadra told me in September 1989 that his thinking on this matter had changed substantially over the years and that he is now highly critical of Church-government alliances. That, he said, is why he is against the "popular Church," which he deemed to be a servant of the Sandinista government. Cuadra is director of *La Prensa*, which was one of the bitterest critics of the Sandinista government, and is a close friend and advisor to President Violeta Chamorro.

What did the official Church look like to a Nicaraguan revolutionary? Alejandro Guevara, a resident of Solentiname who became a member of Father Ernesto Cardenal's community on that island and later joined the Sandinista struggle, recalled "a dynamic but very reactionary" priest who came to the island every six months to celebrate Mass. He seemed to share with quite a few other Nicaraguan priests a disedifying business mentality regarding the sacraments. Furthermore, "Father Chacón was a National Guard chaplain," Alejandro continued. "His whole sermon was just scolding. He was a Somocista. When Pedro Joaquin was put in jail, he said, 'Pedro Joaquin, such a lively, intelligent boy, in jail for being an idiot!'"[96]

Another member of the Solentiname community, Manuel Alvarado, recalled that those who taught a religion of fatalism and "said that we shouldn't hate anybody had us supporting Somoza's government. Religion taught us that we had to have a dictator there, for God has put him there, that we had to spend our time praying for this man to be healthy. That's what religion taught us, to accept the conditions of life that we had." Olivia Silva added: "I got to the point where I could not live resigned to eating next-to-nothing, bringing up my children in such poverty."[97]

Francisco Rivera Quintero, who as "El Zorro" (the fox) had led the insurrections in Estelí, told Sergio Ramírez of his early experiences with religion. When his mother died in 1967 and the family brought the body to church for the funeral, the priest, already vested, asked from the altar what her relation was to Filemón Rivera, who had joined the Sandinista guerrilla movement. "My father told him proudly that Virginia was the mother of Filemón Rivera," Francisco recalled. "And the priest said that he could not pray for the mother of a terrorist." The group was sent away without a prayer. (Filemón was killed in combat in 1975.)[98]

As a young man Francisco began to ask whether God existed and, if so, why didn't He change things, why did He allow a few "to screw the

96. As cited by Margaret Randall, *Christians in the Nicaraguan Revolution* (Vancouver: New Star Books, 1983), p. 52. Randall explained: "Pedro Joaquin Chamorro, leader of the anti-Somoza bourgeoisie and editor of La Prensa newspaper, was imprisoned a number of times for his political activities and finally murdered by the Somozas on January 10, 1978."

97. Ibid., p. 71.

98. Francisco Rivera Quintero, *La marca del Zorro*, as told to Sergio Ramírez, op. cit., p. 27.

rest. The priests with their catechism, and the grandparents, explained that there are poor and there are rich because that is the will of God, and that the world is the way it is, and that the destiny of each one is set from birth," Francisco recalled. "And if some went to Mass in rags, without shoes, with patched clothes, while others sported nicely starched shirts, shiny rings, and gold chains on their necks, religion could do nothing about it. It didn't matter that later those same bosses who were beating their breasts in church, with bellies so fat that they had a hard time kneeling down, exploited their peasants on their haciendas or splashed mud on people walking, without even beeping their horn so people could get out of the way, as they proudly sped along in their new pick-up trucks."[99]

Another Sandinista leader experienced the same kind of religion in the service of the rich. "I knew a God who joyfully rang the church bells and dressed up when General Somoza would visit León," wrote Tomás Borge in a 1969 letter to Father Ernesto Cardenal asking for a meeting with the priest. "A God who proudly received the candle offered by the calloused hand of a *campesino,* but refused to redeem him from his poverty, placing himself on the side of the landlord. A God who forgave the heavy sins of the rich, but forbade poor young women pregnant with 'natural' child from entering the church."[100]

Father Cardenal, who had founded the Christian community at Solentiname in 1966 and who was becoming known for his revolutionary theology and poetry, met with Borge, who had helped to found the Frente Sandinista in 1961. Borge would become the Minister of the Interior in the new government formed in 1979, and Cardenal (who played a key role in the revolutionary struggle) the Minister of Culture.

The personal religious beliefs of many of the leaders of the Nicaraguan revolution have been the object of much speculation over the years. "Would you define yourself as a believer, an agnostic, an atheist?" Borge was asked by Uruguayan journalist Mario Benedetti in 1989. "I was a believer, a fervent Catholic," he responded. Attributing this fervor largely to his mother's influence, Borge also noted that he was once about to enter the seminary to become a priest.

---

99. Ibid., pp. 49-50.

100. *Christianity and Revolution: Tomás Borge's Theology of Life,* edited and translated by Andrew Reding (Maryknoll, N.Y.: Orbis, 1987), p. 14.

"Afterwards I experienced a period of not believing," he continued, "curiously enough as a consequence of the sermons of Msgr. Isidro Augusto Oviedo y Reyes, who specialized in the cruelties of hell. If this were true, I thought, then there could not be a God as I conceived of him—not only just but also generous. This was more or less the analysis I made as an adolescent.

"Later I became a believer again and remained one until about the age of 20, when I became an atheist. Nonetheless, my religious background is so powerful that I have become a kind of religious atheist. I admire Christ; my office in the Ministry of the Interior is decorated with images of Christ; I read the bible and it moves me not only as a literary work but also in many other aspects."

Benedetti asked Borge: "What did religion give you? What do you retain from that stage of your life?" Borge responded: "Love of humanity. I don't believe that one can be a revolutionary without loving one's neighbor, without a certain forgetting of oneself, without a capacity for self-giving."[101]

J. E. Arellano pointed out that one bishop during the Somoza period was an "exemplary exception" to the general rule of hierarchical support for the dictatorship: Bishop Octavio José Calderón y Padilla of Matagalpa. "From the late 1950s to his death in 1972, his basic message was: The Catholic Church loves peace—not a peace imposed by bayonets, but a peace which comes from concord and love among human beings."[102] The bishop defended the rights of labor unions against Somoza's repression. When Somoza García was killed in 1956, the bishop decided to visit the rural missions of his diocese rather than participate in the pontifical requiem Mass.[103] According to González Gary, the bishop "had a critical and anti-Somocista position regarding the economic and military excesses of the dictatorship, not allowing himself to be bought off by the dynasty."[104]

---

101. *El Nuevo Diario*, March 21, 1989.

102. *Breve Historia*, p.90.

103. Ibid., p. 98.

104. Op. cit., p. 221. See also Angel Arnaiz, op. cit., pp. 103-104.

The bishop's critical position was shown in a pastoral letter he wrote in 1959 just two weeks after the archbishop of Managua had published a pastoral letter supporting the authority of the dictatorship. Archbishop González y Robleto had written that "all authority comes from God and . . . he who resists the authority resists God." Armed resistance even against tyrannies "would amount to the consecration of anarchy." The prelate called the government a "benefactor of the Church" and claimed that it never persecuted or punished those who did not involve themselves in revolutionary activities." (The pastoral came some two months after an unsuccessful armed invasion).

Two weeks later Bishop Calderón y Padilla published a pastoral letter in which he said that "the authority is null when there is no justice." He added that when the civil authority is in open opposition to divine law, man is free to oppose the civil authority. In such cases, resistance is a duty and obedience a crime.[105]

Another important exception among the clergy was Father Azarías H. Pallais (1884-1954) of León, author of six books of poetry and two of prose. In González Gary's words: "This priest gave himself passionately to the option for the poor; he was a prophet whose poems showed his rejection of imperialist domination and his recognition of Sandino's struggle. Faithful to the gospel, he denounced the injustices of what he called 'the demagogic tyranny' and he proclaimed his 'hunger and thirst for justice.'"[106]

The changes launched in the Church with the Second Vatican Council (1962-1965) and the Latin American bishops' conference at Medellín (1968) were received enthusiastically by a small group of clergy and laity, but the Nicaraguan Church in general was not prepared for the challenge of renewal. "The Church was not prepared to embrace this option for the poor and to break its old alliance with the rich and powerful."[107]

---

105. Philip J. Williams, op. cit., pp. 21-22.

106. Op. cit., p. 226. See José Arguello, "Azarías H. Pallais: Profeta de la Iglesia de los Pobres," in *Nicaragua: Trinchera Teológica* (Managua: Centro Ecumenico Antonio Valdivieso, 1987).

107. González Gary, op. cit., p.239.

Edgard Parrales, who as Minister of Social Welfare and then Nicaraguan ambassador to the Organization of American States was one of the priests in government, recalled his European-style seminary formation. "Some of the Spanish professors in the seminary had an underlying conquistador mentality," he told me, "considering themselves superior to us Nicaraguans. There was very little study of Nicaraguan history and culture."[108] It was not until he studied in Rome in the late sixties that Parrales found people interested in Nicaragua, and this encouraged him to study and appreciate his own country. Parrales and many others also point to the Spanish civil war as an important influence on the mindset of many priests and sisters, especially Spaniards, in Nicaragua.

Nicaraguan Franciscan Sister Luz Beatriz Arellano recalled that the new social ferment "came about in a conservative church which did not seem to realize what was happening in the country."[109]

The author described the Somoza-era Church as emphasizing the sacraments and inviting people "to think only of the next life, the salvation of the soul, and the happiness of a world after death." Preachers stressed God as the punisher, Jesus as the crucified Lord "with whom the people identified in their own sorrow and death," and the Virgin Mary as the sorrowing mother. The Church was the place of salvation; reading the bible was confined to the Mass, "with few people having a bible to which they could refer."

The clergy understood their mission "as a duty to form the middle and upper class destined to assume power. . . . Up until this time we had been told: the church does not mingle in politics. Nevertheless . . . the church was, directly or indirectly, committed politically to the interests of the privileged sectors of the country because of the classist character of the church at that time."

In 1969 the First Pastoral Meeting was held in Managua, involving 258 people, among them bishops, religious and secular priests, nuns, and lay persons. The first presentation was an analysis of the objective reality of the Nicaraguan Church by then Jesuit priest Noel García, sociologist at

---

108. My interview of Edgard Parrales, July 1989.

109. "Twenty Years After Medellín," *Amanecer*, Oct.-Dec., 1988. *Amanecer*, the magazine of the Antonio Valdivieso Ecumenical Center in Managua, is published in English by New York Circus Publications; P.O. Box 681; Audubon Station; New York, N.Y. 10032.

the Central American University. The study, based on a survey of priests and lay persons, found the bishops to be "advanced only in age . . . , conservative. . . , apathetic . . . , negative . . . , disunited . . . , non-accessible to the people, . . . and incapable of effective and constructive leadership."[110]

Reinaldo A. Tefel, a committed lay Christian who later became head of the Sandinista government's Department of Welfare and Social Security, observed that "the Catholic clergy, especially the hierarchy, had kept a great distance, not to say abyss, from the marginal people, closing their eyes to the problems which afflicted the people who supposedly were their parishioners."[111]

García's study found the diocesan clergy to be few in number, not very open to dialogue, without a spirit of renewal, and ideologically hidebound. Rather than being concerned about the problems of the faithful, they were mainly interested in their own economic well-being.[112]

Thus they were not giving true priestly witness. There were exceptions among the young priests, who assimilated the Vatican II ideas very well and lived in constant tension with the hierarchy, who tried to put the brakes on their impetus for renewal.[113]

García found that the parish priest had little to do with the faithful. He was notably absent from community life and could only be seen at Sunday Mass, which was attended by very few. The liturgy, preaching, and apostolate in most parishes were untouched by Vatican II. Most Sunday sermons were monotonous, lacking the message of Christ and seeming to be insufficiently prepared. Catechetics was reduced to mere memory work without understanding.

There were three categories of weddings, thus contributing to the class spirit and making distinctions between bourgeois and proletarian weddings, the Church of the rich and that of the poor. García urged examination of fees and stipends which for so long had created the image of money-minded priests and parishes. His characterization, he noted, ap-

---

110. Cited by Foroohar, p. 185; J. E. Arellano, *Breve Historia,* p. 101.

111. Cited by González Gary, p. 234.

112. In an interview in December 1988, García told me that this was the perception of many of the lay respondents.

113. J. E. Arellano, *Breve Historia,* p. 102.

plied equally to parishes staffed by religious and diocesan priests. J. E. Arellano commented dryly: "There were very few parishes which were developing projects of social promotion."[114]

As for the religious clergy, García found that most of them were working in schools. They were isolated and did not work much as a team. They were quite individualistic, working more for their order or congregation than for the Church. There was very little cooperation with the diocesan clergy, with a lack of confidence evident between the two groups. They were also criticized "for living very comfortably in their spacious schools and parish houses," according to García.

As for women religious, the study found them to be even more isolated. "Nevertheless," García observed, "a certain apostolic spirit is beginning to be seen within the various teaching congregations. They are showing social concern, insisting that their students get involved in social promotion." J. E. Arellano noted that this tendency would grow in the ensuing years.[115]

Another concern of the pastoral conference was to analyze the injustices of Nicaraguan society and to urge a Christian response. This was expressed in the paper delivered by Dr. Ernesto Castillo of the Central American University, who in the years before the triumph would become a member of "the twelve"—a group of respected citizens who openly supported the Sandinistas. After describing the many ills of the nation, Castillo concluded that "a traditional structure sustains underdevelopment. Therefore, the solution is not technology, but rather a revolution or destruction of the structure."[116]

Castillo argued: "The question is not whether there will be revolution or not, but rather, a peaceful revolution or a violent one. As Christians we cannot but desire a peaceful alternative. Christ came to bring us peace, and people by nature want peace for themselves and others. However, the revolution could be peaceful only if the ones maintaining the system let the necessary changes happen peacefully, and only if they recognize the rights of the poor masses. But if the ones in power oppose

---

114. Ibid., pp. 102-103.

115. Ibid., p. 102.

116. Cited by Foroohar, op. cit., p. 188.

change, the people will have to use force . . . to implement the much-needed changes."[117]

He urged Christians in Nicaragua to do everything possible "to achieve a political reform which has been prevented by a despotic and corrupt government, [a regime] which doesn't tolerate any renovative action of the Church which would condemn its crimes, frauds, robberies, and injustices." He specifically urged the hierarchy and priests "to fulfill their great obligation, to condemn the dictatorial regime, to abstain from collaborating with a government sustained by violence, and to demand that all privileged classes give their firm support to the oppressed sectors in their struggle for political change."[118]

These conclusions "proved to be too difficult for the conservative Nicaraguan Church to digest," commented Foroohar. "The hierarchy was not even prepared to criticize the existing unjust social system, let alone propose a revolutionary alternative." Bishop Pablo Antonio Vega of Juigalpa emphasized that Castillo's "points of view, judgments, and proposed options are his own" and that the presentation was not a "doctrinal exposition or a pastoral statement." Vega asserted that "it is not a priestly function to predetermine the political options of a layman."[119]

At the end of January 1969, Castillo and several others launched *Testimonio*, a monthly newspaper which would criticize both the Somoza regime and its clerical allies. The second issue presented the controversy between the paper and the bishop of Granada over the very expensive new National Theater. While the bishop considered it a response to "modern demands," *Testimonio* denounced it as an outrage "in a country where thousands of children do not have grade-school education because of scarcity of resources."[120]

In the fourth issue *Testimonio* criticized a large sector of the clergy for their complete identification with the government, an identification which was described as collusion, submissiveness, respect, and servility. The article noted that this sector included priests with military rank who en-

---

117. Ibid.

118. Ibid., p. 189.

119. Bishop Vega's comments cited by Foroohar, op. cit., p. 190.

120. J. E. Arellano, *Breve Historia*, p. 107.

joyed duty exemptions on luxury imports, made an ostentatious display of cars and houses, and lent money at usurious rates.[121]

The seventh issue was devoted to the problem of land ownership, which *Testimonio* labeled "a situation of institutionalized violence." The eighth issue included a strong criticism of U.S. imperialism: "an 'underdeveloped' country is one that is oppressed by a dictatorial government (generally military) sustained, directly or indirectly, by U.S. imperialism. . . ."[122]

At the end of 1969 *Testimonio* stated: "We sadly recognize that we have not moved ahead very much. The Church as institution continues to be compromised by its alliance with power and money and is far from living out the gospel poverty and authenticity necessary for its mission. Most Nicaraguans continue to call themselves Christians, but every day the differences between rich and poor grow deeper."[123]

In their sixteenth issue the editors expressed their feeling of frustration and isolation, noting that the movement for Church renewal was not sufficiently united. And with its eighteenth issue, in November 1970, the prophetic paper shut down its presses. Luis Rocha, who was one of the editors of *Testimonio* and who is now with *El Nuevo Diario*, told me that one of the main problems was lack of financial support.[124]

Somoza-era theology never seemed to ask: Why, after all, was Jesus condemned and executed? The death of Jesus, "separated from his human life and from the historical causes of his human death, was turned into a myth to quench the latent flames of struggle in a class society under the yoke of imperialism," wrote the author of an introduction to the proceedings of a seminar held in Managua in September 1979 under the auspices of the Jesuits' Instituto Historico Centroamericano (Central American Historical Institute).[125]

---

121. Ibid., p. 108.

122. Ibid., p. 110.

123. Ibid., p. 112.

124. My interview of Luis Rocha, May 1989.

125. *Fe Cristiana y Revolución Sandinista en Nicaragua* (Managua, 1979), p. 16.

"Moreover, the creed of Christians in our country paid no heed to the epic liberation struggle of Exodus in which God called a people to forge their own national history," the introduction continued. "The God in circulation like religious money to be used by the oppressed masses was the God of the philosophers, the God of the ideologists of the bourgeoisie, a mixture of an all-powerful God outside history and of a God mysteriously responsible for the established order of exploitation and domination, an eternal God immunized against the long-suffering of human beings. The God who was preached was not the God known in the struggle for justice on earth but a God known in the religious confines of the church, a God who has nothing to do with the building of a just society."

Given such preaching, it is no surprise to learn, as I did from a Delegate of the Word in the rural outskirts of Masaya, that in some churches the rich, who were the special friends of the pastor, had their reserved pews (with padded kneelers) up front.

Part Three

The Church in the 1970s

5

Christian Base Communities

"Christians should experience the communion to which they have been called in their 'base community.' . . . The Christian base community is the primary and fundamental nucleus of the Church. . . , the initial cell in the Church body, the focus of evangelization, and presently the prime mover in human promotion and development"
—Latin American bishops at Medellín, Colombia, 1968.[1]

"The Christian base communities, which in 1968 were just beginning, have matured and multiplied, above all in certain countries, so that now they are a source of joy and hope for the Church"
—Latin American bishops at Puebla, Mexico, 1979, #96.

"The first thing we discovered was that the parish is not just the church building or a certain geographical space with all its inhabitants, but rather a community of brothers and sisters who visit one another, pray together, and help one another in hard times, as members of the Family of God," said Félix Jiménez, the keynote speaker at the 20th anniversary celebration of St. Paul the Apostle parish in Managua in 1986.[2]

---

1. Documento Pastoral de Conjunto, #10.

2. Talk published in *Nicaragua: Trinchera Teologica*, editors G. Girardi, B. Forcano, J. Ma. Vigil (Managua: Centro Ecuménico Antonio Valdivieso, 1987), pp. 63-82. For a discussion of Christian base communities in Nicaragua and Brazil, see Arthur F. McGovern, S.J., *Liberation Theology and Its Critics* (Maryknoll, N.Y.: Orbis, 1989), Ch. 10, "A New Way of Being Church." See also Phillip Berryman, *The Religious Roots of Rebellion: Christians in Central American Revolutions* (Maryknoll, N.Y.: Orbis, 1985).

This parish has a unique historical distinction in the growth of the Nicaraguan Church: it was the birthplace of the country's *comunidades eclesiales de base* (Christian base communities).[3] An exact translation of the Spanish term would be "ecclesial (Church) base communities," which brings out the important Church aspect in the communities' self-identity. Because of the awkwardness of the literal translation, however, I will use "Christian base communities," hereafter abbreviated as CBCs.

These communities were so named because they are "primarily comprised of lower-class, grassroots people, the base of society, as opposed to the pinnacle of power in the social pyramid . . . . The members of these communities," Leonardo Boff noted, "are generally poor and from the base of society (the lower classes) and from the base of the Church (the laity)."[4]

The CBCs, usually initiated by priests and sisters but designed to outgrow their dependence on "professional" religious personnel, constitute perhaps the most significant and well-known phenomenon in the Church throughout Latin America.

The Managua-based coordinating committee of the communities published a small leaflet summarizing their development, which began in the late sixties. "Almost all the communities started out with a strongly spiritual approach, involving bible study and personal and family conversion." Many Christians who joined the revolution had their first experience of a vital, personal, and meaningful Christian life in the charismatic movement.

Miguel Ernesto Vijil, for instance, who was from a wealthy family and who became Minister of Housing after the triumph, said at a seminar in September 1979: "Jesus Christ for me was the beginning of my participation in this revolutionary process, because he was the one who gave me the strength to change a whole set of internal structures that I had, which had been imbued in me since childhood and which in a way had turned me into a self-centered man. With Jesus Christ I have learned to focus on others. That personal change is what has given me the ability to participate in the revolutionary process. This is a change which will never end; I will be involved in it all my life."[5]

---

3. See Father Uriel Molina, ibid., p. 57.

4. *Church: Charism and Power*, trans. by John W. Diercksmeier (New York: Crossroad, 1985), p. 125.

Many others have told me that as they became more familiar with scripture and with the teachings of the Church in Latin America, they came to the conclusion that they had to move beyond an individualistic spiritual experience and beyond the comfortable small group to reach out to the poor and to fight the structural sins of injustice.

"But time and the lived experience of oppression required us to move forward, and so we developed *cursillos* (short courses) of conscientization to analyze our reality," the communities' leaflet continues. "We in the Christian base communities were led by our faith to take part in prophetic actions denouncing the injustices and announcing that God wanted liberation for the oppressed. Because of our faith and the Christian commitment which the gospel demands, we got involved in various ways in the pre-insurrectional phase and in the final insurrection. In love we accepted the risk and reality of giving our lives for others and for the transformation of Nicaragua."

Roots in Vatican II Renewal

The Second Vatican Council (1962-65), with its emphasis on the role of the laity in the Church and the social responsibility of Christians, would have a profound impact on the Nicaraguan Church (as well as the rest of the Church in Latin America). The year 1966 has special significance for the Church in Nicaragua. Father Ernesto Cardenal founded the Christian community on Solentiname, an island in the southern part of Lake Nicaragua. The biblical reflections and courageous actions of this community would become an inspiration not only to other Nicaraguans but throughout the world.

The same year saw the death of the Colombian priest-revolutionary Camilo Torres, whose words and witness challenged the Latin American Church. And 1966 was the year of ordination of Gaspar García Laviana, a Spanish priest who would come to Nicaragua in 1970 and later follow the example of Camilo.

In 1966 Father José de la Jara, a young Spanish priest teaching in the seminary in Managua, asked the archbishop to assign him to develop a

---

5. *Fe Cristiana y Revolucion Sandinista,* op. cit., p. 116.

pilot project for the pastoral care of about 60,000 people in an east side district of Managua. St. Paul the Apostle parish was created, with Father José as pastor. Given the large number of people within the parish boundaries, pastoral teams made up of lay people as well as religious were organized and gradually began to form Christian communities. Maryknoll Sister Maura Clarke, who along with three other women was murdered by troops in El Salvador in 1980, worked in this parish, and people still speak of her unique ability to bring out the best in them.

The goal was that each member of the community be known and loved as a brother or sister and helped when in need. Obviously such a community could not consist of thousands of people, and so the parish was divided into sub-groups, each having representation in the parish council. In this way it could avoid the danger of being merely a "sacramental gas station," in the words of one of the subsequent pastors who spoke during the celebration.

Lay people took courses to become Delegates of the Word and could then preside over celebrations of the Word, with or without the presence of a priest. The development of lay leaders has been especially necessary in the Latin American Church, due to the acute shortage of priests and religious. In many areas, if a Christian community wishes to meet and pray together more frequently than once every few months, it has to develop ways of proceeding which do not involve total dependence on the presence of a priest. But the growth of lay leadership and responsibility is seen as a very positive development in itself, consistent with Vatican II theology, and not just as a necessary stopgap measure. (Priests with a sensitivity to the role of the laity are warmly welcomed in the CBCs, not only to celebrate Mass but also to take part in discussions and projects.)

"It was striking to see how workers, nearly illiterate, interpreted the bible and applied it to their reality," noted Jiménez. "They were planting the seed of what would be theology of liberation in Nicaragua."

Some of the speakers at the anniversary celebration told how women have played an important leadership role in the communities and how this has contributed to the growth of their sense of dignity and equality. One woman said that previously she had spoken with priests only in the confessional and was afraid of them. But in the small community where the priests treated her with respect and care she was able to be at ease in communicating with them, and they and the rest of the community helped her to become a lector and public speaker. This kind of personal liberation has been experienced by people in many communities.

Marriage renewal was also an important program at St. Paul the Apostle. Jiménez stressed the role played by San Miguelito parish in Panama (staffed by priests from Chicago) in the formation of the people of St. Paul the Apostle.[6] In 1966 the pastor and several married couples went from Managua to San Miguelito to study the "Family of God" movement. Jiménez noted: "The influence of San Miguelito on the parish of St. Paul, in terms of pastoral religious contents and ways of organizing, was such that the first encounters at St. Paul were directed by priests and lay people from San Miguelito."

The Chicago priests developing new forms of ministry in Panama and the people of their parish also had a significant influence on Father Ernesto Cardenal and his community in Solentiname through St. Paul parish in Managua. Ernesto explained: "This is how that commentary, *The Gospel in Solentiname*,[7] began. Father de la Jara, an outstanding Spanish priest, came to Solentiname and suggested to us that I should not be preaching the gospel but rather that the people should discuss it and comment on it. He had done that in his parish in a working-class neighborhood of Managua. I told him that I thought the peasants, who are very quiet and introverted, would not speak. He told me that the workers were also introverted but that in his parish they gave extraordinary commentaries on the gospel. He had learned this method of commenting on the gospel from the parish of San Miguelito in a working-class neighborhood of Panama where a priest from Chicago had arrived with this method. Because of his advice, I tried it, and right away the people began to comment very well on the gospel."[8]

The biblical discussions in the Solentiname community were based on a deep personal spirituality. Ernesto Cardenal has described his relationship with God in simple but striking terms: "God is beyond every idea or imagination. But for me it is an experience, something lived, and a love. It is a union." He recounted that it was God who led him to the Trappist

---

6. See also Father Uriel Molina, *Nicaragua: Trinchera Teológica*, p. 57.

7. Maryknoll, N.Y. : Orbis, Vols. 1-4, 1977 and other years.

8. *Nicaragua: Trinchera Teologica*, p. 339. For a description by St. Paul parishioners of a visit to Solentiname, see *ibid.*, p. 68.

monastery in Gethsemani, Kentucky, where Thomas Merton was his novice director. Later, God drew him to Solentiname, he recalled, and then to participation in the Sandinista movement for liberation, and to being Minister of Culture. "I see all that as a single path," Ernesto said, "obeying a will."

His personal love of God is joined intimately with his commitment to justice. "I believe that God is the force behind social change and revolution. In other words, the force of love. And that is the biblical concept of God." He went on to describe the kingdom of God as the kingdom of justice. There is also a strong cosmic dimension to Ernesto's experience. "I believe that God is the author of everything. And in a certain sense He is immersed in His work, not removed from it."[9]

From my experience with many Delegates of the Word and members of CBCs, I can say that their spirituality, with its deep social dimension, is just as authentic and personal as that expressed so well by Father Cardenal. Soon the members of St. Paul the Apostle parish began reaching out to other parts of Managua and Nicaragua, helping in the formation of communities.

Sunday Celebrations

Jiménez recalled that "the most important moment of the week was the Sunday Eucharist," characterized mainly by a spirit of joy as reflected in songs and smiles. People brought their bibles and took part in the "dialogue homilies" which in those days scandalized some priests and laity. In 1968 the community, inspired by the Panamanian Mass which they had heard in San Miguelito, composed the "Nicaraguan People's Mass," which Father Uriel Molina has described as "the first expression of revolutionary liturgical music."[10] (The "Peasant Mass," composed in 1975 by Carlos Mejía Godoy, with the help of Ernesto Cardenal and the Solentiname community, speaks more dramatically of social conflict as part of the process of liberation.)

---

9. As cited by Margaret Randall, op. cit., pp. 111-112. This book provides valuable reflections by members of the Solentiname community and by members of the student community in the Riguero neighborhood of Managua at Father Uriel Molina's parish.

10. *Nicaragua: Trinchera Teológica*, p. 352.

Discovering the Bible and Social Responsibility

At the anniversary of St. Paul the Apostle parish people spoke of their discovery of the bible and the impact this had on their lives. Reading and discussing Exodus, for instance, helped them to see that injustice and exploitation are *not* according to the will of God. Thus they broke with a passive, immobilizing spirituality and began to see their role as co-creators with the Lord of a more human social order. Several people noted that they had become socially active and politically concerned more through their shared reflection on scripture than through any exposure to sociological or political analysis.

However, their social action gradually led them to see the need for a broader political and economic analysis and for a concrete political movement to free Nicaragua from the brutal and corrupt Somoza dictatorship. In 1968 the Latin American bishops met at Medellín, Colombia. "For the first time in the history of the Church magisterium," said Jiménez, "a religious document speaks about the *integral liberation* of the person and about economic, social, and political change of structures."

"Medellín speaks of God working in the history of our people when they advance from less human to more human conditions," he emphasized. "This means that the liberation of Latin America is sacred history and that the Christian's task is to struggle for that—for social change, for a new society. And all of this is part of Christianity, just as going to Mass, receiving communion, and reading scripture."

Cursillos (literally, "short courses") began to be called "cursillos of conscientization." That word, used frequently in Latin America, was defined briefly by the speaker as "becoming aware of what is happening from the standpoint of Christian faith and relating biblical themes to the socio-political reality of the country."

As the formation of lay leaders became a top priority, the parish council selected 12 people to take a three-month course including topics such as Bible, Christology, Church History, Medellín, and group dynamics, taught by Fathers Uriel Molina, Fernando Cardenal, and others. Later, others were chosen to take similar programs. Those who finished the course would then go to other areas to form communities or assist in the development of communities in the parish.

As the connection between faith and real life was emphasized and acted upon, some people dropped out of the community, claiming that "religion and politics don't mix." Others left because they were afraid to make a social commitment, and others because their economic interests were tied in with the Somoza dynasty.

Uriel Molina noted that the meshing of the option for the poor with involvement in the revolutionary struggle "meant conflict not only within the Church but with the middle and upper classes who were also working for the overthrow of the Somoza dictatorship but who could not see the option for the poor as a class option."[11]

Leonardo Boff has expressed the dynamism of the Latin American CBCs: "They are gaining a critical and transforming consciousness in terms of both the Church and society. They are taking history into their own hands, becoming masters of their own destiny." The community assists in the discovery of the dignity "inherent in the human person, a dignity debased by the ruling classes, which is leading to an emphasis on the rights of the poor."

Members of these communities discover that they have rights as citizens, "that they are the image and likeness of God, children of the Father, temples of the Holy Spirit, and destined for complete personalization at the end of history, yet also anticipating that reality in the present through their practices of freedom."[12]

Taking Action

Around 1970 the first large mobilizations of people against increases in bus fares and in prices of basic foods came out of this parish. The CBCs, much like community organizations in the United States, were dealing with neighborhood or city-wide problems.

The Sandinista National Liberation Front (FSLN) had been founded in 1961, and gradually over the years its leaders and activists were not only making their presence felt but were establishing themselves as committed, honest Nicaraguans dedicated to the removal of what they saw as the root of the country's social problems: the Somoza dictatorship, which monopolized most of the nation's resources and brutalized the poor in order to keep them down.

---

11. Op. cit., p. 60.

12. *Church: Charism and Power*, p. 118.

"Around 1974," Jiménez noted in his summary of parish history, "most of the young people in the parish youth movement were getting involved in an organized way with the Sandinistas in the revolutionary struggle; and their participation has been very important, both before the 1979 insurrection and in the revolutionary process since then. Many of them took leadership positions in the people's organizations and in the government."

From 1975 on, religious discussion in the parish communities was not just some abstract theorizing about human rights, justice, and equality. Rather, people spoke about Nicaragua in particular and about the *cause* of the injustices: the dictatorship.

When a member of Somoza's National Guard coldly shot and killed a boy who was climbing over a stadium wall to see a baseball game, the people of the parish organized a silent march in protest. When the Capuchins denounced the National Guard's slaughter of peasants, the people of St. Paul the Apostle parish echoed the protest in the capital city. And during Lent 1979, just a few months before the July 19 triumph over Somoza, the parish Way of the Cross procession was seen as "subversive" by the dictatorship and was patrolled by heavily armed troops. The local historian summarized: "Many members of the parish communities worked closely with the Sandinista movement, offering their houses as 'safe houses' or as places to keep weapons, literature, and medicine."

After the Victory

After the overthrow of Somoza, CBC members continued to join or support the Sandinistas in building a new Nicaragua. Since the Sandinistas have a special commitment to the poor, it was not surprising that the members of the poor communities generally supported the new government, while the upper-class Christians (including some members of the clergy and hierarchy) saw their self-interest threatened by the "revolutionary process." An older woman who spoke during the anniversary event said: "Politics and Christianity go together, since both have to do with promoting the common good and social justice."

Between speeches and songs during the anniversary celebration, people would call out the now familiar refrain: "Between Christianity and revolution there is no contradiction!" That statement has been demonstrated empirically in the people's experience. Christians, and their community structures and networks, played an integral part in the revolution against the Somoza system and continued to take an active role with the revolutionary government in the construction of a new, more just society—and in the defense of that society against U.S. hostility.

Jiménez identified three factors as contributing to something of a letdown in the parish's rhythm of work since the triumph. First, "many of the founding leaders of the parish dedicated themselves completely to the activities of the revolution" because of the urgent needs of the new government. Jiménez did not consider this in itself as something negative; these leaders felt they were fulfilling their Christian commitment in their work for a new society, and this left little time for much involvement in the Christian community.

Secondly, the two priests who had worked with the St. Paul communities since 1968 left the priesthood and got married. Jiménez said that this had a negative effect on the organization of the communities.

The third problem was the Catholic hierarchy and especially Cardinal Obando, who "have tried to deprive the Christian base communities of their legitimacy, accusing them of being the 'popular Church,' saying they are separated from the Church and allied with the Sandinista government. Obando was never in agreement with the pastoral approach of the parish, although during the dictatorship he allowed the priests and the communities to function.

"However, after the triumph, as happened with other parishes and priests in Managua, the conflicts became clear," Jiménez continued. "In its twenty years of existence, the parish was visited twice by Obando, once in 1974 and again in 1982. The second visit included a 'dialogue' with the parish council which brought out the basic differences."

According to Father Uriel Molina, in the post-triumph phase "some Christians lost the faith, considering it perhaps a step in the learning process toward higher levels of awareness. Others preferred to put a veil around the religious problem because of the conflict between the revolution and the hierarchy. Others found that some pastors would not talk seriously with them as legitimate members of the Church. For being Sandinistas they were considered as separated from the Church." But, he added, the vast majority of the members of CBCs "continue being Christians and continue actively in the reconstruction of the country.

"Little by little the hierarchy kept isolating the communities, without building any bridge toward those Christians who were involved in the revolutionary structures. Rather, the hierarchy centered its attention on spiritualistic movements and utilized popular religiosity in an effort to get an anti-revolutionary consensus in the Christian masses."[13]

In closing, Jiménez noted that in spite of all these problems the St. Paul communities have continued in the political and ecclesial struggle. In a recent interview Fermín Torres, long-time community member, echoed Jiménez's reflections about Obando's antipathy toward the base community. In Fermín's view, Obando has frequently confused the community's option for the poor and its commitment to class struggle with "fomenting class hatred." Fermín emphasized that the struggle, both during the seventies and eighties, has not been motivated by hatred but rather by love for the poor and even for the rich, who need to be confronted with the truth and liberated from their position as exploiters.

After four years of talking with government officials, soldiers, the families of those who were killed and those who returned alive, students, and others representing a broad range of the Nicaraguan people, I share the conclusion that hatred is not a significant part of the equation, and I believe that pointing the finger at this alleged class hatred is an unfair argument which is really aimed against a radical option for the poor.

The late Nora Astorga, Nicaragua's ambassador to the United Nations, also brought this out clearly in an interview seven months before her death in February, 1988: "The Nicaraguan people are not bitter. We're not a people who hold resentments for a long time. Above all, there is love and generosity in this country. That does not mean we aren't firm when we need to be, but there isn't a lot of bad feeling among us."[14]

A striking example of forgiveness and compassion was given in August 1990 when a member of a CBC in Managua, whose son had been killed by the contras four years earlier, hosted a blind ex-contra for a weekend visit with her and her family. Other members of the same CBC, who conduct a bible class with the blind and arrange home visits, had asked her if she would receive the former contra soldier; she had previously received other blind persons. During the visit she had many good

13. *Nicaragua: Trinchera Teológica*, p. 61.

14. *Envío*, April, 1988.

conversations with her guest but did not talk much about the war. She did learn that he had been blinded by a grenade about four years ago.

A beautiful painting on a wall in Masatepe, about twenty miles south of Managua, depicts a body riddled with bullets and proclaims: "From this grief it is not hatred or vengeance that is born but the will to defend the resurrection of Nicaragua."

In Closing

Father Molina began his presentation to the large assembly with a litany of Christians who gave their lives in the insurrection and in the war against the invading contras. After he pronounced each name, the people responded "presente!" Father Molina noted that faith really means following Christ in a practical way and that it was that kind of faith which led the people during the dictatorship to get involved in the protest against increased bus fares and in the "transformation of society."

He observed that the Christian task was to consolidate the revolution and to continue to build the new Nicaragua. For the Christian, he added, every political order, including that of the Sandinista revolution, is relative and must be criticized and corrected when necessary. A similar attitude is expressed by the Jesuits, who describe their task as giving "critical support" to the revolutionary process in so far as it promotes the well-being of the poor majority. Thus Christians, while participating in the revolution, avoid absolutizing or idolizing it.

The day's events came to a close in the parish hall. The walls were lined with pictures of members of the parish who had been killed in the struggle against Somoza or against the contras. U.S. citizens in the congregation were particularly moved as the people sang, with commitment and determination: "No pasarán"—"They shall not pass." We sang, because we believed in the justice of Nicaraguan self-defense. But we sang with heavy hearts, because the song's "they" referred to young Americans who, we felt, might be sent to kill Nicaraguans and die in an invasion.

6

Father Gaspar García Laviana

"I have decided to write to you, as my brothers and sisters in Christ," Father Gaspar García Laviana stated in a public letter to the Nicaraguan people, "to share with you my resolution to join the underground struggle as a soldier of the Lord and a soldier of the Sandinista Front for National Liberation." The 37-year-old Sacred Heart missionary, who had moved to Nicaragua from his native Spain in 1970, wrote his message at Christmas 1977. Within a year he would be killed in battle as a soldier in the struggle against Somoza.

Father Gaspar's letter, published in early 1978, continued: "When I came to Nicaragua, I dedicated myself with a passion to my apostolic work, and I soon discovered that the hunger and thirst for justice of this crushed people whom I served as a priest demanded more than the consolation of words—it required action."

After describing some of the injustices which were rampant in Somoza's Nicaragua, Gaspar declared that the revolutionary war led by the Sandinistas was a just war as far as his Christian conscience was concerned "because it represents a struggle against a state of things which is hateful to the Lord our God. Somocismo is sin," he continued, "and liberation from oppression is liberation from sin. With gun in hand, filled with faith and love for the Nicaraguan people, I must fight to my last breath for the advent of the reign of justice in our country." In the letter he mentioned the traditional teaching of the Church justifying insurrection in the case of a clear and prolonged tyranny which seriously violates the fundamental rights of the person and which does not yield to non-violent efforts.

Gaspar's public letter, as well as another message addressed to bishops and priests, had a profound impact on the people, significantly enhancing the status of the Sandinistas and their struggle. Gaspar, who became a capable and respected commander in the revolutionary army, was killed in battle on December 11, 1978. The massive uprising of all sectors of the people continued to grow; and on July 19, 1979 the Somoza dictatorship, which had taken 50,000 lives in its efforts to retain power, was defeated.

Identification with the Poor

Gaspar, ordained in 1966, had spent some years as a worker-priest in Spain before beginning his missionary work in Nicaragua. Reminiscing about Gaspar, his friends and associates recall his deep love for the people and his conversion to a simple life style in keeping with gospel poverty. Ricardo Zuñiga, who worked closely with Gaspar and who is now the director of the Center for Agricultural Education and Promotion (CEPA), told me that Gaspar "had a great compassion for people and desire to help. He would readily deprive himself in order to give to others in need."

Father Fernando Cardenal, who also joined the Sandinistas and played an active role in the revolution (though not directly in the armed struggle), told how he took Gaspar's place several times at his parish in Tola when Gaspar's work with the peasants took him to other parts of the country. "I was surprised by the Franciscan poverty of his residence, if we can call it that, in Tola. Gaspar took on himself the sufferings of the people. His love for the peasants was beyond measure, and after much effort he came to identify with them."[1]

Gaspar's identification with the poor prompted him to share the administrative responsibilities of his parish. "For the financial management of the parish," Zuñiga noted, "he organized a lay council, which paid him a very modest salary—less than that of a grade-school teacher. Of course, a priest always receives help from other sources, like families in the parish. Still, the small salary was a sign of his commitment to live poverty. What's more, he shared everything with people in need, and that showed his detachment."

This detachment, Zuñiga added, enabled Gaspar "to be free of the upper classes, who usually try to buy the priest. He was never afraid to

---

1. Father Cardenal, Minister of Education in the Sandinista administration, is quoted in *Gaspar Vive,* an excellent biography of Gaspar written by his fellow Sacred Heart missionary, Manuel Rodriguez Garcia, published in Costa Rica in 1981.

denounce the rich for their injustices." As Gaspar began to speak out against the injustices he saw, he was subjected more and more to the label of "communist" and troublemaker.

Identification with the Struggle of the Poor

The young priest, who was especially outraged by the lack of medical care for the peasants under Somoza, regularly spent his mornings visiting the sick in his parish and in the hospital in Rivas. There he became a close friend of two of the doctors but was a threat to others by his constant discussion of the inadequate state of health care in the region.

He complained about the scarcity of medicines, about the illegal selling of medicines at inflated prices, and about the lack of medical attention for his people. Gaspar's biographer wrote: "He did not hesitate to name those responsible: a government which keeps the country in a state of slavery and which looks only to its own enrichment while forgetting the needs of others. Among the medical personnel," the author added, "were some openly professed Somocistas who accused Gaspar of being a dangerous rebel. But this did not stop him: he knew that a hospital should take care of the sick, and he would see to it that it did so."

When he was pastor of San Juan del Sur, he returned home one night to learn that an elderly man in a mountain village was in urgent need of medical care for tetanus. Gaspar drove through a heavy downpour over roads which are barely passable even when dry to find the man in critical condition. During the slow and difficult trip to the hospital, Gaspar watched the man die at his side.

"Is it because they live in the mountains," he blurted out upon arrival at the hospital, "that they have to die like rats, without any kind of care? Aren't they persons like us? Why don't they have medicines, or doctors, or teachers? Why can't they read and write? Why are they so abandoned?"[2]

---

2. In a February, 1988 article on the revolution's accomplishments as well as persistent problems in health care since 1979, Envío noted that during the Somoza era "in terms of available medical attention, the gap between the city and the country became ever greater. A large part of the peasant population was obliged to travel 80 kilometers or more to the closest city, because there were no health centers of any kind in the countryside. . . . In 1979 there were only 1,311 doctors, more than 80% of whom worked in urban areas."

Carlos Fonseca had described peasant conditions in this way: "The terribly big landowners monopolize the bulk of the land. For most of the year, the peasants kill their hunger with salted corn. They know nothing of cooking oil. If they have a cent, they spend it to eat boiled beans. And if some time they buy a little meat, they make soup out of it. In the department of Matagalpa, more than 100 people have died of hunger in a few days. A frequent sight there is that of children with bellies swollen by hunger, with a yellow look on their faces. In the town of Darío . . . there is also night blindness caused by lack of proteins. Goiter is endemic there. In other regions of the same zone, there have been cases of collective insanity caused by hunger. Whole population groups eat only old corn, because it is cheaper, but it has lost all its nutritional value, and so they become crazy with hunger and start killing one another. This happened in the little settlement of Malacahuás."[3]

Gaspar expressed his love for the peasants, and his outrage at the way they were oppressed, in a number of poems, which were published in 1979 under the title, *Songs of Love and War,* the first book published by the revolutionary government's Ministry of Culture. In a poem called "Peasant," he wrote:

Your premature death from quiet hunger hurts me.
Your bones wrapped in thirsting skin hurt me.
Your downcast eyes plowing the earth hurt me.
Your ignorance and eternal sadness hurt me.
But what hurts me most of all is your powerlessness.

In a poem entitled "Anguish," he wrote:

The anguish of my soul
is not calmed by the rosary, the Mass, or the breviary.
My anguish is mitigated
by schools in the valleys, the peasant's well-being,
freedom in the streets, and peace on the country paths.

In his introduction to the book, Father Ernesto Cardenal, then Minister of Culture, wrote: "These are poems filled with love, and by the same token poems filled with anger. This is the poetry which led him to the guerrilla struggle and to death."

---

3.   *Carlos Para Todos*, by Eduardo del Rio (RIUS) (Managua, 1987), p. 69.

In another poem Gaspar spoke of "the young face, the old features, the fresh skin, the dead eyes" of the 14-year-old prostitutes in the town of Tola. The exploitation of these young girls was another factor in Gaspar's decision to take up arms, according to Zuñiga. "He was a priest who struggled against exploitation and injustice," Zuñiga said. "Perhaps the worst and most visible sin, as far as he was concerned, was the kidnapping of young girls for prostitution, some even less than 14 years of age."

Zuñiga explained how the system worked. The owner of a house of prostitution would go to a poor family and offer the young girl what appeared to be an honorable job. Then they would sell her some nice clothes, on credit at high interest. When the girls got deeper and deeper into debt, which they could never pay off, they were told that they could not leave with their debts unpaid. They were trapped.

"Of course there were laws against this," noted Zuñiga, "but since Somoza's army was behind it, no one dared to bring charges in court. That would have been to challenge one of the key businesses of the Somoza regime and to expose one of the nerve centers of the system's corruption."

From the pulpit Gaspar denounced the houses of prostitution and their National Guard partners and protectors. One day in February 1977 two young girls escaped and told Gaspar that other minors were in the house of prostitution and that whenever they disobeyed the owner their feet would be burned or they would be whipped. With this testimony Gaspar went to the local judge, who went to the house with the intention of closing it down and fining the owner. He could only accomplish the latter, since National Guard troops stationed themselves at the door to keep the place open.

Gaspar continued his public denunciations of the situation, but in vain. Some time later the Guard helped move the establishment to another town. In attacking this system of vice and corruption, the priest was making himself a public enemy of the dictatorship. "The control of the bars and houses of prostitution," explained Zuñiga, "was really one of the most important businesses for the National Guard. For instance, in the seventies, the municipal commander of the port of Corinto, which abounded in houses of prostitution, had a monthly income of U.S. $30,000, due to bribes and commissions. Other top military positions, like Managua's chief of police or the nation's chief of mining, were also big prizes which Somoza bestowed on his friends so they could get rich quickly."

Throughout the first half of 1977 Gaspar received threatening phone calls and noticed that he was being followed by Somoza's forces, who accused him of being associated with the Frente Sandinista. In March a National Guard colonel reminded Gaspar of the recent assassination of Salvadoran Jesuit Father Rutilio Grande, telling the priest that he should be careful, that the "mafia" could kill him, and that he should get some protection. "From that moment I knew clearly that the Guard was preparing my death," Gaspar said. For several years he had been assisting the Sandinistas by carrying messages and helping to transport people in addition to educating and organizing the peasants. Camilo Ortega, whose brothers Daniel and Humberto became Nicaragua's President and Minister of Defense respectively, frequently stayed at Gaspar's rectory, where the revolutionary leader was known as a visiting seminarian. Camilo, like Gaspar, would not live to celebrate the triumph of the revolution.

The Need for Structural Change

Gaspar had come to the conclusion that helping the poor with their individual problems was a band-aid approach which only helped the corrupt social and political system maintain itself in power. He devoted himself to educating the peasants to the *systemic* nature of their problems and to their need to get organized to change the unjust structures.

Father Fernando Cardenal told me of his communication with Gaspar in late 1976. "In Tola, where he was pastor, we had a long conversation during a National Congress of Peasant Delegates of the Word," Father Cardenal said. "He told me that in his pastoral work he had been in contact with the Frente Sandinista. But that was not the subject of the discernment process he was involved in, since he had no question about the justice of the Sandinista cause. Rather, he was deliberating as to whether he should agree to the Frente's proposal that he join in the armed struggle."

How to Help the Revolution?

Cardenal recalled: "I simply advised him to make a profound analysis of the pros and cons of the issue from the point of view of his Christian commitment. At no point did I suggest what he should do but simply tried to help him to see the issues clearly. On the one hand, a priest joining the armed struggle would be a call to conscience for many Christians. Father Camilo Torres had done this in Colombia," Cardenal pointed out, "and was killed in 1966, but a similar commitment here in Nicaragua would have a much stronger and more immediate impact on Nicaraguan Christians. The Somoza dictatorship had done everything possible to present the Frente's struggle as something bad, something in which a Christian could not be involved. A strong argument against this would be the fact that a priest would join the struggle.

"On the other hand," Cardenal continued, "such a decision would have the disadvantage of limiting his pastoral work by removing him from the areas where he had been working." Gaspar's decision was to join the armed struggle. "One of the main reasons," according to Cardenal, "was that, as he told me, every day he felt more and more pressured by the Guardia due to his denunciations of injustice and more and more limited in his pastoral work. He opted for the path of armed struggle as his way of continuing to work for the liberation of the peasants."

Cardenal explained why it was important for a priest to join the armed struggle. "The bishops never wrote one word in favor of the Sandinista revolution or in favor of the Frente. Some of their letters contained clear denunciations of the violations of human rights by the dictatorship, but in these letters they also said that they were against all violence, no matter where it came from. That statement is completely unfair. They were putting the criminal violence of the oppressor on the same level as the revolutionary violence of those who defend themselves, the poor who take up arms to defend their own lives, their community, and their just cause of liberation." He added: "In June 1979, shortly before the start of the final offensive, the bishops justified the people's uprising against Somoza, but they did not speak directly about the Frente."

Gaspar's public letter, cited at the beginning of this chapter, helped the Frente Sandinista "gain its citizenship papers throughout the country," according to Gaspar's biographer. "The people were very interested in the contents of the letter." The biographer also noted that through Gaspar and many other priests and thousands of other Christians who got involved in the struggle the Church gained the respect of the Sandinistas. Gaspar's decision influenced countless young people to join the Frente.

"We Grew Together in Our Understanding"

Father José Alvarez Lobo, O.P., came to Nicaragua in 1967 and began teaching in the Dominican high school in Chinandega. He was also superior of the Dominican community. "I met Gaspar through some meetings on national pastoral planning," Father José recalled in a recent interview, "and I got to know him more personally through our involvement in a rural pastoral group which met once a month.

"Gaspar at first was involved in development projects financed from abroad, thinking he could do something by building schools and health centers. But little by little he realized that this was not the way, that it was just putting a little paint on a house that was falling apart. That approach was not contributing to the elimination of the causes of the problems but rather to the toleration of those causes.

"Little by little, through his contact with the people, the workers, the poor, seeing their hunger and how they were mistreated, he concluded that armed struggle was the only way to change the situation. He came to that decision painfully but considered it consistent with his love for the poor and his desire for their liberation. I believe that only those of us who lived that situation here in Nicaragua can understand what it was like.

"Gaspar was a happy and jovial person, and also frank and open. He was enthusiastic and an extrovert. When he saw young people dedicated to others and risking everything in the struggle for liberation, he knew that was the way. He recognized that it was not always those who called themselves Christians who were the most generous and committed."

Father José spoke of his and Gaspar's disappointment over the official Church's lack of involvement in the real struggles of the people. "Gaspar felt that to work for a different kind of society in Nicaragua would be to work for a purification of the Church—a purification from its love of the government, from its love of power, from its love of its personal advantages. Thus the Church could become the servant of the people. I personally believe that we Christians in the Church are not exempt from culpability for the maintenance of social, economic, and political conditions which cause the majority to suffer; we share in this social sin. Thus we had to take risks and make sacrifices to change this situation. Gaspar was very much aware of this. He gave himself to the liberation of the people not only out of love for the people but also out of love for the Church.

"In December 1978," Father José recalled, "just a few days before his death, Gaspar told me that he had never felt so much a priest, so much a builder of the new society and the new person, as then. He told me that after the triumph, which he expected soon, he would continue to be a priest, though not in the traditional parish setting. He would work with the peasants in cooperatives. He continued to be motivated by faith and love."

"He Chose to Struggle"

Father Jesús Martín Mateo, S.J., came to know Gaspar in the National Rural Pastoral Team. In October 1977, when Father Martín was returning to his native Spain for further studies after serving as director of CEPA, he went to say good-bye to Gaspar, "who was a close friend and co-worker. Another friend who was with me took a picture of Gaspar with a monkey on his neck, hugging Gaspar! When Gaspar was killed, this friend sent me the picture. I made three enlargements of it. It demythologizes Gaspar, showing him as a human being more than other photos do.

"When I was getting ready to leave Gaspar, with the jeep running, he said: 'You'll see, you'll see; this is at the caramel point (boiling point).' I said: 'No way; the tiger is well,' meaning that Somoza had all power in his hands. It seemed to me that Somoza had the support of the U.S. government, the whole Guard behind him, and also the bourgeoisie who were allied with him economically even though they dissented politically. I felt it would be a long process. Gaspar said: 'You don't know, you're not on the inside of all this.' At that time Gaspar was involved in the preparation of the attacks on San Carlos and Rivas; however, the weapons which were coming were intercepted in Costa Rica. Gaspar was implicated and felt that his involvement would be exposed. He left the parish and joined the forces of the Frente.

"About a year before, he had come to CEPA, saying that he wanted to talk about something. 'I'm going to the mountains,' he announced. 'It's impossible for me to work any more; they've closed the doors on all sides; they've destroyed everything I've tried to do; there's no other way except to take up the gun.' We tried to discourage him from that, pointing out that by joining the armed ranks of the Frente he would implicate the other members of the Team. We felt that as long as we had a platform in which to work above ground that was much more effective.

"Gaspar, in his own impulsive and outspoken way, said that we were cowards, but we remained firm in our position, and he in his. Gaspar, like others from his region of Spain (Asturias), was enormously generous and felt passionately about things. He was the most demanding among us as to the measures which must be taken. Often we had to calm him down, urge him to show a little patience and not act precipitously. Indeed, his strong feelings were accompanied by good sense; with us he blurted things out but then thought them through. He was very selfless and very consistent. He did not see the step he had to take as an attractive one but was convinced that it was necessary.

"It is clear that Gaspar did not take up the gun because of any attraction to violence; he had lost hope in the ordinary channels of change. He had tried to organize a union of fishermen but could never get authorization for it; he had also met with all kinds of obstacles in trying to form a cooperative. What kind of obstacles? The sheer force of the National Guard. He saw that legal and political methods were going nowhere and that the liberation of the people could come about only through armed insurrection, which can be seen as a form of self-defense against the violence of the system.

"When he tried to get a young girl out of a house of prostitution and denounced the situation on the radio, he came into conflict with the interests of the National Guard, who labeled him a subversive and communist. The only choice he had was either to give up and leave or to struggle. He chose to struggle. That decision required great courage. Because he was so committed to the people, he took on this enormous risk, which was also the risk of being misunderstood. He knew that many would not approve of his being a priest and revolutionary soldier at the same time; they would consider him crazy."

In the Ranks

After Gaspar had become a revolutionary soldier, he wrote to his brother, Silverio, in Spain: "In spite of the fact that I am in a war, I am at peace with myself and I am happy. There is nothing as worthwhile as giving one's life for the liberation of the people. The commitment I am making is what Nicaragua needs at this time, not just sermons. God wants the liberation of all people, and throughout history he raises up situations and people to fulfill their destiny. As a priest," he added, "I must lead my people, and in a situation as desperate as this there is a need for people to stand up against evil. You can be sure that my witness will encourage many."

Daniel Ortega first heard about Gaspar through his brother, Camilo Ortega. The priest and the future president did not meet, however, until Gaspar had joined the revolutionary army. On the first anniversary of the triumph of the revolution, Daniel Ortega, then coordinator of the governing council, spoke of Gaspar as a martyr of the revolution and a "model of self-giving and love for the people." Daniel spoke for several minutes about his priest friend: "He told me once: 'the injustice suffered by the people hurts me more than if the Guardia beat me.' If I refer to him in all my speeches," Daniel continued, "it is to indicate that the Nicaraguan revolution is Christian, has a Christian vein and Christian leaders. The Church is a necessary part of the political process of liberation, and it should continue to help that process.

"The presence of Gaspar in the Sandinista ranks strengthened Sandinismo and gave support to the Christian spirit which Sandinismo has always had and which Sandino always had. We must remember that Sandino himself spoke of faith as a liberating element and wrote against priests who preach resignation to the people. We all came to love Gaspar as a brother," Daniel concluded, "and we could communicate easily with him."

Gaspar was also fondly remembered by another Sandinista government official, the late Nora Astorga, who served as Nicaragua's ambassador to the UN until her death on February 14, 1988. Nora worked with Gaspar in the Sandinista struggle, and they became close friends. In an interview in July 1987 she spoke of her friendship with Gaspar, recalling especially how he and others in the ranks took care of her when she was about to give birth to her third child.

She remembered Gaspar's words to her: "It is possible that I may not live to see the victory. But if you cry when I die, I will be very annoyed. The only thing I will permit is that once in a while you bring me some little flowers, but they must be from the countryside. And don't go around crying; I will always be present in this struggle."

Nora was so shocked at the news of Gaspar's death that she could not really take it in. Nor could she cry, until two years later when she and her son visited Tola. Nora sat in the church where he had been pastor, and she visited his tomb, and the long pent-up grief burst forth in tears. "I don't know how many hours I cried," she recalled. "I know that Gaspar would not have liked me to cry, but," she paused, "that was very unfair of him to give me that order!"[4]

Gaspar's Impact

When the Frente Sandinista issued its official statement on religion in 1980, it recognized the important role Christians had played in the insurrection: "Christian patriots and revolutionaries are an integral part of the Sandinista revolution. . . . The participation of Christians, both lay and religious, in the FSLN and in the Government of National Reconstruction is a logical consequence of their outstanding involvement with the people throughout the whole struggle against the dictatorship."

The statement indicated that many FSLN members were motivated by their faith and that many of these shed their blood for the cause. "Special mention must be made," the statement continued, "of the revolutionary work and heroic sacrifice of the Catholic priest and Sandinista militant, Gaspar García Laviana, in whom Christian commitment and revolutionary consciousness found the highest degree of synthesis."

Gaspar's biographer conducted a survey among the peasants and workers who knew Gaspar. "Who was Father Gaspar?" he asked. One response was: "He was a prophet of the 20th century. He announced the Good News and denounced injustices. He made the people of Nicaragua see clearly the dignity we have as children of God."

In response to the question, "What do you think of his work as a priest?" one person answered: "He brought us peasants together and helped us to see what brotherhood means. He showed us how to work and act in a communitarian way. Thanks to him the communities work together now."

---

4. *Envío*, Vol. 7, No. 82, April, 1988; also published in *Tayacán*, Feb. 22, 1988.

Zuñiga observed: "He never stopped thinking of himself as a priest. He saw his involvement in the armed struggle as part of his priestly ministry and as part of his work for a more human world."

In a poem written to Gaspar, Bishop Pedro Casaldáliga wrote: "Let's have a talk, Gaspar, you and I, alone. Let's open our hearts, Gaspar, with no other witness than the Love which you are now living face to face. The big landowners were the ones who crushed your poor and who are crushing my people. It is the gospel itself, exasperated love, which burned in your hands more than the strange gun, my brother. Tell me, Gaspar, what would you do if you came back?⁵

Gaspar Lives

Gaspar lives on in the hearts of the people and of the revolutionary leaders, as an example of Christian dedication to liberation. But there are also many tangible results of the revolution for which he gave his life. Streets, plazas, organizations, and even whole neighborhoods are named after him. The hospital in Rivas, where he had a few doctor friends who worked with him but where he was usually shocked by the inadequacy of health care, was named after him, as was a rehabilitation center in Managua where most of the disabled are casualties of the war against the U.S.-backed contras. Health care, especially in the rural areas, became one of the top priorities of the revolutionary government. In the early years after the triumph, infant mortality was dramatically reduced, and polio was eliminated thanks to the involvement of the people themselves in massive vaccination campaigns.

Gaspar's concern about prostitutes did not die with him. In one of its first decrees the revolutionary government banned any use of the human body for selling products, so that advertising in Nicaragua could not contribute to the notion that the human body is a thing to be exploited. While prostitution has not been abolished completely, the phenomenon is nowhere near as rampant as in other Latin American countries, and the Sandinista government did not protect it and share in its profits as Somoza's regime did. In fact, the government worked with the Antonio Valdivieso Ecumenical Center in a social and educational program to help prostitutes get a new start in life.

---

5. *El Vuelo del Quetzal*, op. cit., p. 148.

But the basic social injustice which led Gaspar to become a revolutionary was the inequitable distribution of land. During the Sandinistas' tenure in office more land was redistributed in Nicaragua than in all the other Central American countries combined. Twenty percent of the nation's land belonged to Somoza; when he left, that became government property and was put to use as state farms or cooperatives. Large landholdings which were not being used productively were given to the peasants, either in the form of cooperatives or individual plots.

As Gaspar wrote in his letter explaining his decision to join the Sandinista revolutionary army, "the hunger and thirst for justice of this crushed people whom I served as a priest demanded more than the consolation of words—it required action." He took action to bring a revolutionary government into power; and the actions and policies of that government, with all its limitations, were a tangible response to the people's hunger and thirst for justice.

In April 1990, between the election and inauguration of Violeta Chamorro, a group of Christians in Tola participating in a nationwide fast for peace and for the disarming of the contras told a *Nuevo Diario* reporter: "The ideals of Gaspar are more important now than ever."

7

The Hierarchy, Somoza, and the Sandinistas

A New Archbishop

Miguel Obando y Bravo, who had been auxiliary bishop of Matagalpa for two years, was named archbishop of Managua in 1970, the same year Father Gaspar arrived in Nicaragua from Spain. Both clerics would begin to speak out against injustice and oppression, but they would have very different journeys. The priest would make the hard choice to become an active revolutionary; the archbishop would adopt a reformist stance.

In May 1970 the new archbishop was feted with a party thrown by Anastasio Somoza Debayle, the son of Anastasio Somoza García. In the presence of several bishops, the dictator toasted the new archbishop: "On behalf of the National Guard, I offer homage to a most illustrious son of Nicaragua, who has the same ideas and the same mission as we have, the difference being in our uniforms. Both organizations are moved by one sentiment: love of all Nicaraguans."

In response, Obando gave profuse thanks for the event in his honor, recognizing "the most noble Christian values which inspire each one of the members" of the National Guard and praising the Christian "fervor" of Somoza. He spoke of the "fraternity" which could be felt as they "broke and shared bread together, as family," and of the closer "bonds of friendship" being formed that night. "Our word of encouragement goes out to the Army of the Republic," Obando assured them, "and its high officials, that they may always remain constant in their duty, looking out for the safety, freedom, and peace of the country."

He urged the soldiers to "imitate Cornelius and his companions, St. Paul's companions in struggle in the preaching of the gospel—soldiers both of Catholic action and of earthly military service. As such, they proved that, without betraying conscience and while giving to Caesar what is Caesar's and to God what is God's, it is possible to be a perfect Christian while being a perfect citizen."[1]

Denouncing Injustice

Toward the end of 1970 the new archbishop began to address social issues: "As part of its mission of liberation the Church must denounce injustices and commit its members to the peaceful transformation of unjust structures, so that people can become free to forge their own destiny."[2]

The archbishop quoted parts of Pope Paul VI's encyclical *Populorum Progressio* on the legitimacy of revolutionary insurrection in cases where there are clear abuses of fundamental rights and of the common good, but he also quoted Paul VI in Colombia in 1968 denying that armed revolution was a proper means to remedy the evils of society.[3] Foroohar observed that "Obando's vacillation between legitimizing the use of violence by the people to bring down the structure based on *institutionalized violence*, and condemning any kind of violent revolution, continued throughout his pastoral letters and public statements."[4]

In 1971 Somoza gave Obando a luxury model Mercedes-Benz; when a wave of protest broke out, the archbishop returned the gift, thus putting an end to the policy of such gift-giving by the dictatorship to the Church, "at least at the level of the archbishop."[5]

Later that year Somoza engineered a pact between his Liberal Party and the Conservatives, characterized by J. E. Arellano as a "political maneuver to perpetuate the socio-economic domination by those parties, with a guarantee of repression by the National Guard." Obando refused to take part in the official ceremony celebrating the new arrangement.[6]

---

1. Novedades, Managua, May 9, 1970, as cited by González Gary, op. cit., pp. 249-52.

2. J. E. Arellano, *Breve Historia*, p. 123.

3. Ibid., p. 124.

4. Op. cit., p. 204.

5. J. E. Arellano, *Breve Historia*, p. 123.

6. Ibid.

In 1972 Obando, in a speech at the national university, discussed various aspects of the question of violent revolution. Although he himself expressed his option for non-violent means, he recognized that in certain circumstances it is possible to justify armed insurrection.[7] (In 1989 Obando recalled this speech "on active non-violence in the style of Gandhi and Martin Luther King" as one which led Somoza "to think that I was a communist.")[8]

The bishops differed in their views of Somoza's regime. "A small group was overtly pro-Somoza," according to Foroohar. "On the other end of the spectrum stood Archbishop Obando y Bravo, an outspoken anti-Somoza figure. However . . . Obando always kept his distance from the radical opposition led by the FSLN."[9]

In their 1971 and 1972 pastoral letters, the bishops of Nicaragua began to speak of the political responsibilities of Christians and the need for structural change. Philip J. Williams attributes this step forward to "a fairly complete generational change which occurred between 1968 and 1972 within the episcopal conference, signalling the exit of the 'old guard' and the entrance of 'new blood.' Of the nine bishops in 1968 only three remained bishops in 1972. Four new bishops were ordained during this time, leaving a total of seven bishops in 1972."[10]

The devastating earthquake which destroyed downtown Managua in December 1972 helped to convince the Church and other sectors of the cruel corruption of the regime, as relief assistance was shamelessly pocketed by Somoza and his cronies. During the social turmoil following the earthquake, the archbishop, "although maintaining and even intensifying his criticism of Somoza's regime, modified his position on social revolution significantly and carefully kept his distance from radical revolutionary groups advocating armed struggle. . . ."[11]

On the first anniversary of the earthquake, the hierarchy celebrated a commemorative Mass in Managua's central plaza, in front of the now unsafe cathedral. During the Mass, with Somoza present, the Christian

---

7. Ibid., p. 125.
8. Interview of Obando in *La Cronica*, May 24-30, 1989.
9. Op. cit., pp. 212-13.
10. Op. cit., p. 27.
11. Foroohar, p. 216.

base communities "made their presence felt. . . . Hundreds of signs, brought secretly into the plaza, displayed anti-Somoza slogans. Somoza got up and left."[12] The event brought out the deep division within the Church between the moderate hierarchy and the prophetic Christian communities.[13] "They were united in being against Somoza but separated by their strategies," noted González Gary.[14]

In April 1974 Obando issued a statement complaining that capitalism had told the Church to "stay in the sacristy and busy itself with private life, preach resignation and patience, focus exclusively on the after-life, and take care of the afflicted. But it should stay well out of the social and economic area, acknowledge its incompetence in such affairs, and preach that the established order, the classes as they exist, the prevailing structures and the political order in power reflect God's will for man."[15] Obando called that mentality "old and outdated," reminding his readers that "the Church can never be politically neutral."

The bishops showed their lack of political neutrality in their pastoral letter of August 1974. They affirmed the "right to dissent," describing this as the right "to object in the name of conscience against injustices and arbitrariness. . . ." However, they did not miss the chance to cast aspersions on the FSLN: the right to object "is no unreasoned insurrectional or armed protest, but a coherent, conscience-founded claim." After citing this, Foroohar commented: "Supporting the political opposition as 'a coherent, conscience-founded claim' as opposed to 'unreasoned insurrectional or armed protest,' the bishops drew a clear line between the political position of the Church hierarchy and the radical policies of the FSLN, a line which was also drawn by the private sector opposition by excluding the FSLN from their efforts to organize a broad coalition against Somoza (UDEL—Democratic Union for Liberation)."[16]

12. González Gary, op. cit., p. 269.

13. Dodson and Montgomery, "La Iglesia en la Revolución Nicaragüense," in NICARAUAC, April-June, 1981.

14. Op. cit., p. 297.

15. Foroohar, op. cit., p. 238.

16. Ibid., pp. 241-43. See also González Gary, p. 271.

The Christian Revolutionary Movement

Along with the Christian base communities, the student-based Christian Revolutionary Movement also took a radical stance toward the dictatorship. The seeds of the movement were planted in the late sixties when progressive religious and priests, in their youth ministry particularly in the schools, began to promote the approach of "seeing, judging, and acting." Youth groups would apply this method to Nicaragua in the light of the bible.

In July 1970 students at the Jesuit-run Central American University (UCA) occupied the campus. While the protest was directed at campus issues (e.g., greater student participation), it took on a political character since the Jesuit rector, Father León Pallais, was strongly pro-Somoza and had the support of his cousin Somoza. Father Fernando Cardenal, S.J., who had been appointed vice-rector three days earlier, publicly stated that the demands were just; he was fired shortly thereafter and began teaching in the national university. When the demands of the strikers were met, large numbers of Managua residents (including Pedro Joaquín Chamorro of La Prensa) joined in a Mass on campus celebrated by Fathers Fernando Cardenal, Uriel Molina, and Edgard Parrales.

In Father Cardenal's judgment, the event was historically important in that for the first time Christians took an active role in the student movement. Several months later UCA students launched a hunger strike demanding that Church officials be allowed to see some recently arrested political prisoners in order to ascertain their physical condition and that the prisoners be brought before a judge for due process; Father Cardenal accompanied the students, about 100 campus leaders, in the cathedral downtown. The priest has described the protest as "the first public political action by Christians, as Christians." The bells were rung every fifteen minutes; members of the Christian base communities, the Cursillo movement, the Christian family movement, and many others came to express support. Many other churches throughout Nicaragua were occupied in support of the fasters. Somoza gave in, releasing student leaders and Frente Sandinista members.

Giulio Girardi considers the non-violent occupation of the cathedral as "perhaps the event which touched off the active and collective participation of Christians in the Nicaraguan liberation process."[17] The hierarchy threatened to suspend priests involved in the action if they did not leave the cathedral immediately. On October 7 Obando and four other bishops condemned the act as "disrespectful of the dwelling place of the Most Blessed Sacrament."

"We have never been nor will we ever be in agreement with torture and violations of human rights and dignity," the bishops said. "But it is another thing to say that we are obliged to protest publicly in each case. . . ."

The bishops went on to speak of a just wage and to cite the social encyclicals' teaching "that the work contract should be softened such that workers participate in a certain way in the ownership, administration, and profits. How beautiful this doctrine is," they exclaimed, "but misused it would lead to a revolution and we would be called communists. It cannot be put into practice without a slow process of work and persuasion, directed above all to our legislators."[18]

A few days later hundreds of people signed an open letter to the bishops, protesting their harsh condemnation of the cathedral action and noting that Jesus placed the good of human persons above sabbath laws and temple regulations. In their letter the bishops had said that they could no longer keep silent about the cathedral protest; the people commented that the bishops had kept silent throughout a long series of human rights violations by authorities but now felt obliged to speak out against a "just and peaceful protest" in defense of human life.

The people recognized the respect due to churches but defended action in defense of human persons, "the living temples of God" who were being desecrated by torture and massacres (citing 1 Cor. 3: 16-17). They insisted that the Church must "apply the norms of the gospel in each concrete case, including individual cases." They strongly objected to the slowness and gradualness proposed by the bishops in working toward justice for workers, saying that this made justice a "very distant and almost impossible dream."[19]

---

17. *Revolución Popular y Toma del Templo* (Managua: Centro Valdivieso, 1989), p. 9. Girardi goes on to develop a series of theological meditations bringing out the significance of the occupation of the cathedral.

18. Letter cited by Girardi, ibid., pp. 85-88.

19. Ibid., pp. 93-97.

Father Ernesto Cardenal also wrote an open letter to the bishops, criticizing them for "wanting to remain in the good graces of the government" and likening their letter to the pharisees' charge that Jesus' cures had profaned the sabbath. "Aren't you forgetting," he asked, "that for Christians the presence of God is not enclosed in material buildings but rather the new temple is Christ and all of us as people make up the Body of Christ? You protest because the faithful have occupied churches, which are theirs because the churches belong to the ecclesial community; but you do not protest when the true temples of God are violated and profaned." Girardi put it this way: "The defense of the temple comes out of an ecclesiocentric theology; the defense of the occupation of the cathedral is the seed of an anthropocentric theology" (p. 206).

Reminding the bishops that the sabbath is for people, Cardenal said that their attitude was responsible for the growth of atheism. "The faithful must respect and obey the bishops," Cardenal said, "but the bishops must also obey the gospel and cannot do whatever they want." They are opposed to all change, he said, in the Church and in politics.

Bishops and priests "must be faithful to the gospel and rid themselves of all ostentation and wealth or appearance of wealth, and they should change their residences and cars and suits in order to be able to understand the need for change in society and in the Church. And in order to go along with those changes."[20]

The Christian student movement grew. In 1972 eight students (including Luís Carrión and Joaquín Cuadra) decided to live in a community in the working-class neighborhood of Riguero, where they were received by Father Uriel Molina, OFM, in his parish. In December 1972, in the midst of a severe drought which caused serious suffering especially for the peasants, preparations were being made for a highly commercialized Christmas celebration. Christian students saw this as "an insult to the Christ child who was born in poverty," Father Cardenal recalled, and about 120 began a "prophetic fast" in the cathedral to protest the seasonal display of luxury in a situation of acute poverty for the masses. "Christ came to liberate the poor," a large banner proclaimed, while the fasters demanded a "Christmas of equality for all" and the liberation of Sandinistas in prison. They were also protesting Nixon's bombing of

20. Ibid., pp. 98-100.

Vietnam. The cathedral was severely damaged when the December 23 earthquake devastated Managua; the protesters escaped unharmed.

A few months later Father Cardenal, who had moved in with the students in Riguero, and a large number of student activists met in a retreat house and founded the Christian Revolutionary Movement. As members deepened their revolutionary commitment, the vast majority joined the Frente Sandinista (as individuals). Cardenal emphasized three important aspects of the Movement. First, its members were motivated by their faith to enter the struggle. Secondly, they were from wealthy bourgeois families but chose to insert themselves in the poor neighborhoods, in the factories, and in the peasant communities. Members of the Christian Revolutionary Movement took part, through CEPA, in the formation of Delegates of the Word (such as Edgardo García, who became the head of the Sandinistas' peasant organization) in many regions of Nicaragua. The third characteristic of the movement was that it afforded its members the opportunity to study Marxism "in real depth," as Cardenal put it.

"In the Frente's struggle, the most important sector was the students," noted Cardenal, "and in that sector the Christian Revolutionary Movement had gigantic importance." Many of its members took leadership positions in the revolutionary government: for example, Luís Carrión became vice-minister of the Interior and then head of the ministry of the economy, and Joaquín Cuadra and Alvaro Baltodano became members of the Army high command.

"The hierarchy opposed the Movement," recalled Cardenal. "Obando had a complete lack of trust in us but could not stop us since the Movement was an independent student initiative."

Archbishop as Mediator

In December 1974 Obando served as mediator between the government and the Sandinistas after the latter took a number of top Somocistas and other dignitaries hostage during a party at the home of José María (Chema) Castillo. The action, in which the party's host was killed, marked a significant escalation of the revolutionary struggle.

In his recent *Agonia en el bunker*,[21] Obando recalled the date, attributing considerable significance to it and to his own role in the events which were to unfold: "It was the night of the 27th of December, 1974, the date which our Lord Jesus Christ had chosen for this his servant to begin his participation as direct witness and mediator" in the beginning of the Somoza regime's agony. Obando had described his role as mediator in an earlier book, *Golpe Sandinista,* published in May 1975; that account is the basis for the following summary.

After agreeing to Somoza's request that he help, the archbishop visited the scene and learned the Sandinistas' demands: the publication of their political manifesto, the release of a number of political prisoners (including Daniel Ortega) and their safe passage along with the commandos to Cuba, and five million dollars.

In a discussion Somoza told Obando: "These kids (muchachos) are making a mistake. This problem will be solved today." The dictator wanted to take drastic action which would have resulted in a bloodbath.[22] Obando replied: "God willing that it be resolved without bloodshed! I know that five million dollars is a very large amount, but the life of a human being has no price."

When Somoza agreed to the Sandinistas' demands, Obando and the papal nuncio went to the house for the last time, accompanied by the Spanish and Mexican ambassadors.

The hostages were released at the airport, and their captors and the released prisoners boarded the plane along with Obando, the nuncio, and the two ambassadors for security. During the flight to Cuba, the Sandinistas said that they would like to speak with Obando, and they did so in turns.

(In August 1978 the archbishop would once again serve as mediator between the regime and the revolution when the Sandinistas took over the National Palace.)

Mediators, But Not Allies of the Revolution

The Sandinistas during this time did not consider the hierarchy an ally in the revolutionary struggle. In 1975, with repression growing, Christians in the FSLN began to try to remove the ideological roadblocks which the bishops had been putting in their path. "Faced with a situation of social sin, and in the midst of the class struggle which is developing in

---

21. (Managua: Archdiocese of Managua, 1990), p. 13.
22. My interview of Cardinal Obando, October 1989.

our people, we must clarify our role as Christians and contribute in the most effective way to the struggle to eliminate the structures which generate exploitation. . . .

"The high clergy," they continued, "have not taken up the role which they should as apostles of Christ. They are playing the game of the dominant classes inasmuch as they remain on the level of the most timid protests or, what is worse, justify the actions taken against the people."[23]

In 1976 the Capuchins publicly denounced the torture, disappearances, and other abuses committed by the National Guard against hundreds of peasants in northern Nicaragua, many of whom were Delegates of the Word educated by the Capuchins.

In January 1977 the Nicaraguan Bishops Conference stated in a letter: "The accumulation of land and wealth in the hands of a few continues to increase. Poor peasants are thrown off their lands. Many crimes go unpunished, and the number of persons detained without trial is growing." The bishops also denounced the regime's interference in the work of the Church and gave official voice to the specific charges which had been made by the Capuchins, thus provoking a tirade of verbal attacks and threats against Obando and some priests, especially in *Novedades*.[24]

Although the bishops used strong language in this letter, they distanced themselves from the radical opposition. Posing the question, "Can violence be the remedy on the path for a renewed change of our institutions?" the bishops denounced the "lawlessness" of "so-called freedom movements" which also "stir passions, lead to personal vendettas and end up as 'new lords' who take charge of government without regard for human rights."[25]

Conor Cruise O'Brien has summed up Obando's stance in this way: "Until 1978-1979—when Somoza was visibly collapsing and bereft of American support—the Archbishop seems never to have attacked him in the fundamental way in which he has attacked the Sandinista regime, or with the same accents of Holy War. To denounce abuses of power is not so radical as to deny the legitimacy of power."[26]

23. FSLN, "Por la incorporación de las grandes masas cristianas al proceso revolucionario," extracto de La Gaceta Sandinista, Managua, October, 1975, as cited by González Gary, p. 290.

24. J. E. Arellano, *Breve Historia*, p. 132.

25. Foroohar, op. cit., p. 343.

José M. Ruíz Marcos, in an article on "The Bishops of Nicaragua in Relation to Somoza" (*El Nuevo Diario*, August 18, 1986), commented on the bishops' January 1977 statement: "Thus the revolutionaries are implicitly compared with Somoza, and it is claimed that both are bad. This comparison in itself was an insult."

Ruíz noted that "outside Nicaragua much importance is given to the Nicaraguan bishops' position toward the revolutionary process, because it is thought that these bishops have moral authority from having struggled against the Somoza tyranny, supporting the revolution; it is thought that they are censuring the 'excesses' of a revolution gone astray.

"However," he continued, "their position against the FSLN and its revolutionary project is not new; it is the same as ever. It was the people of God who surpassed their bishops and left them behind in history, alone with their sage advice. In criticizing the FSLN and the revolution today, the bishops are following the same line they have since 1970."

On the basis of his analysis of official statements by Obando and the bishops' conference during the seventies, Ruíz concluded that the bishops were equivocating and overly respectful in opposing the tyranny, not presenting the prophetic message of Jesus. Many Christians considered the hierarchy's critical statements too little, too infrequent, too inaudible, and in some cases too late.

Commenting on the same statement by the bishops, in which they said that the acts they were denouncing "place the authorities at the margin of the nation's laws," Father Alvaro Argüello, S.J., recognized its importance in "de-legitimizing" the regime. The bishops' allusion to the FSLN as the potential "new lords," however, struck Argüello as revealing a "lack of clarity and an ambiguous attitude" on their part. They were "de-legitimizing Somoza but at the same time de-legitimizing the only group which was the historical alternative to the dictatorship."[27]

Betsy Cohn and Patricia Hynds characterized the Nicaraguan bishops as "ambivalent about Somoza. . . . They spoke out occasionally against Somoza abuses and in January 1977 even questioned the legitimacy of the regime. Yet, in July of that same year, they offered a solemn Te Deum and Mass for Somoza after his heart attack."[28]

---

26. "God and Man in Nicaragua," op. cit.

27. *Fe Cristiana y Revolucion Sandinista en Nicaragua*, p. 94.

In October 1977 Obando and two other bishops became members of a pro-dialogue commission. In opposition to the FSLN, the private sector was looking for ways to turn the dictatorship into a Western style democracy "with the least disruption of the socio-economic structure of the country."[29] In close contact with UDEL, the political arm of the bourgeois opposition, "and having repeatedly declared his support for the political program of the organization as opposed to the revolutionary armed struggle," Obando issued a statement on October 19 urging a search for "civilized ways" and for a national dialogue.

The timing of the statement was significant: it came just a few days after some successful armed actions by the FSLN, including the attack on the National Guard barracks in San Carlos in which some people from the Christian community at Solentiname participated as FSLN fighters, and just shortly after a pronouncement by "The Twelve" supporting the FSLN. Obando's statement fit into "the uninterrupted opposition of the Church hierarchy to the armed struggle and to a radical socio-political alternative to the existing structures, a policy that the bishops had pursued unanimously and clearly since the end of 1972."[30]

In a statement published in *La Prensa* on December 21, 1977, Obando asserted that "active non-violence permits [the people] to be revolutionary without renouncing Christianity, and to be faithful to Christ without renouncing the revolution."[31]

The hierarchy, like the private sector opposition, was critical of the regime but still recognized its legitimacy as a potential partner in dialogue. "On the other hand, siding with the radical opposition, the Christian base communities and the progressive sector of the Catholic Church didn't recognize the legitimacy of the regime and rejected dialogue with the dictator."[32]

In a letter issued on January 6, 1978, the bishops' conference spoke out against social injustices, repression, and official corruption. However,

---

28. "The Manipulation of the Religion Issue," in *Reagan versus the Sandinistas*, ed. Thomas W. Walker (Boulder: Westview Press, 1987), p. 99.

29. Foroohar, op. cit., p. 350.

30. Ibid., pp. 350-351.

31. Ibid., pp. 360-61.

32. Ibid., p. 364.

they also addressed the government in a clearly reformist tone, quoting from previous Church documents: "We honor your authority and sovereignty, respect your function, recognize your just laws, esteem those who make them and apply them; but . . . only God is great, only God is the source of your authority and the foundation of your laws. . . . It is up to you to be the promoters on earth of order and peace among men."

They also addressed the workers: "It is not hatred which saves the world. It is not only the bread of the earth which can satiate the hunger of man." Calling upon the youth to reject hatred and violence, the bishops urged all Nicaraguans "to work for the integral development of our people in a climate of harmony and freedom, where ruler and ruled are brothers in serving the common good." They supported the notion of a "sincere and realistic dialogue" to prevent further bloodshed."[33]

Seeing dialogue as a tactic of the bourgeois opposition to retard the movement for revolutionary change, the Sandinistas declared in a statement published in *La Prensa* on January 9: "The dialogue is a lie against the people, because it is posed at a precise moment when the dictator is fatally wounded."[34]

With the assassination of *La Prensa's* Pedro Joaquin Chamorro on January 10, 1978 the notion of dialogue became more and more unthinkable. On January 11 UDEL pulled out of the national dialogue and on the 24th, in the midst of the general strike promoted by the private sector, demanded Somoza's resignation. The next day the Conservative Party of Nicaragua joined the demand for his resignation, receiving support from *La Prensa*. Many other parties and organizations made the same demand.[35]

Following the assassination of Chamorro, the bishops' conference published a document calling on the government to investigate the crime and punish the guilty parties; they also warned the people not to turn to violence: "To those who seek to solve problems through weapons and blood, we say that these problems can only be solved in an atmosphere of justice and national concord. Ideas are fought with ideas. . . ."[36]

---

33. "Mensaje al Pueblo de Dios al Iniciarse el Año 1978."

34. Cited by Foroohar, op. cit., p. 370.

35. Ibid., pp. 371-378.

36. "Mensaje ante el Infausto Deceso del Dr. Pedro Joaquin Chamorro," January 10, 1978.

In an interview with *La Prensa* on January 27, Obando expressed his "complete support for the General Strike as a peaceful means to demand justice."[37] The next day the bishops' conference expressed its agreement with those who "try to solve the country's problems through the use of civilized means."[38] On January 29, 1978, the bishops' conference called for a "change of structure to benefit the people in general, especially the poor who are the privileged ones of Jesus."[39]

Somoza reacted to the general strike with increased repression. Street demonstrations were increasing, some of them involving violence, and many people were becoming radicalized. As the private sector with its reformist program lost ground in the leadership of the mass movement, the FSLN stepped up its armed actions, gaining strong support among the people. On February 2 the FSLN attacked the cities of Granada and Rivas.[40]

In an interview in *La Prensa* on February 9, Obando expressed his own option for non-violent means but added that "there are theologians and moralists who believe collective armed resistance is permitted" under certain conditions.[41]

On February 22 the bishops' conference spoke out against the use of churches for disseminating news reports banned in the press (a practice known as "journalism of the catacombs"). The bishops protested such "disrespect" shown to the churches, which are "destined especially by Consecration or Benediction for divine worship." Churches are "signs and symbols of heavenly realities, where the Most Holy Eucharist is celebrated and kept, where the faithful are made holy, and where the presence of the son of God is adored."

The bishops also expressed concern that "these situations promoted division among the faithful." They ended by noting that "the living temples of God are more important than temples of stone" but that the Lord wants the latter to be respected.[42]

---

37. Foroohar, op. cit., pp. 378-79.

38. "Mensaje ante la Grave Crisis de la Nación," January 28, 1978.

39. J. E. Arellano, *Breve Historia*, p. 135.

40. Foroohar, op. cit., p. 386.

41. Ibid., p. 387.

On February 24 theologian José Argüello wrote an open letter to the bishops expressing disappointment that at such a crucial time they did not "take a strong position with regard to the atrocious repression which was victimizing the people." Instead, "the bishops this time have taken a step backwards, contradicting what they said in their pastoral letter" of January 6, "and showing publicly that they are intimidated by the threats of the Somoza government." The bishops were taking the side of the government by "practically denying Nicaraguans their right to information."

In their January 6 letter the bishops had said: "We cannot keep silent when freedom of expression is not complete." On February 9 the archdiocese of Managua had spoken favorably of the "journalism of the catacombs." How is it possible, then, Argüello asked, "that from one day to the next this suddenly becomes an act of disrespect and even of profanation of the temple of God?" He attributed this change to "an excess of prudence which has nothing or very little to do with the gospel of Jesus."

The bishops had said that "we cannot reduce our mission as pastors to the sacramental or catechetical sphere." But now, Argüello said, they were "falling again into that obsolete theological position which separates religion and worship from the life of the people of God. . . ." Citing Matthew 12:3-4, he asked whether the bishops were not "going against the absolute freedom adopted by Jesus with regard to the Jewish traditions and norms which absolutized the value of the cultic regulations."

As for the danger to Church unity, Argüello said: "Unity based on the lack of commitment of the Church and its pastors is nothing more than a pious yawn by people who do not want to throw themselves into a continual gospel-inspired questioning of our traditional ways of thinking and acting." The bishops should have criticized the National Guard for specific violations of human rights and certain violations of church space, Argüello said. He chided the bishops for being "timid and insecure" in the aftermath of the assassination of Pedro Joaquin Chamorro, failing to say anything about the judicial cover-up. He ended by urging the bishops to get back on track in the defense of the rights of the people.[43]

---

42. Letter cited by Girardi, *Revolución Popular y Toma del Templo*, op. cit., pp. 89-90.

43. Ibid., pp. 101-105. Letter published in *La Prensa*, Feb. 28, 1978.

In March Obando went to Masaya to try to mediate in the uprising in the Monimbó neighborhood. In a meeting with young revolutionaries Obando was asked to provide them with weapons. "That is something I cannot do," he replied. "I am a pastor of the Church; and my mission is not to supply weapons which cause death but rather to seek solutions which lead to peace," he explained. "Secondly, with the money I have, the most we could buy would be a revolver," he added. He offered to talk to government authorities in an effort to find a peaceful solution, to get medicines for the wounded, and to work for the freedom of some prisoners.[44]

(By 1986, in very different circumstances, he would be helping the *counter*-revolutionaries get considerably more than a revolver—namely, $100 million in U.S. government aid. See Chapter 9.)

On August 2 the bishops' conference called for "a new socio-political order" and "reorganization of the Army." They still had some hopes to stop the violent revolution: "Centuries of Christian faith and cultural values should not be swept away in a wave of hatred and madness, in a collective self-destruction."[45] They rejected violence, noting that "the mission of the Church is distorted both by those who would confine it to the sanctuary and by those who take up the gun." The latter is "doubtless a reference to the public decision of some priests to join the FSLN, a decision which clearly showed support for the people's armed struggle."[46]

The bishops made a "veiled accusation," according to González Gary, against the FSLN by saying: "Nor can we hope that authentic liberation will come from systems which prescind from God and from respect for the most sacred values of the human person."[47]

On August 3 Obando and his priests' council suggested that Somoza resign "in order to promote the formation of a national government which, with the support of the majority of the people, would keep Nicara-

---

44. *Agonía en el bunker*, pp. 81-82.
45. "A Los Hombres de Buena Voluntad."
46. González Gary, op. cit., p. 332.
47. Ibid., p. 331.

gua from falling into the power vacuum and anarchy which is always a threat in the processes of change."[48]

But "the most significant document," in J. E. Arellano's opinion, was a letter sent to President Jimmy Carter in September 1978, signed by the priests' council of the Archdiocese of Managua and the board of the Conference of Religious (CONFER), asking Carter to halt all aid to the Nicaraguan government. "Even aid for educational and agricultural purposes," they said, "is used in the final analysis to repress the people."[49]

In September the papal nuncio showed that he was on friendly terms with the dictator. "His picture, lifting a glass of champagne with Somoza in a toast on September 15, 1978 (national holiday), while the dictator's planes were destroying Estelí, sufficiently symbolizes his nefarious work. With this kind of nuncio, the pope's prolonged silence about Nicaragua is explained, if not justified."[50]

On October 5 in Lisbon, Ernesto Cardenal criticized the pope for not denouncing Somoza's "genocide" and noted: "Throughout the long years of the dictatorship, all the apostolic nuncios have supported the Somozas. . . . The nuncio is a Somocista and was always pressuring the Nicaraguan bishops to refrain from opposing the dictator."[51]

Cardenal joined Carlos Tünnermann (also one of The Twelve, who became Nicaragua's Minister of Education and later ambassador to Washington) in sending a telegram to the pope in December: "Nicaraguan Catholics are surprised by the Vatican's silence in the face of the tragic situation of the people of Nicaragua . . . who have been atrociously massacred by the government of Gen. Somoza."[52]

With the armed insurrection escalating and the FSLN emerging as the leading force in the struggle, the non-violent strategy for a reformist solution was fading from the picture. However, "the imminent triumph of the Sandinistas and their overwhelming support among the Nicaraguans pre-

---

48. J. E. Arellano, *Breve Historia*, p. 136.

49. Ibid.

50. *Fe Cristiana y Revolucion Sandinista en Nicaragua*, p. 95.

51. González Gary, op. cit., p. 357.

52. Ibid., p. 361.

paring for a final offensive didn't change the archbishop's hard line on armed struggle."[53] In an interview with *La Prensa* on April 8, 1979, Obando asserted: "Violence seeks the death of the other, the gospel always seeks life; and violence is always unjust because it is against liberty." He advised Christians to take "the same attitude towards violence as towards any other evil and resist the temptation to justify violence."[54]

Bishops Justify Armed Rebellion

With the Sandinista triumph fast approaching, bourgeois groups were rushing to prove their revolutionary spirit and their long-time advocacy of radical socio-political change.[55] In Foroohar's interpretation, "the fervor also affected the Church hierarchy," and on June 2, 1979, the bishops' conference stated that the people's uprising was legitimate: "We are all hurt and affected by the extremes of revolutionary insurrections, but their moral and legal legitimacy cannot be denied in the case of obvious and prolonged tyranny which seriously violates the fundamental rights of the person and harms the common good of the country."[56]

In Foroohar's view, "the long-time anti-Marxist stand of the hierarchy finally was replaced with an unprecedented ideological tolerance in . . . a desperate attempt to secure a share for the bourgeois opposition in the upcoming revolutionary triumph."[57] Perhaps more importantly, the hierarchy wanted to secure a share for itself in the now inevitable revolutionary victory. Counsel and urging from many priests and religious also had a significant influence on the bishops' decision to publish their statement on insurrection.

From September 1978, "when the people launched their struggle to the death against the dictatorship," the bishops' conference had kept a "prolonged silence." In spite of the growing evidence of "genocide," the bishops waited ten months before issuing their statement on June 2,

---

53. Foroohar, op. cit., p. 410.

54. Ibid.

55. Ibid., p. 412.

56. "Mensaje al Pueblo Nicaragüense."

57. Op. cit., pp. 412-13.

"practically when the Sandinista people's insurrection was at the portal of certain victory."[58]

Many priests and religious, and vast numbers of lay persons, had been miles ahead of the bishops in supporting the revolution. "Making a clear connection between faith and revolution, the people insistently pressured the bishops to put an end to their vacillation. Also, the critical attitude of the Nicaraguan youth toward the hierarchy gradually bore fruit" in the June 2 statement.[59]

The Nicaraguan bishops "did not publish the statement because they supported the FSLN," noted Penny Lernoux. "Like a majority of the Latin American bishops, they belonged to the political center, wanting reforms but not revolution. As in Chile, the hierarchy had hoped for a moderate government run by the Christian Democrats or another party in the political center. But by mid-1979 it was clear that the only group that could beat Somoza was the FSLN and that a majority of the population supported the guerrillas. . . . The Nicaraguan bishops did not intend to repeat the experience of the Cuban hierarchy, which by opposition to the revolution removed itself from the process. They recognized the necessity of working with the Sandinistas, and that is why they issued their unusual statement in support of armed rebellion."[60]

Obando in Venezuela

In keeping with his political preferences, on July 17, just two days before the triumph, Obando was in Venezuela trying to work out a "solution" to the crisis which would preserve something of the old structure and prevent the Sandinistas from coming into power as the dominant force.[61]

More specifically: "On July 17, 1979, Archbishop Obando was in Caracas, meeting with Venezuelan Christian Democrats and members of Nicaragua's traditional political parties and large businesses, in the hope

---

58. González Gary, op. cit., p. 359.

59. Ibid., p. 370.

60. *People of God*, p. 368.

61. *Pax Christi* Report, October, 1981.

of forming a social-democratic force to replace the collapsing Somoza regime."[62]

As Irene Selser has pointed out, Obando was accompanied at that meeting by Enrique Dreyfus, then president of COSEP (the private enterprise council) and now Minister of Foreign Relations in the Chamorro government, and by Humberto Belli, now Minister of Education. Obando "wanted to expand the provisional five-person junta (Daniel Ortega, Sergio Ramírez, Moises Hassan, Violeta Chamorro, and Alfonso Robelo) to include a representative of the Social Christian Party (PSC) and Adolfo Calero, manager of Coca-Cola in Nicaragua and CIA collaborator since 1961."[63] Calero would later become one of the civilian directors of the contras. Leaders of the Social Christian Party told me that at the Caracas meeting there was talk of including a representative of their party in the junta.[64]

Sergio Ramírez has commented on that meeting: "Imperialism had decided to get all its players lined up in Caracas in a move against the FSLN, thinking that the moment for taking power was not yet imminent."[65]

Celebrating the Triumph

In spite of all the maneuvering against them, the Sandinistas emerged as the leading force in the revolution which overthrew the Somoza regime on July 19. Undeterred by the devastating effects of the war, the people celebrated their liberation with fiestas and liturgies. In Ciudad Sandino (part of Managua), the preface of the eucharistic prayer began: "We praise you, Father, because today more than ever you have been present in our history, and we give you thanks because we captives have become free. . . . So we want to celebrate this paschal day, this day of resurrection of your people."

---

62. *Envío*, December, 1983.

63. Irene Selser, *Cardenal Obando* (Mexico, D.F.: Centro de Estudios Ecumenicos, 1989), pp. 43-44.

64. My interview of PSC leaders, June 1989.

65. *Barricada*, June 30, 1984, as cited by González Gary, op. cit., p. 372.

Special thanks was given for Sandino, Carlos Fonseca, Gaspar García Laviana, and other "men and women you raised up among us." The Lord had given the whole people "courage for the struggle, unfailing generosity, and love for a better future unseen" and had "raised up the people from daily discouragement, making us believe in the hope and the possibility of a free country."

The prayer acclaimed Jesus as "the first of the captives freed, the humiliated one who was exalted, the repressed and censored rebel whose Good News we proclaim today." The prayer concluded: "Father, we commemorate the raising up of the one they wanted to erase from memory by killing. The quality of his life has remained engraved in us, and his resurrection shows us that there is reason for hope. In this celebration we express our faithfulness to his way. This is the sacrifice which pleases you and by which you save us. We hope to live with Jesus in the new land of freedom and love where we will give you glory forever. Amen."[66]

The victory, far from being a threat to people's belief or a rival for their loyalty, confirmed and nourished their faith. "There is no doubt that the revolution increased the religious fervor of the masses, their faith in the God of life who gives and defends life."[67] An article in *El Nuevo Diario* (September 28, 1980) noted: "Part of this new Nicaraguan culture is the religious experience of a God who emerges from the heart of the oppressed, with the oppressed. Here we have a new, living experience of a God, a Christ, who struggled alongside the oppressed and against the oppressors; the people feel that their victory is also the Lord's."[68]

In its October 1980 "Official Communiqué on Religion," the FSLN recognized the important role which had been played by Christians individually and even by the Church as an institution in the victory: "A large number of FSLN militants and combatants found motivation in the interpretation of their faith to join the revolutionary struggle and consequently the FSLN. Many of them . . . shed their blood to make the seed of liberation bear fruit. How can we ever forget our beloved martyrs . . . and the Delegates of the Word assassinated by Somoza's Guard in the mountains and so many other brothers and sisters?"

---

66. González Gary, op. cit., pp. 379-83.

67. Ibid., p. 377.

68. Ibid.

The FSLN noted that these people "knew how to fulfill their responsibility as patriots and revolutionaries without getting tangled up in long philosophical discussions." There was also recognition of the many Christians (lay persons and religious) who were not militants in the FSLN but "who preached and practiced their faith in relation to our people's need for liberation; included in this is the Catholic Church and some evangelical Churches, as institution, which took part in the people's victory. . . ."[69] González Gary noted that Bishop Manuel Salazar y Espinoza, president of the bishops' conference, took part in the July 20 celebration in the Plaza of the Revolution where the people welcomed the victorious leaders.

Summary

Father Juan Hernández Pico, S.J., has suggested that the religious experience of the Nicaraguan people is influenced much more by symbols than by the official theological and moral statements of the hierarchy.[70] He summarized the major symbols which helped Christians integrate faith and revolution: "the presence of priests in the student movements repressed by the Guardia; the occupation of churches to carry out hunger strikes as a way of applying religious pressure in defense of the political rights of revolutionary prisoners; the revolutionary biblical poetry of a priest-monk who founded a utopian peasant community (Ernesto Cardenal in Solentiname); young people from bourgeois families choosing to live in community in the poor barrios of Managua; popular religious songs to invoke the God of the poor and to free people's hearts from the yoke of slavery; priests who risked their lives denouncing the violations of the peasants' right to life; Delegates of the Word who brought together in their own lives the clandestine struggle and celebration of the faith; religious women who used their residences as safe houses and first-aid centers for revolutionary fighters; priests who offered their churches as communication centers [regular meetings were held in certain churches where reporters presented the otherwise-censored news]; one priest, Gaspar García Laviana, who became a military commander in the liberation

---

69. Ibid., p. 374.

70. "Religión y Revolución en Nicaragua," Cuadernos de Sociología, Universidad Centroamericana, Managua, Enero-Junio 1989, p. 70.

struggle and others who with noted lay persons and non-believers formed the revolutionary political Group of Twelve; and even an archbishop whose service as mediator in the liberation of revolutionary prisoners got him stigmatized by the official radio as 'comandante Miguel.'"[71]

71. Ibid., p. 73.

Part Four

Trends in the 1980s

8

The Church of the Poor in the Revolutionary Era

A.
Definition and Development of the Christian Base Communities

The Christian base communities (CBCs) of Managua have given the following self-description: "We are a group, not very large, of Catholics who live our faith and Christian commitment in a way which incarnates us in the life of the people at this particular historical moment. We want to be salt and yeast." Evident here is a recognition of the numerical limitations of the movement.[1]

In Managua, for instance, a city of about one million people, 22 grass-roots Christian (Catholic) communities form a well-organized network of support, planning, and cooperation. (There are a few other communities which are not part of this network.) The average size of the core group of committed members of each community is about fifteen. Similar communities exist in the various regions of Nicaragua; about 90 representatives take part in the annual national assembly of the communities.

---

1. The limited sampling taken by Roger N. Lancaster must have consisted in a disproportionate number of Church of the Poor supporters: "A substantial majority of the population in Managua's popular barrios affiliates with, identifies with, or supports the activities of the Popular Church to one degree or another. Of course, degrees vary, and the milieu may be characterized as a 'pluralism of religions'" (op. cit., p. 86).

Later, in his observations of two "economically marginal shantytowns" in Managua, he claimed that "roughly half of these two *repartos* adheres to the teachings of liberation theology" (op. cit., p. 103.) While terms can be defined variously, this seems a vast overstatement.

Chilean theologian Pablo Richard addressed the issue of size. "The Church of the Poor," he wrote, "does not look for great institutional power. Only part of the spiritual force of the Church of the Poor is made visible in the pastoral and evangelizing work of the CBCs, of the Christian militants, and of the centers and publications. But that spiritual power within the revolutionary process goes much beyond what is seen outwardly.

"The Church according to the Christendom model can be measured quantitatively: how many parishes, priests, sacraments, vocations, etc.," he continued. "But the Church of the Poor cannot be measured quantitatively. Its presence is felt and is powerful, but it cannot be measured by computers. One priest committed to the Church of the Poor in Nicaragua today has a much greater impact for liberation and evangelization than 100 spiritualistic and uncommitted priests. Prophetic testimony has spiritual power and great impact in a society which is in a revolutionary process."[2]

The very existence of the Church of the Poor, no matter what its size, as a sector of the Church committed to working critically within the revolutionary process is a sign to Nicaraguans and to the world that Christians can and do support the movement for radical change.

In Managua each community sends two representatives to the regular Monday night meetings of the network. In addition, each community has its weekly Mass plus a meeting for prayer, reflection, and planning. Furthermore, the communities encourage their members to be "salt and yeast" by taking an active part in civic life (neighborhood organizations, health and educational campaigns, volunteer work especially at harvest time or in neighborhood improvement, and other projects) and in this way to carry out their Christian social obligations. Since the communities supported the programs of the Sandinista government, they saw no need to set up rival social programs which might gain points for the Church in comparison with the Sandinistas. This perspective helps to explain the phenomenon presented so negatively by René Mendoza. After alleging that the Sandinistas did not deal seriously enough with local problems, he stated: "Nicaragua's Church of the Poor, too, emphasized the universal, the abstract, instead of looking at local reality. It spoke of the poor, of justice, of imperialist aggression, but barely spoke of, much less engaged

---

2.   "Nicaragua Vive y La Iglesia de los Pobres Tambien," *Iglesias* (Mexico), March 1989.

in, fights for water, health, education or economic development" (op. cit.).

As the economic crisis worsened, however, the network initiated some modest social programs like workshops on natural medicine and on the use of soybeans, also starting some sewing schools and buying cooperatives. This development also stemmed from the recognition of the importance of specific, practical social projects in the dynamics of creating and sustaining Christian communities.

The communities' self-definition continues: "We are *community* because we relate to one another as brothers and sisters, and in our weekly meetings and liturgical celebrations we share our achievements, hopes, joys, and also our sorrows." This aspect of the life of the community carries a built-in limitation on the size of each group. In order to expand the number of communities, the network has been intensifying its outreach work in the last few years.

Pastoral outreach to the "new barrios" (squatters' settlements) is one of the priorities. One approach which has been used with considerable success involves showing a filmstrip on the life of Jesus, usually in some outdoor location. If this seed falls on fertile soil, a missionary team is ready to assist in the formation of a neighborhood community.

The formation of youth groups, sometimes but not always including the catechists of the community, is another pastoral priority, along with support for the Mothers of Heroes and Martyrs (mothers of those killed in the insurrection against Somoza or in the war against the contras).

At a meeting of Managua communities devoted to writing their history in preparation for the tenth anniversary of the triumph, a priest who works with one of the communities spoke simply of "the joy of being together" as a key element in the communities' experience and a sign of God's presence. Citing 1 John 1:1-4, he said that the communities have heard, seen, and touched the Word of life and announce their experience to others.

"We are *ecclesial*," the communities' document continues, "because we are part of the universal Church, and we follow the example of the early communities (Acts 2:42-47)." That example of common ownership inspires not only the development of Christian community but also Christian involvement in cooperatives and in the construction of a fraternal society.

"We are in communion with our pastors, the bishops, and we take part in the Church's missionary work of proclaiming the gospel while working together to build the Kingdom." Some of the communities are part of their parish structure, holding their meetings in a church facility and participating in the parish Mass. Others have been forced out of the parish by militantly anti-Sandinista pastors who made life in the parish unbearable for those whose Christian option for the poor led them to support the revolutionary government. And some new communities have been founded by missionaries from the older groups without explicit reference to a parish structure.

In all cases, however, the people feel themselves to be in communion with the Catholic Church; where they are at variance with some bishops and priests, it is primarily on questions of political options and judgments. Their joy in being members of the Catholic Church is clear during the pastoral visits of bishops from other countries who come to listen to the people and to strengthen their faith and commitment.[3]

"We are at the *base*," they continue, "because we are poor and humble people who organize ourselves in faith and hope in the Lord Jesus to transform society, to make it more just and fraternal and based on love." Some of the members recall the words of Pope John XXIII at the start of Vatican II: "The Church presents itself as it is and as it wants to be: the Church of all and particularly the Church of the Poor."

None of the Managua communities is located in a wealthy neighborhood; one is in a middle-class section, while the others are in lower-middle, working class neighborhoods or in the "new barrios." The latter are the poorest areas, populated by relatively recent squatters and consisting of small shacks without indoor plumbing.[4]

---

3.   Roger N. Lancaster (op. cit., p. 27) spoke of "the well-known schism between the conservative church hierarchy and the revolutionary Popular Church." While "officials" of the Popular Church present it as part of the established Church, the people at the base speak quite openly of a schism, according to Lancaster. His sampling must have been quite tilted toward the more radical individuals. Furthermore, the fact that "the liberation theology movement clearly has its own organizational structure, both inside and outside of the official church," does not place it in schism.

Similarly, I think that the author goes too far when he speaks of the "strong anti-clerical sensibility and content" of the Popular Church and even considers it "anti-ecclesiastical" (pp. 55-56).

4.   Father Uriel Molina noted: "In Nicaragua we do not find CBCs of the upper middle class. They are all of the lower middle class, very poor" (*Nicaragua: Trinchera Teologica*, p. 58).

A new and important development in evangelization has been the understanding that the good news is proclaimed not only to the poor but by the poor. Fifteen Mexican bishops, in an April 1989 letter on CBCs which has been studied extensively by the Managua communities and found to be a source of much support, testified: "In being with the CBCs, we ourselves, who are evangelizers, have been evangelized by the poor. Our close relationship with the communities has made us feel more intensely than ever God's project and also the project of death working against God."[5]

The Mexican bishops described the CBCs' procedure as: "see, think, act, celebrate, evaluate." These are the steps of evangelization, which means "to communicate through works and words the Good News of the arrival of the Kingdom of God. It becomes ever clearer to us that the Kingdom draws near by means of historical projects which are part of God's plan and which help to make God's values present."

This evangelization, as "the life and central task of the CBCs," must be "integral" (complete): oriented toward "restoring relationships with God, with other people, and with nature" and having a "transforming effect on personal, family, and social life." It must also have an impact in the "strictly political sphere" where, as in the other areas, there is need for a "careful and constant process of personal and community discernment."

The bishops urged people to cooperate in the "emergence of the new society, being present as proclaimers of the Good News in the genuine movements of the people, strengthening efforts for justice and liberation. As members of the Church, place yourselves at the service of the poorest," the bishops said, also encouraging the CBCs to support efforts at renewal in the parishes and dioceses. The message, signed by three archbishops and 12 bishops, ends with an exhortation to the whole Church "to recognize the Spirit which gives life and strength to the CBCs."

---

5. "Aliento, Esperanza y Compromiso: Mensaje de 15 Obispos Mexicanos sobre las CEBs," issued in Guadalajara, Jal., April 7, 1989.

An important insight was offered by a visiting theologian at a national assembly of representatives of the CBCs in Nicaragua. "The CBCs," he said, "are not a 'movement' within the Church; rather, the community *is* the Church at the local level, in communion with the universal Church." The fifteen Mexican bishops made the same point in their letter: "The CBCs are not a movement in the Church, but rather the Church in movement." Citing Puebla, they described each community as "a cell of the large community."

Thus the communities are essentially different from a bible class or prayer group or social action organization in a parish or school. One community chose the following slogan as particularly significant: "CBCs: the Church being born again."

The theologian also described the typical parish as a pyramid within a vast pyramid representing the whole Church, whereas he drew a circle to represent a CBC as part of a larger circle of communities, with coordination through the central hub. The struggle of the laity, he said, is not to take the place of the priests in the pyramid but to form true communities of brothers and sisters in the service of the Kingdom. (It is significant that at almost all community meetings or assemblies the chairs are arranged in a circle, even when the crowd is very large.)

He also pointed out that the Church must always be about the double task of solidifying community and going out on mission. Perhaps the latter is the special contribution of the Church of the Poor in a modern, revolutionary situation.

Nicaraguans would share the definition of CBCs offered by Mexican Cardinal José Salazar López at the First Regional Meeting of CBCs in Guadalajara in 1982: "The CBCs are groups of people with common interests and objectives, brought together in Christ through a primary human relationship among themselves."[6]

---

6. Ibid.

B.
Critical Support for the Revolutionary Process

On March 24, 1981, the first anniversary of the assassination of Archbishop Romero, *El Nuevo Diario* carried a challenging document entitled "Christian Fidelity in the Nicaraguan Revolutionary Process," the fruit of an ongoing monthly reflection process involving Christians—lay, religious, and priests. The document was part of a series of statements by Christians interpreting the revolutionary process.

The document and a remarkable public panel discussion involving revolutionary Christians and government officials were significant expressions of the Church of the Poor's *critical* support for the revolutionary process. If author and former U.S. embassy attaché Edward R. F. Sheehan had made more than a few brief visits to Nicaragua before going public with his vitriolic judgments, he might have learned something about this document and conference sponsored by the Jesuits' Central American Historical Institute. Sheehan characterized the Jesuits of the Institute and of the Central American University as "Marxist Jesuits" and "erudite true believers so identified with the Revolution they had lost their independence." They insisted on their "critical distance," he said, but no evidence of this could be seen in public.

Sheehan also labeled the Institute's publications "verbose apologies for everything the Sandinistas did."[7] He has obviously not kept up with *Envío* in recent years, where he would have found serious criticism of some of the revolution's economic policies. Perhaps the most controversial article was "The New Economic Package: Will a Popular Model Emerge?" in the August 1988 issue.

In the introduction to "Christian Fidelity," the authors recognized that "previous reflection papers were characterized by support for the people's revolutionary process (a support based on the fact that this political project is in line with our duty to build the Kingdom in history as an expression of our option for the poor)." This document would be new in offering a "critical perspective based on our fidelity to God and the poor, the only absolutes in our commitment. All the rest is relative, imperfect, and subject to improvement, beginning with our own judgments and options."

---

7. *Agony in the Garden* (Boston: Houghton Mifflin, 1989), p. 292. The book's subtitle, "A Stranger in Central America," is a curious indication of the author's lack of experience and depth in his subject.

They asked government leaders, the "vanguard" of the people, to "live with and always trust in the people whom they lead, letting themselves be accompanied and counseled by the people." Power should be put "at the service of the people in such a way that the people participate freely and increasingly in power."

Seeing the moral challenge of the revolution in relation to Lent, they said that "God is asking for radical changes in our heart and in our mental, affective, religious, social, and political structures." These changes would lead to "generous hearts detached from wealth, hearts of the poor" and also to structures of solidarity and justice "free of deadly selfishness."

Leaders of the revolution were invited "to join with the poor in their sacrifices," living, working, and eating "with visible austerity and generous solidarity."

The authors reiterated their support for the revolutionary state in its efforts to organize society for the good of the majority, urging ever greater participation by the majority in that process. "The support we give to the state should contribute at the same time to revolutionary vigilance over bureaucratic excesses, which are not only a legacy from the past but also an inevitable weight borne by every modern state." Such bureaucracy is "a source of coercion and rigidity always tending to consolidate and perpetuate itself instead of making itself superfluous."

And when the state takes a leadership role in the economy, these bureaucratic tendencies are "very strong and need constant correction." They noted that "twenty-one ministries, some of which are in competition for spheres of action and resources, are a source of quite a bit of concern. The state should not assume functions which can be carried out by the people's organizations. The "strengthening of the state" must be accompanied by the "flowering of autonomous and creative initiatives.

"As Christians we must remember that no state apparatus has its reason for being in itself; to attribute that to itself is its constant temptation. Its only reason for being is service, which should consist in the organization of social life for the good of the majority. Any tendency by the state to consider itself identical with the majority is never healthy." In fact, when the state is the organizer of a class alliance, "it should realize that there can be conflict with the poor classes."

When the state recognizes its mistakes and has the "revolutionary humility" to accept the just criticism of the masses, it gains greater legitimacy than by acting defensively, "which shows insecurity and sometimes leads to arrogance." In ensuing years the Sandinista leadership showed its considerable ability to admit mistakes, accept criticism, and change policies (e.g., regarding land reform, Atlantic Coast issues, etc.).

The authors insisted on the development of a "people's democracy" in which the increasingly articulate participation of the people is just as important as technical expertise. "Not by bread alone do the masses want to live, but perhaps more by the dignity which comes from responsible participation."

In this challenge the words of Archbishop Romero were invoked: a Church or government leader is "a servant of the people of God. That must never be forgotten!" Their attitude must never be: "I give the orders here. What I want is what is done."

The authors were not shy about expressing their support for the Frente Sandinista, although they recognized clearly that their option cannot be deduced directly from the gospel. "The gospel is not a catalogue of concrete solutions which exempts people from the hard work of making history." But hard analysis was what had led this group to make its Christian love effective by joining or supporting the FSLN. "Other Christians will analyze the situation differently and will feel their faith drawing them to other responses. But the criterion for every Christian's political option must be: the cause of the poor as the cause of Christ."

The authors reasoned that failure to support the FSLN "in its close relation to the poor classes would be equivalent to choosing for this country a political project which would not radically change the society of exploitation and domination which we have inherited." They wanted more than a mere change of names in government or curbing of the traditional corruption: "We want a firm and solid move forward toward a new society not based on capitalism."

But the revolutionary project, they noted, does not have its future "assured mechanically." The vanguard well knows that it is nothing "apart from the poor classes." It is well aware that if it does not live as a vanguard in the midst of the people "as the fish in water it will have nothing from which to draw life and will be perceived as a privileged group." The right relation between vanguard and people is one of "mutual education and dialectical complementarity." And the more FSLN leaders are from the lower classes, "the more the people's interests are assured in the party."

The authors noted that "the best aspects of our Christian faith lead us to believe that the greatest danger for every revolutionary party, and thus also for the FSLN, is to take heroic pride in its own merits and to think that it always knows better than the poor classes what they need." They suggested that the problems of the Atlantic Coast "can be material for reflection in this regard. It is precisely because of the revolution that the Coast has awakened. Roads have been opened up, and TV and phone service inaugurated. The literacy crusade was carried out in native languages. Previously no one from the Pacific side did so much for the Coast. But the demands of the people there are also ethnic and have many social and cultural aspects. The demand for authentic revolution coming from the Coast must be listened to." [See discussion of Coast issues in the next chapter.]

The authors gave high marks to the post-triumph revolutionary process for "the growth in revolutionary consciousness in the masses." They observed that this development was especially noteworthy because of "the tremendous work of de-politicization done by the dictatorship, the manipulation and paternalism by the patróns [godfather-type landlords], and the fact that before the triumph the revolutionaries concentrated more on training people for insurrection than on political consciousness-raising." The authors urged that the post-triumph work of raising political awareness should continue as a priority and that more efforts should be made to organize the very poorest.

Seeing that the bourgeois sectors were pressuring the state more and more in defense of their interests and were looking to the right-wing sectors of the U.S. government for help, the authors urged the poor classes to redouble the defense of their interests in the revolutionary process.

The authors recognized "the inevitable ambiguities of revolutionary processes in history." These ambiguities underline the need for constant improvement, they noted, "but should not paralyze constructive support for the process."

The government has not impeded religious education or evangelization, the authors pointed out. The FSLN has recognized the role of religion as a motivating factor for many revolutionaries and has accepted believers on an equal footing with non-believers as members. But there is no doubt, they continued, that the 1980 FSLN statement on religion would have been enhanced "by an explicit directive indicating that party structures not only are no place for religious proselytism but are no place for anti-religious proselytism either." [See our discussion of this matter in the section, "Fear of Marxism," in Chapter 10.]

The authors insisted that "a Christian judgment on the revolutionary process should not have as its main criterion the well-being of our churches as institutions. What is decisive is not how the Church feels in the process but how the poor are faring. This does not mean that the Church is separate from the people but that its priorities are on the good news announced to the poor. It means seeing the Church as the servant of the Kingdom of God, in the midst of people 'as one who serves' (Luke 22:27).

"The Church is not centered in itself but in the glory of God as manifested in Jesus Christ, who told us how he would be present to all people whether they knew it or not: 'Lord, when did we see you hungry and feed you?' (Matthew 25:31-46). We believe that Jesus, united forever to the Church and speaking from his identification with the poor, invites the Church to complete faithfulness to His cause." [See our section on the Church and the Kingdom in Chapter 11 for a fuller treatment of this issue.]

This document was published in *El Nuevo Diario* and distributed widely in Nicaragua and abroad. A popular version, with drawings and questions, was produced to be used for reflection in the CBCs. After two months, a panel presentation was held before a full house in the auditorium of the Jesuits' Central American University, with six members of CBCs challenging six representatives of movements or institutions of the revolution. Radio newscaster Freddy Rostran spoke positively of the weekly "Face the People" sessions in which top government leaders dialogue with various sectors of the population, but he complained that "citizens meet brick walls when trying to present their problems to officials at lower levels." He mentioned various social problems and urged greater participation by the people in the state structures so that they do not continue in their "tendency to become gigantic." By criticizing "mistakes and abuses," he concluded, Christians are defending their revolution.

Emilio Baltodano Jr., then General Secretary of the governing junta, affirmed the need for criticism and said that the government welcomed criticism from the point of view of the option for the poor. People's participation is essential, he emphasized, because the government is only one of the "basic elements" in making the revolution. He agreed that there is a problem of bureaucracy, which manifests itself sometimes in "lack of effectiveness" and other times in "lack of efficiency." He pointed out, however that the government's 21 ministries and 9 institutes came into being because of the revolution's commitment to respond to "the broad gamut of problems." He recognized the possibility of reducing the size of the state but noted the problem of massive layoffs which that would entail. (In 1988 the Ministry of Housing and Ministry of Culture felt the axe of "compactación," with some of their functions being assumed by other departments, while deep cuts were made in the entire government budget.)

Maria del Socorro Barreto of "Christians in the Revolution" noted that during the years of guerrilla struggle Sandinista leaders shared the hard life, risks, and conditions of the masses. Thus they were able to "gather and interpret as their own the aspirations of the poor." Now the leaders need certain conditions for their own security, but how do they keep in touch with the people? She also called for a "better pedagogy to further the people's political consciousness" and reiterated the previous complaint about middle-level government officials, calling some of them "arrogant and irresponsible."

Minister of the Interior Tomás Borge responded bluntly: "I must confess that bureaucracy is becoming a strait jacket in the revolution." As an example he offered the case of a woman who was seven months pregnant but who had to present proof of pregnancy to some government office. He also recognized the "lack of sufficient austerity" and the arrogance of many government workers. "We have to make every effort," he said, "not only to be the vanguard of the poor but to be part of the poor." He said that in a recent conversation most of the top leaders of the FSLN expressed interest in living in poor neighborhoods but had to recognize that security measures and other necessities of their work would still separate them from other residents.

He agreed that government leaders should move more directly among the poor, adding that the criticism that middle-level officials are too removed from the people should be directed also at the top leadership.

Indiana Acevedo of the CBC of the San Judas neighborhood expressed "a danger in that the leadership of the mass organizations want to give us norms and priorities in a top-down approach." She asked whether it would not be better if tasks were based on the people's own aspirations, thus bringing the people to a greater degree of real power-sharing.

Patricia Elvir of the Sandinista Youth explained that part of the problem is due to the failure of many people to take an active role in their neighborhood, student, or other organizations.

University student Salvador Chamorro of the Christian Revolutionary Students asked how unity in the Church could be a reality in the midst of a struggle in Nicaragua between the "project of the poor majority and that of the rich minority." He spoke appreciatively of the bishops' November 1979 document on the revolution but observed that "now we are not seeing clear guidance about the option for the poor. At times we even feel that the Church is making an option for the rich."

Father Amando López, S.J., who was then rector of the Central American University in Managua and who was martyred along with five fellow Jesuits in 1989 at the Central American University in San Salvador, noted that unity cannot be imposed on the Church but rather is a task and a challenge and must be based on the Church's option for the poor. He mentioned that Bishop Pedro Casaldáliga of Brazil was accused by a fellow bishop of being a communist and that Archbishop Romero was "denigrated by his own fellow bishops, one of whom is a colonel in the army which rules El Salvador." He noted the difference between the documents of the Brazilian Bishops Conference and those of other national conferences. There has been conflict in the Church ever since the time of the apostles, he said. He concluded by urging all Christians to speak out on important political issues, not being so preoccupied with the statements or the silence of bishops.[8]

Father López had been asked to participate in the dialogue when "the Catholic hierarchy declined to take part in the event."[9]

The document which had served as the basis for discussion "reflected a characteristic shared by other writings which began to emerge in 1981 and which continue to be published today: critical support for the process," *Envío* observed. "It should be stressed that those who seek to portray the 'Popular Church' as a small group of Christians manipulated by

---

8.   The document, "Fidelidad cristiana en el proceso revolucionario de Nicaragua," and the text of the panel discussion were published by the Central American Historical Institute and the Antonio Valdivieso Ecumenical Center in 1981 in a booklet entitled *Los Cristianos Interpelan a la Revolución: Fidelidad Crítica en el Proceso de Nicaragua.* (See our discussion on Church unity in Chapter 11).

9.   *El Nuevo Diario,* May 27, 1981. This lengthy article reported to the public most of the criticisms which had been offered.

the government ignore the critical nature of these Christians' support, expressed in meetings, courses, and publications."[10]

Another example of "critical support for the process" can be seen in the way some Christian intellectuals analyze the problem of the "top-down" approach of some Sandinistas, a problem noted in the working document and in the panel discussion. It can be pointed out that in the final stage of the insurrection what was needed was clear, definite leadership to channel the uprising of the masses in a militarily effective way against the dictatorship. The "consciousness-raising" and political education had already been done, at least sufficiently to bring the people to the boiling point; what was required was not further discussion, voting, or arriving at consensus, but the discipline of an army to combat the National Guard.

That is what the Sandinistas provided, and it was effective. Once in power, they soon found themselves increasingly under attack from the bourgeois sectors and then from the Reagan administration, and so once again they were in a military situation. These factors may have contributed to the tendency on the part of some to have a top-down approach, to "lay down the line," as the saying goes, even though they may believe that it is not the ideal either for the FSLN or for the nation.

C.
Third Annual National Assembly

A major event in the life of Nicaragua's CBCs was held in May 1988: the third annual national assembly. Sixty representatives came together for the three-day meeting in Managua around the theme of "the missionary Church." (Previous years' assemblies had involved larger numbers, but the intention for 1988 was to have a smaller working group of representatives.)

The first session of the assembly involved taking stock of "the Church of the Poor." Reports from the various regions indicated that this sector of the Church had experienced a slight growth over the last few years—not so much in the sense that the communities had grown in size but

---

10. *Envío*, December 1983.

rather that some new groups had been founded by the "missionary" Church.

After this the assembly divided into three groups, with each tackling one of the following topics: religion and politics; the efforts by the right-wingers to discredit the "Church of the poor"; and the communities' style of work and ministry.

Religion and Politics

The theme of "religion and politics" has been on the front burner in Nicaragua ever since the birth of the communities in the late sixties. One point which was emphasized at the 1988 assembly and which the communities have come to grasp more clearly in recent years is that we should never lose sight of the distinction between religious celebrations or meetings and outright political sessions. Everything has a political dimension, but explicit discussion of politics does not have to dominate every gathering of the "Church of the Poor." It was felt that perhaps some insensitivity to this distinction has alienated some people from our communities. Many of our own people still have a need for a deeper knowledge of Scripture and of the nature of the Church and for a more personal participation in liturgy as well as for a more thorough grasp of the relationship between their faith and their social and political commitment.

Liberation theologians have stated clearly that theological reflection is a *second* moment, coming after social commitment and action. The Church of the Poor in Nicaragua finds itself to a great extent in that second moment. The Antonio Valdivieso Ecumenical Center, in its working paper inviting people to a 1985 seminar to explore the topic of liberation theology in Nicaragua, said: "Revolutionary practice is richer and more advanced than the corresponding theoretical reflection. That is, revolutionary practice coexists with a theology which is traditional or vaguely progressive."[11]

Reflection along the lines of liberation theology is needed "to accompany and nourish the faith of those believers who have committed themselves to the struggle but who nevertheless experience a growing distance between their new political consciousness and their level of Christian re-

---

11. *Nicaragua: Trinchera Teológica*, p. 41.

flection, between the forms taken by their political militancy and those taken by their Church participation."[12]

One of the participants in the seminar, María López Vigil of the Central American Historical Institute, stressed the need for a catechism of the Church of the Poor rather than an academic treatise on theology of liberation: "We can make beautiful statements about faith and revolution, but every day we see that the majority of the people still have not associated religion and commitment—and I'm not referring to revolutionary commitment, but rather to community commitment."[13]

Father Juan Hernández Pico, S.J., has noted that the religious protest against the injustice of the Somoza dictatorship was based on an "intuition which could be expressed in a very simple consensus: God cannot want this situation of oppression and unjust misery to continue. This implies an image of God as combining love and justice, an implicit image of sin as incompatible with God, and an identification of oppression and unjust misery as sin."

In the subsequent struggle to defend the revolution, this intuition developed to some extent: people believed that God wants peace; those who gave their lives for the revolution are honored as martyrs who acted out of love for their people; resistance against imperialism is considered an expression of the dignity of the children of God, especially of the poor; faith must be validated by action, especially the building of the fraternal society.[14]

With a good biblical and liturgical background and acquaintance with Church history and teachings, the more committed members of the CBCs, many of the Delegates of the Word, and Christian intellectuals went far beyond these basic intuitions in grounding their action in their faith. But a great need has remained for deepening people's capacity to relate commitment in the world to their Christian life. Attending to this need in our own communities and in the Christian population as a whole is a specifically *pastoral* contribution to the revolutionary process.

---

12. Ibid., p. 42.

13. Ibid., p. 156.

14. Juan Hernández Pico, S.J., "Religión y Revolución en Nicaragua," Cuadernos de Sociología, Universidad Centroamericana, Enero-Junio 1989, p. 72.

This does not mean that we are going to "avoid politics" in our preaching and discussions and celebrations. Indeed, many noted that for our critics "politics" is any and every aspect of ordinary human life: health, education, housing, war and peace, jobs, food, the future for the children, and other "material" concerns. Including such matters in discussion or prayer is branded as "meddling in politics." In this way some seek to keep the social system "untouchable" and thus protect their personal interests. Religion is confined to the purely "spiritual," and the gospel has no application to daily life in society.

This is obviously unacceptable to the Church of the Poor. While being attentive to the distinction between religious themes and political issues, we will not steer clear of controversial justice issues in our preaching and prayer in some desperate attempt to keep all feathers unruffled.

Another reason why some Christians feel that they must keep themselves pure and unspotted from "politics" is that the word has such a dirty past in Nicaragua (as well as in other countries). During the U.S. military occupation, politics was a puppet show; and during the Somoza dictatorship it was a corrupt racket. The people never saw political involvement as a viable way to struggle for justice. A new framework was created in 1979 (not without its human and technical limitations, of course), but old thought patterns remain.

Related to this attitude is the notion that, if the Church is going to relate to politics at all, it must be in a strictly prophetic, critical way—denouncing injustice from a critical distance. But with the triumph of the revolution the CBCs decided to *announce* a new society and participate in the building of it. But this more positive attitude clashed with the older one of denunciation and condemnation.

Assembly participants studying this question recognized that in time of war it is difficult to know just how to be critical of the revolutionary government in a constructive way which would not help the enemy's efforts to reverse the entire process. Many acknowledged that perhaps some have been too quick and facile in defending every aspect of the revolution and that this has kept some people away from our communities, seeing them as unconditional defenders of the Sandinista government. Such a posture is not of any service to the revolution and is not worthy of disciples of Jesus, the one and only Lord of all creation. The assembly renewed its commitment of *critical* support for the revolutionary process.

Efforts to De-Legitimize the Church of the Poor

Participants in the 1988 assembly of communities pointed out that efforts by the more conservative sectors to discredit the Church of the Poor were intensifying, with some clerics urging their faithful to scrutinize the "credentials" of priests, sisters, Delegates of the Word, and catechists. Ministers not officially authorized by the diocese or parish were meeting increasing resistance.

What the assembly found particularly unjust about this is not that bishops and pastors wanted to exercise their authority but that the main criterion for certifying "legitimate" ministers was one's relationship to the revolution. If a Delegate of the Word, for instance, was a member of a Sandinista farm cooperative, or if in his ministry he expressed support for the revolution and opposition to the U.S./contra aggression, he would be denounced as too political or materialistic, and an attempt would be made to replace him by one of the delegates "of the bishop."

The assembly agreed that the CBCs should strive to hold their ground ("maintain their space") in the Church. One's personal political option is no grounds for excommunication. The Church of the Poor does not claim that all Christians must support the revolution, but it does affirm that such support is a legitimate option for Christians and wants to have that legitimacy recognized.

The Church of the Poor is often accused of fomenting disunity in the Church and even of wanting to set up a parallel Church. "There is a great international and national campaign," wrote Pablo Richard, "to smear and delegitimize the Church of the Poor in Nicaragua. That campaign feeds on disinformation and lies. The Church of the Poor wants to avoid confrontation in the Church. No Catholic in Nicaragua today wants to break the institutional unity of the Church or create a Church parallel to the bishops. I have never heard anyone in Nicaragua expressing a desire for that. What the Church of the Poor in Nicaragua has always wanted and wants today is only to proclaim the gospel to the poor."[15]

---

15. "Nicaragua Vive y La Iglesia de los Pobres Tambien," Iglesias (Mexico), March 1989.

Style of Work and Ministry

Representatives tried to take a good hard look at their style of ministry and the life of the communities in an effort to see where improvement is necessary. Some pointed out that the communities have experienced the aging process in various ways. Some meetings have fallen into a dull routine—song, prayer, scripture, reflection—with little or no attention given to programming over a period of time. And in some communities members have been seeing essentially the same faces and hearing the same homogeneous views for many years.

In short, the communities in Nicaragua face the same pastoral challenge of how to maintain vitality and enthusiasm as communities everywhere face. (Omar Cabezas, after becoming national coordinator of the neighborhood organizations known as Sandinista Defense Committees, criticized the committees for a similar kind of hardening of the arteries which had set in in some of them over the years.)

Another challenge for some groups lies in maintaining a spirit of active participation and shared responsibility. It is all too easy to fall into the same passive dependence on a lay coordinator which previously characterized the people's relationship with their priest-pastor.

People felt that liturgical celebrations, on the other hand, have kept up a spirit of joy and meaningfulness, although some communities need to work on the quality of their liturgical music. It was recognized that the Church of the poor has some built-in limitations as to the technical excellence (electronics, aesthetics) of its celebrations, and there is no desire to "compete" with the bourgeois parishes or movements in attracting people with gimmicks or external trappings. Within a few months after the assembly, one of the Managua communities had made remarkable progress in the development of its choir, which soon began to receive invitations to help with the singing in other neighborhood communities.

D.
Fourth Annual National Assembly

In May 1989 ninety representatives of communities throughout Nicaragua met for the fourth annual assembly. Following a method which has become common in the CBCs, the three-day process began with a morning session devoted to social and economic analysis. People first met in regional groupings to identify the problems they were experiencing, mentioning low salaries, slippage in health and education, rising crime rates, and even malnutrition. While there was a general awareness of the external causes of these phenomena (the abated but continuing war, the credit and trade embargo inflicted by the United States, the regional Central American crisis, the 1988 hurricane), people also mentioned the human faults of their government and urged correction where necessary.

After pooling their observations in a plenary session, the people listened to an expert's analysis of the economic situation and took part in a lively dialogue with him. He explained that Nicaragua's grand total of $200 million in annual export earnings fell far short of the country's needs and demands, making belt-tightening unavoidable. Thousands had lost their jobs, and subsidies in almost all areas had been practically eliminated.

The next working session dealt with the reality of the Church, and once again the process began with people's own experiences in their particular region. One bishop was reported to be aware of the work of the CBCs in his diocese, and he was "letting it continue" without interference. Representatives from the Matagalpa region affirmed that Bishop Carlos Santi had met with the mothers of youngsters kidnapped by the contras and had expressed his desire to help. Others reported that tensions continued high in their areas between the "official" Church and the Church of the Poor.

The assembly then heard a theologian's response to the observations which had been shared and his analysis of the general ecclesiastical situation. "Some bishops are able to dialogue with government officials," he noted, "especially at the local or regional level, but they have a limited goal in view: maintaining or gaining space in society for the Church as institution. They are not open to any kind of dialogue, however, with the CBCs." Some participants suggested that the bishops (taking their main cue from the pope and from Obando) may be more opposed to the ferment of participation in the Church than to the revolution in society. Others said that the bishops saw both processes of change as intertwined and mutually reinforcing.

The theologian also noted that some bishops and pastors were forming "communities" within parishes but with a notably charismatic and middle-class complexion, "churchy" groups which avoid involvement in the real struggles of the poor or which promote at best a Christian Democratic reformist approach.

The speaker offered three "challenges" to the CBCs: to deepen the ethical formation of the people so that the communities can confront the human faults of the revolutionary process from within; to proclaim the values of Jesus in such a way as to rekindle enthusiasm for revolutionary values; and to devote more time and energy to the role of the laity in the practical construction of the new society rather than in activity within the Church community.

In one session of the assembly the representatives from the various regions were asked to identify the biblical texts which had been especially meaningful to the people in recent times. I will merely note them here, without prioritizing, as theological raw material from the people's experience:

1) Romans 12. People feel that as revolutionaries struggling for a world of justice, peace, and love they "are not conformed to the standards of this world," which are selfishness, competition, and exploitation, but are being transformed inwardly by God. Each member of the body has immense dignity and talents for the service of the people. We should "share generously," loving and respecting one another, and those in authority "should work hard," not simply lording it over others.

One group said that vv. 12 and 13 were especially important to them in this difficult time: "Let your hope keep you joyful, be patient in your troubles, and pray at all times. Share your belongings with your needy fellow Christians, and open your homes to strangers." The spirit of sharing was felt to be implemented in the programs of the revolution. The spirit of revenge was being defeated in the attitude of the revolution toward the former National Guard (who were not massacred in a bloodbath and who were practically all released) and toward the contras who were offered amnesty. The need to "pray at all times" is recognized by the communities, and their practice of prayer is evident to visitors.

2) Acts 2:42-47. Learning and sharing in the fellowship meals and prayers are the very heart of the CBCs, but they also seek to develop a society where "property and possessions are shared" according to each one's needs, as among the early Christians. People in the assembly emphasized that Christian sharing must be material as well as spiritual.

3) Matthew 6:24-34. The words of Jesus, "you cannot serve both God and money," are seen as an indictment of the self-centered materialism which characterizes capitalism. The birds of the air survive quite nicely without gathering a harvest and putting it in barns; what Jesus did not mention was that they are not limited by the fences of private property! The disciples are counseled not to worry about food, drink, and clothing but rather "to be concerned above everything else with the Kingdom of God and with what he requires of you, and he will provide you with all these other things." People understand this to mean that they should place top priority on struggling for the Kingdom of peace and justice, not "worrying about tomorrow," but being willing to risk all in the quest for a fraternal society.

4) Luke 24:13-35. The disciples on the road to Emmaus were dejected because of the execution of Jesus, a prophet who was thought to be "the one who was going to set Israel free." Gradually they recognized Jesus in his unfolding of the Scriptures—"like a fire burning in us"—and in the breaking of the bread. Returning to the community in Jerusalem, they gave and received new strength and hope. Ten years after the triumph over Somoza, many Nicaraguans were dejected because the revolution had not yet produced freedom from want and from external oppression. But CBC members knew, as Sandino had said, that freedom is not won with flowers, and they tried to keep the flame of hope burning as a light to a troubled society.

5) Luke 9:57-62. The disciple is always on the move, looking and working toward the goal. The Son of Man has no place "to lie down and rest." Faced with the exigency of proclaiming the Kingdom of God, there is not even time to bury the dead or to say good-bye to one's family. "Anyone who starts to plow and then keeps looking back," Jesus said, "is of no use for the Kingdom of God." Thanks to the wreckage caused by the U.S. strategy of "low-intensity warfare," many Nicaraguans, perhaps most, felt that they were better off materially under Somoza. They lived then in dread and humiliation, seeing no real hope for significant change within the system of oppression, but perhaps their caloric intake was somewhat higher. Nevertheless, they recognized the external factors responsible for their present plight and tried to keep their eyes on the prize.

One of the visiting theologians at the assembly said: "Yes, you are suffering here in Nicaragua, but with hope; in other countries, people are suffering even more, and without hope." To lose hope, he added, would be a "mortal sin" in the literal sense of the term: it would be death-dealing not only to Nicaraguans but to other Third World peoples who look to Nicaragua as a pioneer. Nicaraguans in the CBCs felt hopeful because they had achieved the first stage in the transformation of their society: having a government on the side of the poor majority. The second stage, freedom from imperialist interference, remained an elusive goal.

6) Exodus 14-16. People recalled that during the struggle against Somoza the liberation theme of the early chapters of Exodus was paramount in their spirituality; in 1989 they identified with the desert exerience of the liberated people, asking the Lord to nourish their hope and perseverance.

7) Isaiah 40 and following chapters. In spite of the growing misery in Nicaragua, people believed that the Lord had "good news" for them, that their time of suffering would soon be over. They looked to the upcoming 1990 vote, confident that it would be fair and that the United States and other nations would have to recognize the legitimacy of the process. They felt that the Sandinistas would win, since most Nicaraguans recognized the external causes of their suffering (the war, the economic embargo, etc.), and that life would improve as hostile action by the U.S. government diminished. (What they did not predict was that most Nicaraguans, whether or not they recognized the external causes of the nation's misery, would vote for what seemed the surer bet to bring peace and material improvement.)

What is important about these texts is that the people themselves identified these passages as life-giving and hope-giving in their present experience.

One of the theologians called Nicaragua a "disquieting sign" for the dominant system both in the realm of politics and in that of spirituality. In the political sphere for two reasons: (1) the Sandinista government represented an option to defend and enhance life for the poor majority, whereas other governments seek only to increase the power and wealth of the elite they represent; and (2) the revolution encouraged the people to be *subjects*—makers and shapers—of the new society, whereas in other countries the driving force is capital and weapons. The assembly recognized that there was still a long way to go before the people are truly subjects, but the participatory process certainly had been launched.

In the area of spirituality, the Nicaraguan experience has been a troublesome one for the high priests of the world because here the presence of God has been felt in the revolutionary struggle of the poor and in the construction of the Church of the Poor. This experience has given hope and encouragement to struggles throughout the world.

The speaker emphasized that God is not only present in history in the struggles of the poor but is "transcendent in history." God is never outside of history, but ahead of us in history, helping us to break personal limits (fear, sense of sinfulness or inadequacy) and the limits put upon us (the chains of slavery and oppression). In Christ God even breaks the limits of death. The following texts were cited: Hebrews 11:l; Hebrews 12:1-4; Ephesians 6:12; and Acts 5:35-39.

Looking toward the year 1992, he emphasized that the last 500 years have been years of struggle and resistance, not only of conquest and exploitation. The 300 million Latin Americans living in "extreme misery," he said, will continue to struggle, and the Word of God can be a sword of liberation for them if they only ask: With whom is God? Against whom is God? What is God's will? "The poor should not return any more bibles to the pope, as one indigenous leader in South America did, but rather appropriate the Word as the good news of liberation."

One theologian stressed the importance of the "institutionalization" of the Church of the Poor—a necessity if it is to withstand the forces of reaction, grow, and include future generations. The assembly identified some of the visible, organizational expressions of the Church of the Poor: the weekly newspaper *Tayacán; Ocote,* a mimeographed newsletter for the CBCs; the network of communities, their coordination, and the annual assemblies; the Delegates of the Word, catechists, and their programs; the Christian formation of youth; courses, workshops, and retreats; visits by bishops and delegations expressing solidarity; the work of Christians from other lands in the service of Nicaragua; personal and material relationships with "sister communities" in other countries.

Also mentioned were: the Evangelical Insurrection sparked by Father Miguel D'Escoto (with his thirty-day fast for peace and life in 1985) and its continuance in various events; the Ecumenical Movement for Peace and Life; Christian centers and institutes for social and theological analysis; organized Christian groups of youth and Mothers of Heroes and Martyrs; international gatherings of representatives; celebrations of the anniversaries of our martyrs and the annual Christian celebration of the anniversary of the revolution; the presence and ministry of priests in the CBCs.

The sins and shortcomings of the Church of the Poor were confessed spontaneously by participants during the penitential rite at Mass. One North American participant living in Nicaragua acknowledged that in spite of all the efforts which have been made by the solidarity movement in the United States and other countries "we have not stopped the violence of the U.S. government against the Nicaraguan people."

During the Eucharistic prayer the people, in the midst of hardship, gave thanks for God's many gifts. When the celebrant pronounced the words of consecration, those who knew him were deeply moved by his personal commitment to work in the contra war zones where he risks his body and blood every day.

The spirit of joy, peace, friendship, and freedom which characterized not only the Mass but the entire assembly seemed to many a sign of the presence of the Spirit. The fifteen Mexican bishops in their letter on CBCs expressed a similar sense of the "joyful experience of the Church" which characterized the Latin American and Mexican meetings of representatives of the communities in October 1988. "People felt warmly welcomed as Church, shared experiences, reflected, prayed, and celebrated their faith together," they recalled. "All of this put before the eyes of anyone who really wants to see the vitality of the CBCs as Church in mission in Latin America today."

The last session of the assembly was devoted to identifying *challenges*. One is to improve our Christian formation programs, especially in scripture; the communities will continue to reflect on scripture regularly, and special courses and retreats are also planned.

Another important challenge is to improve our organization and planning and particularly to work more effectively with the youth. The potential for the Church of the Poor seems great. In an August 1988 survey of Managua students between the ages of 16 and 24, initiated by the theology department of the Central American University in Managua and carried out by the Itztani Research Institute (an independent institution associated with the university), only 9 percent said they didn't believe in God, "and another 4 percent believe in God but don't identify with any religious denomination. Revolutionary conditions in Nicaraguan society hardly appear to have led its youth down the road to atheism." [16] Among

---

16. *Envío*, March 1989.

Catholics, "45 percent identify with the popular current in the Church and 37 percent with the traditional."[17]

Whatever the precise definition of those terms in the minds of the students, their response seems to indicate an alienation from the traditional structures and an openness to new models of Church.

Some participants spoke of the need to strengthen even further the leadership of the laity in the Church of the Poor.

Another challenge is "to renew the spirit of the Evangelical Insurrection so that our evangelization will be incarnate and liberating and thus strengthen the people's revolutionary process." The good news, which is only good if it is being made into a good reality, must be incarnate in history. In contrast, pseudo-evangelization, which has many modern forms, focuses on heavenly mysteries; if it does touch down occasionally, it deals with peace and (less frequently) justice only in generalities, or it concerns itself only with intra-church matters. Our evangelization must also be liberating as opposed to paternalistic or reformist.

Another challenge is to strengthen the people's hope by helping them to organize small-scale social and economic projects to help with survival in a period of crisis. The assembly also pointed out that we could nurture hope by denouncing the U.S. government's "low-intensity warfare" as a major cause of the people's suffering in 1989 and by denouncing inefficiency and corruption wherever they are found (as Sandinista leaders themselves were urging).

---

17. *Envío* comments: "Church groups that would provide a forum for young people who are both Catholics and revolutionaries to express their commitments in religious terms and channel them in concrete activities are not looked on kindly by the hierarchy and thus are not encouraged."

9

Hierarchy-Sandinista Conflicts

Had the contra war not occurred, tensions between the government and the traditional church would still have existed, but they might have been dealt with in a different manner. The war brought out the worst in both sides—which many of Reagan's critics contended was the point of the exercise.
—Penny Lernoux, *People of God*, p. 370.

Just two months after the triumph of the revolution, Father Alvaro Argüello, S.J., recalled a major difference in mentality between the upper-class opposition against Somoza and that of the more revolutionary mass organizations. "Naturally there were bourgeois Christians who joined the struggle against the dictatorship for explicitly Christian reasons," he pointed out, "but for many these reasons did not include an identification with the cause of the poor as their own struggle, as the cause of God. What motivated them was the excessive corruption of the dictatorship, its excessive cruelty, and its genocidal behavior in murdering whole cities.

"They risked their houses in the upper-middle class residential neighborhoods, knowing that the National Guard and its 'ears' could discover what they were doing."

The bourgeois opposition, however, already harbored the seeds of anti-Sandinismo within them. "Now, however, when the reconstruction process in Nicaragua demands so much sacrifice, when the chaos inherited from Somoza is not being put in order as completely or as rapidly as they hoped, their expressions of criticism and their fears are coming out," Argüello noted.

"No one would deny the generosity they showed at a certain time in risking everything. But moral indignation at the excesses of a dictatorship like that of Somoza and a charitable attitude toward the needs of the

163

masses are not the same as an analysis of the system. They do not understand that the seeds of corruption and repression are present in the unbri-
dled liberty to accumulate vast capital, in the absolute freedom to own the
means of production, in a system based on profit and private property
without recognition of a serious social mortgage."

Argüello's tone became invitational: "To be able to share in the joy of
the masses of Nicaraguans it is necessary to take another step: to stop
thinking in terms of the interests of a minority, to take up the interests of
the people themselves (*clases populares*), and thus to put into effect in
the present revolutionary situation that phrase of the bishops at Puebla:
'We invite all, without class distinctions, to accept and take up the cause
of the poor, as if they were accepting and taking up their own cause, the
very cause of Christ.'

"If they do this," he continued, "they will clearly have to take that
arduous and narrow path which leads to the denial of their own class
interests in support of the interests of the majority. Then they will have
to open themselves concretely to the hard saying of Jesus: 'The person
who seeks to save his life will lose it' (Matthew 16:2-5). They will begin
to recognize that a system which historically makes 'the rich ever richer
at the cost of making the poor always poorer' cannot be the choice of any
Christian (Puebla No. 30). Then finally they will understand how other
members of their social class were able to give up their privileged social
position and their material opulence to mingle their sweat and their blood
with the sweat and blood which the poor of Nicaragua have poured out
throughout their history."[1]

This chapter will deal almost exclusively, and in detail, with the period
from July 1979 to the end of 1982. This is partly due to space limitations
but also to the author's perception that the main lines of the hierarchy-
Sandinista conflict were drawn in the early period.

1979

Since at the very moment of the triumph Obando had been involved in
efforts in Venezuela to prevent the Sandinistas from coming to power, he
was not invited to receive the oath of office of the new government in

---

1. *Fe Cristiana y Revolución Sandinista en Nicaragua*, pp. 91-92.

Managua. The bishop of León did. Some observers say that Obando's ego has never forgiven the Sandinistas for that. (In an April 1989 interview the cardinal told me that he had gone to Venezuela at the invitation of the Venezuelan bishops. He didn't mention what the purpose of the invitation was, but he denied that he was there to work politically against the FSLN.)

The new government did not have to wait long to see the seeds of criticism and suspicion come forth. On July 30, just 11 days after the triumph, the bishops' conference issued a statement full of suspicion, doubts, and fears. While the statement expressed some hope for a positive outcome, the dominant tone was negative: "After so much bloodshed and so much sacrifice imposed on our people, it would not be right, nor would it make any sense, that the primary meaning of life and of human values implied in authentic liberation be forgotten once again."

The bishops spoke of an "awakening of new hopes and joys" but added: "We also share the anguish and fears in this stage of transition. We understand that there are serious confusions in ideological aspects as well as in the organization of the new state structures. . . . God is the source of law and social order, and when that source is stopped up, the systems of power try to take its place, building themselves up into absolutes. Thus man, instead of being liberated, is enslaved once again. People become servile, once again losing their personal dignity and freedom. Without God, conscience merely parrots alienating slogans, empty of all critical sense and all human transcendence."[2]

The bishops included a quote from Pope John Paul II (speaking in June 1979 to his native Poland): "Without Christ, man cannot understand who he is or what is his true dignity, or his vocation, or his final destiny."

Rodolfo Cardenal, S.J., saw this letter as an attempt by the bishops "to insure that elements of neo-Christendom would be preserved under the new government."[3] (Neo-Christendom refers to the power, privileges, and prerogatives of organized religion. See Part Five.)

When the junta of the Government of National Reconstruction asked to dialogue with the bishops, suggesting that the language in their mes-

---

2. "Iniciando la Reconstrucción."

3. *Historia General de la Iglesia en America Latina,* op. cit., p. 565.

sage was ambiguous, "the bishops answered that there had been no ambiguity in their language as far as the dictatorship was concerned and that it had well understood the opposition stance of the hierarchy," according to Father Argüello.[4]

Argüello found "nothing to object to in this response, but there were many opponents against Somoza, and unfortunately not all of them were in the opposition because they defended the interests of the poor. Some sought the overthrow of *somocismo* in order to develop a kind of capitalism which the *somocista* system did not allow, since it used the state for its own advantage."[5]

"Will the Churches have the clarity of vision," Argüello asked in that September seminar, "to proclaim justice for the poor as a priority over the formal freedoms (proclaimed in word) by the former regime? Will they have the courage to identify with the poor so that the joys and hopes of the poor, and not the fears of the exploiting and dominating classes, may be the heart's concern of the Churches?

"Will they have the courage to support the sacrifices which will be necessary so that the liberation process not be overwhelmed by impossible immediate demands? That is, will they be united with the poor in an authentic Christian way, contributing to the attainment of that society of austerity, hard work, solidarity, and participation which alone can insure the march to liberation in Nicaragua, given the tough national and international realities? Or will they become the spokespersons for the return to the fleshpots of Egypt?

"As for ourselves," he concluded, "let us give greater weight to hope than to fear. 'There is no fear in love; perfect love drives out all fear' (1 John 4:18). And the person who lives out of fear insures the fulfillment of his own prophecy."[6]

On August 19 the Nicaraguan Conference of Religious (CONFER) had given "greater weight to hope than to fear" in a public message which had a decidedly more positive tone than the bishops' statement of July 30. "With immense joy," they began, "we are seeing the inauguration of a new period in the history of Nicaragua after having passed

---

4. *Fe Cristiana y Revolución Sandinista en Nicaragua*, p. 95.

5. Ibid., pp. 95-96.

6. Ibid., p. 98.

through a long and painful exodus." They spoke of "the joy of libera-tion" which filled the land. "The difficult task of reconstruction is now under way," they continued, "and the whole nation has recovered its hope, especially the great masses who lived in misery. . . . God has passed through Nicaragua, acting with his powerful and liberating arm."

Noting the great significance of the Nicaraguan revolution for the whole world, the conference of religious stated: "God calls us to give the best of our energies and of our lives, accompanying this process of recon-struction, illuminating it from our faith in Jesus Christ."[7]

A colder attitude toward the revolution was expressed by Archbishop Obando in October. "Do you regret having supported the Sandinista struggle?" he was asked. "We knew more or less what was going to come," he answered. "But we have hope that the revolution may redound to the benefit of the Nicaraguans." According to *La Prensa*, Obando de-fined the government as pluralist, adding that it had various tendencies within it. But in the next breath "he expressed his fear that the revolution concerns itself only with aspects related to human development, without seeking the total salvation of man." This was a sign of Obando's belief that government should promote religion and of his uneasiness with the modern concept of a secular state.

The archbishop was also quoted as saying: "There must always be class struggle in the world, but the walls of hatred must be torn down so that the confrontation may be more human." The article continued: "Asked about the persistent rumors circulating in Nicaragua to the effect that the Catholic Church has withdrawn its support for the Sandinista revolution because it considers it materialistic and too radical, Archbishop Obando avoided a direct response and said that the Church has not lost hope."[8]

From the beginning the new government tried to communicate with the bishops concerning its economic planning, only to be constantly ig-nored.

In November the Dominican priests of Nicaragua published a message about the revolution. They spoke positively of the consciousness-raising process experienced by the Church in the struggle against Somoza: the

---

7. *Barricada*, August 19, 1979.
8. *La Prensa*, October 14, 1979.

Church heard "a strong call to stop being an accomplice, through its silence and collaborationism, with the oppressive structures which kept the majority in misery and subjection since colonial times." Quoting a phrase from the Sandinista hymn, they noted that "the people, led by the Frente Sandinista, took up heroically and generously the task of being 'master of their history and architect of their liberation.'"

They saw the revolutionary project as a "confirmation of our faith and hope that God's project in human history is not an illusion: that a society without classes is possible, in which relations between people are fraternal rather than exploitative, in which people do not appropriate things for themselves selfishly but rather share them." They considered participation in this project "an expression of our fidelity to the spirit of Christ in the concrete history we are living. We need the revolution to help us live the fundamental values of the gospel, which the bourgeois society has not allowed us to live in their fullness."

The Dominicans noted an effort by "international capitalism to prevent the Nicaraguan people from gaining their real independence, perhaps because this would mean a break in the domination of some countries over others." True independence would also make it impossible "for some countries to pile up wealth on the misery of others."

Within Nicaragua, "groups until now privileged are resisting the move by the dispossessed majority to take power and to demand equality," they observed. "The Church itself, not much accustomed to deep structural changes, could become part of this resistance if through fear and complicit silence it sets back or puts obstacles in the path of the political project of the poor. We exhort the whole Church, whose mission is to pressure for the coming of the Kingdom, to discern and promote all that is good, human, and just in this revolution, since to keep itself on the margin would mean that it is afraid to join in a process of putting into effect in history the completely gospel values which that revolution announces."

Recalling "the testimony of our Dominican elders, Valdivieso, Las Casas, and Montesinos," they concluded, "we ask the people of Nicaragua to keep committed to strengthening this revolution, which all the disinherited of the earth look to with hope."

Hopes that the hierarchy would heed the call were kindled when on November 17 the bishops' conference, with important input from religious, published a pastoral letter expressing support for the revolutionary process, for the armed insurrection that led to it, for the thought of Sandino from which it drew its inspiration, and for the socialist project it envisioned. The bishops also recognized the leading role of the Sandinistas in the process and spoke positively of the possibilities of a kind of socialism which would be democratic, respectful of human rights, and productive of necessary social change. "We believe that the present revolutionary moment is a propitious occasion to put into effect the Church's option for the poor," they noted.[9]

How did such a progressive document emerge from a socially conservative bishops' conference? According to one explanation, the revolutionary thrust of the new government had not yet gathered momentum.[10] Two representatives of the upper classes (Violeta Chamorro and Alfonso Robelo, now president of Nicaragua and ambassador to Costa Rica, respectively) were still in the five-person governing junta. Reflecting on this early period, Ramiro Gurdián (vice-president of COSEP, the big-business and anti-Sandinista chamber of commerce) pointed out that in the first months Colonel Bernardino Larios of Somoza's National Guard was the new government's Minister of Defense and two COSEP figures were in charge of the Ministries of Agriculture and Industry. And he emphasized that in the Council of State COSEP and the FSLN each had six representatives.[11] Given this situation, perhaps the bishops felt that if some species of "socialism" were emerging it could be attained with the approval and participation of the economically powerful.

The letter was not without its critical tone. "We should affirm that our commitment to the revolutionary process cannot mean that we have a naíve or blind enthusiasm, much less should it lead to the creation of a new idol to which people would bow unquestioningly," they observed. "Like every human process, this one too is found to be subject to possible errors and abuses. Not a few Nicaraguans feel certain concerns and fears welling up within them." The bishops said that their role as pastors was to examine such concerns and bring them to the attention of the government.

---

9. "Compromiso Cristiano para una Nicaragua Nueva."

10. Interview with Father Ernesto Bravo, pastor of La Trinidad, February, 1989.

11. My interview of Ramiro Gurdián, May 1989.

1980

The spirit of national unity is reflected in the tone as well as the content of letters written by Father Jim (Guadalupe) Carney, S.J., to his sister Virginia Smith. Father Carney had been deported from Honduras after many years of work with the peasants and workers of that country. He lived and worked in Nicaragua from 1980 to 1983, when he entered Honduras as a chaplain to a revolutionary contingent and was killed by government forces.[12]

In January Father Carney told Virginia that he found Nicaragua to be "a very interesting country right now because they are making a socialist revolution in a peaceful way. The whole population is more or less in agreement with the revolutionary changes."[13]

In late February Father Carney reported that "there is tremendous enthusiasm among the people in general." He spoke of the upcoming literacy crusade and noted: "Christians work hand in hand with Marxists in this revolution. I'm glad to see this." At the end of March he again mentioned the literacy crusade which was then under way and said: "We all think the revolution in Nicaragua is going along very Christian lines."

A June 6 letter from Father Carney, however, pointed to opposition against the revolution: "Don't believe the horrible campaign in the world's press against our Sandinista government." To counter that campaign, he added: "The Church here, in general, is right in the revolution." Perhaps that qualifier was a sign of the changing times.

As Envío pointed out, "by late 1980 the bishops would downplay the contents of their positive November 1979 pastoral letter and avoid referring to it in public."[14] By then it had become clear that the Sandinistas were serious about their special commitment to the poor majority, and so Alfonso Robelo and Violeta Chamorro had quit the governing junta. Violeta Chamorro's colleague in La Prensa, editor César Vivas (father of Managua's auxiliary bishop Bosco Vivas), told me in May 1989 that Chamorro and Robelo resigned their government posts because the

---

12. See Father Carney's autobiography, *To Be a Revolutionary* (New York: Harper & Row, 1985).

13. Letter dated January 8, shared with me by Virginia Smith.

14. *Envío*, December 1983.

Sandinistas "were giving more representation to the Sandinista Defense Committees [neighborhood organizations] and other mass organizations."

Less than a month after Robelo's resignation in April 1980 the bishops unexpectedly called for the resignation of those priests holding public office. Envío observed: "The announcement seemed to express the same disagreement with the direction of the process that had led to Robelo's resignation."[15] According to Father Angel Arnaiz, "what was clearly at stake was the legitimation of the Sandinista revolution by Christians, whose visible representatives were these priests."[16]

The bishops continued their campaign against the priests in government, with full support from the papal nuncio Andrea Cordero Lanza di Montezémolo. Edgard Parrales, one of the targeted priests, recalled a conversation with the nuncio in 1981. The nuncio told Parrales that the Vatican was going to back the bishops "even if the bishops were wrong," according to Parrales. "Even if they go against the gospel and the truth?" asked the priest. "In whatever circumstances," answered the nuncio.[17]

Penny Lernoux cited as a reason for the bishops' turn against the Sandinistas "the eventual recognition by upper- and middle-class sectors closely allied to Obando and other bishops that the uprising had not been simply a changing of the guard but a genuine class revolution intent on overturning the country's economic and social structures."[18]

It was one thing for the bishops in June 1979 to justify the rising up of the entire population against an unpopular dictatorship; it would have been quite another for them to justify the rising up of the poor masses to gain more and more political and economic power in Nicaraguan society.

They did not share Father Carney's joy over the revolution or his perception of the Christian values at the heart of it. "I'm more enthused than ever about the Nicaraguan socialist revolution," he wrote on August 1. "Real Christianity is even picking up under the revolutionary mystique of forming the 'new person' and the 'new just society' which fills the masses of the people here." In late 1981 Father Carney would write that the major thrust of the Nicaraguan government "is to help the poor." He

---

15. Ibid.

16. Op. cit., p. 141.

17. My interview of Edgard Parrales, July 1989.

18. *People of God*, p. 369.

saw the revolution as an instrument in which many Christians sought to implement "the true gospel Christianity of liberation of the poor."

In his autobiography Father Carney summed up the Nicaraguan phenomenon by saying that "the wealthy no longer control things." He contrasted this with Honduras, where "the power is in the hands of a small oligarchy of rich landowners, businessmen, and military officers who obey the U.S. embassy and the U.S. transnational companies; here there is 'popular power of the people,' and the former oligarchy and the gringos no longer run things. This is why they are crying," he explained, "and lying about what is happening in Nicaragua, and making counterrevolutionary conspiracies."[19]

Edgar Chamorro, a contra leader from 1981 to 1984, has a similar analysis of the nature of the early anti-Sandinista opposition. "The early platforms of disparate exiles, ex-military and oligarchs focused on the importance of private property and a return to the earlier economic privileges and investment opportunities of the old Nicaragua," he wrote. "They emphasized classic capitalist principles and included mention of charity but not of social change."[20]

Father Carney felt a spiritual kinship with Marxist revolutionaries: "We Christian-Marxists who believe in God fight side by side in Central America with the Marxists who do not believe in God in order to form together the new socialist society of brothers and sisters, which will be pluralistic, not totalitarian, that is, which will respect the beliefs of everyone. . . . A dogmatic, anticommunist Christian is not a real Christian; and a dogmatic, anti-Christian Marxist is not a real Marxist."[21]

Lernoux also cited higher ecclesiastical pressures working on the bishops. "One was the growing concern in Rome," she says, "where John Paul took a dim view of priests in government and particularly a leftist one. Another was the influence of Colombian cardinal Alfonso López Trujillo and his fellow conservatives in the Latin American Episcopal Conference (CELAM)."[22] Ever since the crucial Medellín conference in 1968, the cardinal had been campaigning to weaken the Church's option

19. *To Be a Revolutionary*, p. 430.

20. *Packaging the Contras: A Case of CIA Disinformation* (New York: Institute for Media Analysis, 1987), p. 5.

21. Op. cit., p. 440.

22. *People of God*, p. 368.

for the poor and commitment to structural economic and political change. Progressive forces had held their ground against López Trujillo at the Puebla conference of bishops in early 1979, where he did keep the Nicaraguan insurrection against Somoza off the official agenda.

"CELAM has plans to neutralize the progressive priests and religious in all of Central America," Father Carney noted, adding that "there is talk of anticommunist Polish missionaries" being brought to Central America. "CELAM is at present filling the minds of the Nicaraguan bishops with fear of the phantom of communism and, along with the bishops, some priests, nuns, and laypeople, in courses they are sponsoring in Nicaragua."[23]

A statement attributed to López Trujillo appeared in an article in *El Nuevo Diario* (Sept. 22, 1980): "Now they go to Managua as if to their Rome." According to the author of the article, "they" referred to the liberation theologians and to the masses of people whose revolutionary inspirations are formulated by those theologians. "It does not sit well with López Trujillo," the writer continued, "that the era is ending in which the Church's faith has to find support in the power of governments in order to proclaim the gospel."

In November 1979 Mexican Bishop Sergio Méndez-Arceo had visited Nicaragua to participate in the solemn requiem Mass for Father Gaspar García Laviana, the priest who was killed in combat by Somoza's Guard the previous December. "I have come to Nicaragua as I would to a shrine to be with the Lord of history," the bishop said to reporters (*El Nuevo Diario*, Sept. 22, 1980).

In June 1981, at a high-level meeting in the Vatican on Central America, two CELAM officials expressed their concerns forcefully in press interviews. Bishop Antonio Quarracino of Argentina, CELAM's general secretary, said that "the Marxist-Leninist ideological penetration and the international communist influence in Central America is so obvious that one would be blind to deny it." He seemed to recognize the social roots of rebellion in Central America: "Poverty and injustice have provided fertile ground for an extremist revolutionary presence." But he continued firmly: "All you have to do is look at a map to realize what the communist presence in the isthmus would mean for the whole American continent."[24]

---

23. Op. cit., p. 432.

Another participant at the conference, Costa Rican Archbishop Román Arrieta Villalobos, gave classic expression to a reformist Church position: "The only way, the way that the masses of Central America want, is the way inspired by the gospel and based on the social teachings of the Church—the conversion of the privileged sectors of society to justice."[25]

In Milan after the meeting, Archbishop Obando was quoted as saying: "After two years of hope, our revolution is falling into Marxism." Seeming to ignore the fact that Violeta Chamorro and Alfonso Robelo had *chosen* to resign from government, he claimed that the Sandinistas "reduced the governing junta to only three members: a triumvirate that rules with the support of nine Marxist chiefs." He spoke of the number of Cubans in Nicaragua, of the use of the literacy crusade "for other objectives," and of the priests in government.[26]

The massive literacy crusade directed by Father Fernando Cardenal in 1980 had received a cold shoulder from Obando, who declined an invitation to take part in the official closing celebration. (Bishop Sergio Mendez-Arceo gladly accepted an invitation to participate.) "The archbishop chose rather to celebrate parallel Masses with Catholic students from families which were disaffected from Sandinismo," Irene Selser reported.[27]

In an interview in 1989, a bishop of a diocese of Nicaragua complained to me that the literacy crusade had been "political." He mentioned that one group of young teachers had put on a sociodrama depicting the March 24 assassination of Archbishop Oscar Romero of San Salvador. "That's how they were *using* Romero," he shook his head. A priest friend of mine attending the interview expressed amazement and sadness that a bishop would not be delighted that young revolutionaries wanted to honor the martyred archbishop.

In an August 1980 interview discussing democracy, Obando expressed his misgivings about the masses: "The will of the majority should not be exaggerated, because it can become a democracy of masses, and the mass

---

24. *La Prensa*, June 18, 1981.

25. Ibid.

26. *La Prensa*, June 21, 1981.

27. *Cardenal Obando*, p. 53.

is the chief enemy of true democracy, the chief enemy of the democratic ideal of freedom and equality."[28]

Later that year a Canadian Church delegation which included the bishop of Victoria visited Nicaragua, talked with three Catholic bishops and a wide variety of Church and government groups, and the following year issued an extensive report on their findings. They were not as diffident about the masses as Obando had been in his August interview. "The Frente Sandinista wants to give this country a truly Nicaraguan model of society," they said, "socialist in the sense that it is based on the people and conceived in terms of the people, a model created by the people and oriented to the people, that is, to the poor majority who were marginalized previously.

"Because of its own unique character," they continued, "and because of its honesty and its concern for the masses, this Nicaraguan model should grow and be supported."

They also observed: "it seems to us that there is a conflict between two concepts, two models of the Church. One model looks with nostalgia to the power and prestige of the past with its massive processions. The other model is born in persecution and suffering and forged in dialectic and revolution."[29]

In a September 8 letter the bishops of Nicaragua spoke of the challenges presented by the revolution: "The priest today, much more sensitive to the demands of justice, will have to find the difficult synthesis between his commitment to the promotion of the poor and the other activities of his ministry. We would hope that his fidelity to the hierarchy and the gospel would be equal to his fidelity to the task of liberation." They reminded the priests of the need to present an image that would not be "one-sided."

On October 7, 1980 the FSLN published its official statement on religion, recognizing the role of Christians in the revolution and reaffirming the Sandinistas' commitment to respect freedom of religion. "For the first time," Envío noted, "a modern revolutionary movement already in power had broken with the rigid view of religion as an opiate of the people and a brake upon history. This historic novelty did not arise from

---

28. *La Prensa,* August 14, 1980.

29. Published in *El Nuevo Diario,* May 15, 1981.

a new theory of religion but from experiences lived during the liberation struggle, experiences which were very different from those of leaders of other revolutionary movements, such as in Cuba."[30]

The bishops, however, did not seem to appreciate the novelty or significance of the FSLN document. In their response ten days later, they strongly intimated that the good intentions would not be carried out in practice. They emphasized that "a new order must be rooted in man and in the common good, not in new models of 'domination' and 'class exclusivism.'" They asserted that the Church "never surrenders to any enslaving or idolatrous system bent on promoting atheism. Nicaragua has gone forth searching for its historic liberation, not for a new Pharaoh."

The bishops seemed especially disturbed by a tendency to take sides for the poor. "We demand social justice," they declared. "But justice is not 'class privilege.' No class has a privileged place over others." (This statement should be kept prominently in mind when analyzing, as we do in Part Five, the roots of the conflict between the hierarchy and the revolution.)

A group of prominent religious issued a public criticism of the bishops' statement, expressing their "surprise and concern" over the bishops' position. The tone of the document was "excessively polemical," they said, and it was full of fear. They also objected to "generalizations which became accusations and attacks, sometimes very hard, of doubtful validity and not helpful for dialogue." The three-page document, disputing all the points made by the bishops, was signed by the John XXIII Institute of the Central American University, the Antonio Valdivieso Ecumenical Center, the Central American Historical Institute, the Educational Center for Rural Promotion (CEPA), two Jesuits, two members of the National Confederation of Religious of Nicaragua (CONFER), the pastor of St. Paul the Apostle parish, and two religious sisters.[31]

In 1980 the Council for Inter-American Security, in a paper known as the *Santa Fe Report,* urged the incoming U.S. administration to take the offensive against progressive theology: "U.S. foreign policy must begin to counter . . . liberation theology as it is utilized in Latin America by the 'liberation theology' clergy. . . . Unfortunately, Marxist-Leninist forces have utilized the church as a political weapon against private property

---

30. *Envío,* December 1983.
31. *La Prensa,* Oct. 21, 1980.

and productive capitalism by infiltrating the religious community with ideas that are less Christian than communist."[32]

The Santa Fe document was not the first bit of advice offered to a president about the Latin American Church. In 1969 Nelson A. Rockefeller reported to President Nixon that the Catholic Church, recognizing "a need to be more responsive to popular will," had become one of "today's forces for social and political change." It was, he warned, "vulnerable to subversive penetration, ready to undertake a revolution if necessary to end injustice."[33]

In 1975 the CIA is said to have "helped formulate what became known as the Banzer Plan," named after Bolivian dictator Hugo Banzer. The campaign was designed "to sharpen internal divisions within the church, smear and harass progressive church leaders, and cause the arrest or expulsion of foreign priests or nuns who supported social change," linking them with armed struggle and international communism.[34]

The CIA generally sought "to promote Christian Democracy throughout Latin America as a means of domesticating and deradicalizing" social movements. The U.S. government supported the Christian Democrats in Chile in the sixties "with the cooperation of West Germany's Christian Democratic government and the German bishops whose Misereor and Adveniat mission and relief agencies were heavily subsidized by their government. Belgian Jesuit Roger Vekemans, later to emerge as a bitter enemy of liberation theology, served as a channel for at least $25 million a year from the Germans and a further $5 to $10 million in CIA and U.S. Agency for International Development funds."[35]

Vekemans moved to Bogota when the Socialist Salvador Allende was elected president of Chile in 1970. "In the more sympathetic climate of Colombia's ultraconservative church, he teamed up with . . . Bishop Al-

---

32. The Committee of Santa Fe, "A New Inter-American Policy for the Eighties" (Washington, D.C.: Council for Inter-American Security, 1980), as cited by Nelson-Pallmeyer, op. cit., p. 15.

33. *The Rockefeller Report on the Americas: The Official Report of a U.S. Presidential Mission for the Western Hemisphere* (Chicago: Quadrangle Books, 1969), as cited by Cohn, Hynds, op. cit., p. 104.

34. Cohn, Hynds, op. cit., p. 104.

35. Ibid.

fonso López Trujillo, who shared his aversion to liberation theology. In 1972 the previously progressive staff of the Latin American Bishops' Conference was replaced by a much more conservative group under the direction of López Trujillo as secretary general."[36]

Given this background, the Sandinistas could expect the new Reagan administration to try to live up to its promises to roll back the revolution and in that quest to utilize the churches and to "counter" liberation theology. Later on, when U.S. government aid went to the Archdiocese of Managua, the Sandinistas were not being paranoid in suspecting that such support was part of the Reagan administration's strategy to use religion to fight revolution.

In that strategy the administration's "two most important international allies" would be "the conservative hierarchy of the Nicaraguan Catholic church—especially Obando—and the Vatican." Cohn and Hynds considered it wrong "to imply that either was a simple tool of U.S. policy—as Nicaraguans occasionally did when referring to Obando." Rather, there was a "convergence of worldview that often led to cooperative effort. The conservative bishops and the pope were concerned that the hierarchical organization and authority of the church were being threatened by greater grass roots participation in both religion and politics in post-1979 Nicaragua. These fears and a misplaced anticommunism often led Obando and the new Polish pope to pursue policies that dovetailed neatly with those of Washington."[37]

During Reagan's first term the CIA would produce two manuals to guide the contras, urging them to accentuate religious tension. One manual, in comic book style, advised its readers to paint anti-Sandinista slogans, illustrating this idea with a picture of someone writing "Long Live the Pope" on a wall. The other manual urged the contras to express "indignation over the lack of freedom of worship, and persecution, of which priests are victims" and over the participation of priests in the Sandinista government "against the explicit orders of his Holiness, the Pope." The book recommended slogans like "God, Homeland, and Democracy" and "With God and patriotism, we will overcome communism" and "because we love Christ, we love his bishops and pastors."[38]

---

36. Ibid.

37. Ibid., p. 113.

38. Ibid., pp. 105-106.

Operating from Honduras and Costa Rica, contra radio stations, "financed in part with U.S. dollars, used religious themes, heaping praise on Obando—the 'Cardinal of Peace'—and broadcasting his Sunday homilies." Contra posters proclaimed "God is on our side" and "the Pope is with us." The contras' December 1985 bulletin featured Obando's picture on the cover, exclaiming "Long live our Cardinal" and again "With God and patriotism, we shall defeat communism."[39]

1981

In a January 23 letter on education the bishops asserted: "Our people, deeply religious and Christian for centuries, want for their children an education inspired by the gospel and attentive to the orientations of the Church." In this part of the letter they were referring to public education, and problems arose as to what they meant. The government saw itself as a lay state, and the ministry of education did not see its duty as promoting religion or any one church. (The theology behind the bishops' position on education was brought out succinctly in their Christmas 1981 letter when they declared that "there is no authentic humanism without Christ, true God and true man.")

In June and July a seven-member delegation from Pax Christi International visited Central America. The group, which was headed by an Italian bishop, stated: "While the bishops criticize the FSLN for turning Christians into 'political instruments,' they are allowing themselves to be politically manipulated by the opposition. We witnessed the way in which the political opposition declared the archbishop to be a 'prophet and martyr.'"[40]

In its final conclusions the report declared that "Nicaragua is not a Marxist country, much less a totalitarian one." After noting the growing hostility of the U.S. government, the report identified the bourgeoisie's businesses and mass media as "destabilizing factors which the United States can count on to exacerbate economic difficulties. The question is whether the Christian Democrats will get into this game. The Christian unions have become spokespersons for the private sector. The Social Christian Party, one of whose leaders is the coordinator of the Permanent

---

39. Ibid., p. 106.

40. *Envío*, December 1983.

Commission on Human Rights, is the opposition's main catalyst. And Archbishop Obando is letting himself be transformed into the leader of an opposition which does not have any other personage to put forth against the government."[41]

Pax Christi advised CELAM and the Christian Democrats to recognize that the Nicaraguan revolution has the support of the people and is here to stay. "Thus it is an illusion to dream of the coming to power of a Christian Democrat system, which would limit the abuses of economic exploitation but which would maintain the rules of the economic system." The report warned that the attitude of the political opposition and of the hierarchy was actually creating a self-fulfilling prophecy by contributing to a "radicalization of the revolutionary process."[42]

In June controversy broke out when the hierarchy reportedly blocked the return to Nicaragua of Sister María del Pilar Castellano, the principal of a school in the very poor Ciudad Sandino sector of Managua. She had helped in the Sandinista struggle against Somoza and was a supporter of the new government's programs. One neighborhood resident said: "In the past we were never favored by the government, by the rich, and much less by the Church. Now we have a people's government and religious who are dedicated to the physical and spiritual development of the poor, and the bishops want to take this away from us."[43]

A letter signed by 2,000 people, asking that sister be permitted to return to Nicaragua, was presented to the archdiocese. Minister of Education Carlos Tünnermann wrote to sister's superior in Spain to express his concern.[44]

In July the state-run TV system canceled the archbishop's televised Sunday Mass when he rejected their suggestion that the Mass be celebrated on a rotating basis involving other bishops.

In July and August the archdiocese removed two Dominican priests from their pastoral assignments, provoking an outcry from the people who saw the moves as repression against the pro-revolution sector of the Church. In an open letter a group of parishioners expressed their concern

---

41. *El Nuevo Diario,* Nov. 12, 1981.

42. Ibid.

43. *El Nuevo Diario,* June 15, 1981.

44. *El Nuevo Diario,* June 19, 1981.

that behind the transfers lurked "a plan to change our Church into a counter-revolutionary force which would impede the development of a revolution which is being made for the benefit of the poorest and of all the people." The parishioners expressed their hope that there would not be more expulsions of priests and religious "who choose to be faithful witnesses to God our loving Father and not to the god of capital which constantly widens the gap between rich and poor."[45] In early November, during a visit by Obando to one of the churches which had been served by the transferred priest, a group of protesters chanted slogans in support of the priest.

The transfers of priests and sisters demonstrated "one of the constants in the religious conflict: the lack of dialogue," according to *Envío*. "The opposition which these transfers have provoked has always expressed a key demand; that the bishops dialogue with the communities involved."[46]

In August the government of Venezuela honored Archbishop Obando with a prestigious award. Barricada named a number of well-known business leaders and opposition figures in attendance.[47] *La Prensa* devoted a special edition to the archbishop, containing 36 photos of him, many occupying a full page, paid for by private companies and some members of opposition parties. "The *La Prensa* tribute is perhaps the most obvious demonstration of the never-concealed links between the archbishop and the country's wealthy and opposition sectors," *Envío* observed.[48]

1982

When the news broke in January that Franciscan Father Mauro Jacomelli was being removed as pastor of Our Lady of Fatima in Managua, not only his own parishioners but people from the CBCs throughout Managua protested vigorously. *El Nuevo Diario* described Father Jacomelli as a priest who had identified with the people in the struggle

---

45. *El Nuevo Diario*, Aug. 19, 1981.

46. *Envío*, December 1983.

47. *Barricada*, August 29, 1981.

48. *Envío*, December 1983.

against Somoza and whose attitude was one of "critical support for the revolutionary process."[49]

Obando reportedly had pressured the Franciscans to remove the priest from the parish. With a group of parishioners in support of Jacomelli occupying the church, one woman from another parish said: "We are here in solidarity because tomorrow we could be the target, since Archbishop Obando is intent on removing the progressive priests."[50]

A large banner at the entrance of the church proclaimed: "It is impossible to serve the exploited without fighting the exploitation by the rich and supporting the project of the poor." Another sign, using the words of a song, asked: "Christ at the service of whom?"

People in eleven parishes held continuous vigils and prayer services, demanding that Archbishop Obando agree to dialogue with the communities about the personnel transfers. A visiting Delegate of the Word from the northern border region said: "The archbishop should reflect: is he with the poor or with the rich?"[51]

On January 26 the archbishop met with four representatives of the communities, who were surprised to find Obando accompanied by Bishop Bosco Vivas and four priests. Obando promised to begin a series of visits to the parishes where the vigils had been held—a response which the CBCs considered "positive but insufficient." They had been asking for "a broad and profound dialogue about the unity of the Church in the current problematic situation in Nicaragua."[52]

Father Teófilo Cabestrero later reflected on his friend's experience. Father Jacomelli had a "gospel spirituality centered in the Church, and therefore very sensitive to the poor and to their complete liberation. It was a spirituality based on the teaching of the bishops at Vatican II, Medellín, and Puebla; and, logically, it was incarnated in the historical situation of Nicaragua, in the people's revolutionary process—with proper critical distance. In this sense Father Mauro was always irreproachable.

"But," and here's where the trouble began, "he consistently proclaimed the gospel within the process, expressing support for the

49. Jan. 11, 1982.

50. *Barricada*, Jan. 13, 1982.

51. *Barricada*, Jan. 23, 1982.

52. *Barricada*, Jan. 27, 1982.

revolution's achievements which benefit the poor majority in keeping with the gospel. In reward for that the archdiocese removed him from his position as pastor."[53]

On February 18 the hierarchy-state conflict broke out again when the bishops' conference denounced alleged grave violations of the human rights of Miskitos who had been transferred from militarized zones along the northern border. "This charge was issued without any prior discussion about the matter with officials of the government," Cohn and Hynds noted, "and after the bishops themselves had turned down a government invitation to send a fact-finding mission to visit the camps to which many Miskitos had been relocated. Coming as it did at a time of extremely overblown and inaccurate rhetoric from the Reagan administration concerning Sandinista 'genocide' against the Miskitos, this pastoral was seen by many Nicaraguans as essentially aiding and abetting the enemy."[54]

The war which counterrevolutionary bands were waging from Honduras, with $19 million in covert aid from the Reagan administration in 1981, had become intense in the north Zelaya area, with some Miskitos joining the contras or giving them logistical support.

Between November 1981 and January 1982 the contras killed 60 people, including Sandinista soldiers and civilians. On December 14, 1981, 12 border guards and their lieutenant were abducted and later murdered in Honduras. The plan to penetrate Nicaragua and set up a "liberated zone" was known as Red Christmas.

The government responded by evacuating thousands from the Río Coco area "in order to avoid the use of the people as a means of support for the contras and . . . to prevent the Miskitos who were not involved in the counterrevolution from being caught in the cross fire."[55] Although the evacuation was generally considered to be justifiable from a military point of view, the political cost was serious, both among the Miskito pop-

53. *Un Grito a Dios y al Mundo* (San José, C.R.: Editorial DEI, 1986), pp. 163-64. The author noted that his comments were based on his own personal acquaintance with Father Jacomelli and the situation.

54. Cohn, Hynds, op. cit., p. 114.

55. *Envío* monograph, "The Miskitos and the Atlantic Coast," July 1984. This special report provides a good analysis of the complex factors involved in Miskito history and in the counterrevolution in the Zelaya province.

ulation and in international public opinion. The move itself involved extensive property damage since government troops destroyed Miskito villages in order to prevent materials from falling into the hands of the contras. And the Miskitos, with a deep attachment to their land along the river, felt torn from their environment.

In their message the bishops recognized that "armed clashes had resulted in the death of many militia and soldiers of the Sandinista People's Army as well as the death of many of their political adversaries and of some uninvolved citizens." They noted that these events resulted in dozens of arrests and the relocation of the population. "If militarily it is possible to explain the massive evacuation," they continued, "we must nevertheless lament, from a human and Christian point of view, the displacement. . . ."

They also recognized the right of the government "to take the necessary means, including emergency military measures, to guarantee the defense of the country." What they denounced were "some concrete cases" of serious violations of human rights, such as the lack of previous notice and dialogue, the "forced marches for several days without sufficient consideration for the weak, the elderly, women, and children," broad accusations of collaboration with the contras, the destruction of dwellings and animals, and the death of some people in circumstances "which remind us of the drama being lived out by other peoples who are brothers to us." They urged the authorities to take disciplinary measures which would avoid the repetition of such acts in the future.

The bishops' statement was criticized for its vagueness and certain inaccuracies and for its overall interpretation "which in no way addressed the causes of the relocation measure."[56] The correct interpretation of the event, according to Envío, is that "no other means could be found to isolate the Miskito population from the manipulation the United States was exercising from the Honduran side of the border. . . . It was a question of the need to safeguard Nicaragua's territory for the common good and the future of the revolution, the existence of which will, though not necessarily in the short run, benefit the Miskitos and other indigenous peoples."[57]

---

56. Ibid.
57. Ibid.

Envío interviewed Capuchin Father Francisco Solano, who has worked in the Zelaya department for many years, on the issue. "With the sudden evacuation," he recalled, "houses were burned and cattle were killed. There were reasons for doing this: to prevent the contras from using the houses or finding food. This is understandable, but the negative symbol remains: the people saw their houses burned, they saw years of work destroyed in minutes. . . . The Miskitos cannot understand all of this."

Envío asked: "Wasn't there enough time to explain the reasons for the evacuation?" Father Solano said: "I was in the zone at the time. No, there really wasn't time. The choice was between evacuating them or letting them die there." The priest also noted that the government troops' tendency to base themselves in Catholic and Moravian chapels, "the largest and safest buildings, built with cement," was understandable but came as a "tremendous shock" to the Miskitos.[58]

The government issued a strong response on February 22 to the bishops' critique, saying it had "little truth to it and distorted reality." The government also objected to the bishops' failure to use the "official channels of communication agreed upon by the government and the bishops." The government also complained that the bishops had not accepted two invitations to visit the resettlement camps. Among other points in its detailed reply to the bishops' charges, the government said that "those who are victimizing our people, those who committed massacres in the past and still today, cannot be called in any way 'the political adversaries' of our soldiers but rather the enemies of all our people."[59]

Justinian Liebl, who had worked for 25 years in the Atlantic region of Nicaragua as a Capuchin priest, noted in an article that in the sixties when Somoza transferred thousands of Miskitos from their homeland the bishops uttered not a word of protest. He also observed that the hierarchy never spoke out against the physical harm done to Miskito workers by the mining companies or against the rip-off of forest lands, and he criticized the bishops for taking so long even to mention the National Guard massacre of peasants denounced publicly by the Capuchins.

When President Reagan cut off food credits for Nicaragua in 1981, Liebl continued, and began open aggression against Nicaragua, the bishops maintained "an astonishing silence." He noted that they had not de-

---

58. Ibid.
59. *El Nuevo Diario*, Feb. 23, 1982.

nounced the assassinations, sabotage, and other acts of terrorism by the contras. But now, at a moment when an international meeting of political parties was taking place in Nicaragua, they quickly went public. "Decades of silence about the Miskito situation were broken only to use a problem whose roots go very deep to launch a strong and not very veiled attack against the Sandinista People's Revolution and its vanguard, the FSLN," Liebl charged.[60]

On February 23 the bishops issued a strong but brief and vague denunciation of "terrorist guerrilla violence, no matter where it comes from." They cited Puebla in stating that "in no way can crime be justified as a way to liberation."

In July members of the Managua parish of St. Rose learned that their pastor for eight years, Monsignor José Arias Caldera, was being removed from the parish at the end of the month. An archdiocesan spokesman called the move "routine." The previous November the Frente Sandinista had publicly honored the priest for his outstanding work for justice, peace, and freedom. He had been one of the early collaborators with the Frente, giving refuge to Carlos Fonseca among others.

The removal of the pastor, who was known as the "Monsignor of the Poor," was widely attributed to his positive attitude toward the revolutionary government. On July 20 a large group of members of the CBCs of St. Rose occupied the church, protesting the transfer and demanding dialogue with the archbishop.

The response came the next night when an archdiocesan official, accompanied by three seminarians, tried to remove the blessed sacrament from the church. About 80 people gathered around the visitor. Some say he fainted; he claimed to have been roughed up. On July 22 the archbishop denounced the "attack" and excommunicated those responsible, also putting the church under interdict (i.e., that no priest could celebrate any ritual there).

Sergio Ramírez, member of the governing junta, told the press that the events were internal Church matters but had "political consequences. We have been seeing how the more progressive priests, the ones more identified with the revolution, are moved from their parishes and neutralized."

---

60. *El Nuevo Diario*, Feb. 22, 1982.

He said that the papal nuncio had been made aware of the government's concern over "these maneuvers to take away support from the revolution."[61]

On July 24 a contra group savagely assassinated 14 peasants in the town of San Francisco del Norte, writing on the walls of houses that their action was taken "in the name of God." The contras also wounded four and kidnapped eight persons. After mutilating the bodies of the dead, the contras reportedly walked from house to house telling residents "we are Christians, we are democratic."[62] Christians participating in the revolutionary process began to ask the hierarchy to condemn officially such attacks. (Later, in the October issue of their bulletin, *De Frente*, the contras claimed responsibility for the San Francisco massacre and devoted several paragraphs to praising Obando, whom it labeled as "ever more identified with the struggle for the liberation of Nicaragua."[63])

On July 26 about 40,000 people gathered in Managua to honor the dead and to express their outrage over the massacre and their determination to defend the revolution. In front of 14 empty coffins, members of CBCs chanted: "We want a Church on the side of the poor! Long live Monsignor Arias Caldera, the Monsignor of the Poor!" One of their signs addressed Church officials: "We Christians are also revolutionaries. Let the hierarchy define itself as being on the side of the poor or on the side of the bourgeoisie."

When Monsignor Arias came to the microphone, the people applauded and chanted: "Don't go. Don't go." In his speech the priest mentioned some of the revolution's achievements: the literacy crusade, state subsidies for basic necessities, housing for the poor, and defense of the nation's sovereignty. "Are these sins?" he asked. "Why do they want to kill us?

"When people are attached to wealth," he said in response, "when they have an insatiable desire for riches, then their hearts are cold and they are moved by nothing." He said that Christ is present in the dead, who gave their lives for the future of the Nicaraguan people.[64]

---

61. *Barricada*, July 23, 1982.

62. *El Nuevo Diario*, July 25, 1982.

63. *Envío*, December 1983.

64. *El Nuevo Diario*, July 27, 1982.

The same day the Dominicans of Nicaragua issued a public statement based on reports by two members of the order working in the area where the attack took place. They denounced not only the San Francisco massacre but previous atrocities, acts of sabotage, and the increasingly hostile policy of the Reagan administration intent on destabilizing "this process of basic change in favor of the majority of our people."

They expressed particular outrage over "the use of the name of God to try to justify these massacres. That is one more result of the utilization of religion by the rich and powerful who are defending nothing more than their selfish interests. We lament the attitude of silence of most of our pastors concerning these events, and we see that this attitude tends to disorient the Christian people." They noted that the situation is aggravated by the closed attitude of many pastors toward requests to dialogue with the people about internal Church problems.

"As we have done on other occasions," they continued, "we express our support for and confidence in the process of revolutionary change we are living out in Nicaragua." They said they would continue to be involved in the people's struggle "for dignity, social development, and a just peace which can deliver the people from centuries of ignorance, exploitation, and misery. Trusting in Jesus Christ, Lord of life and history, we hope that our Church will hear the cry of the poor and enter into real solidarity with their sorrows and hopes in order to fulfill its mission to evangelize."

Also on July 26 archdiocesan spokesman Father Bismarck Carballo said that the Church in principle condemns murder but could not issue a statement every time something happens.[65] (On Dec. 19, 1982 youth groups from various Central American countries meeting in Costa Rica issued a public statement in which they recalled the excommunication of the people involved in the St. Rose incident concerning the removal of Monsignor Arias Caldera. The drastic measure "was never applied to Somoza and has never been applied to the aggressors of today," the statement observed pointedly.)

Several days later mothers and other relatives of the San Francisco victims arrived at the Fatima parish in Managua, where members of the CBC were holding meetings and prayer services 24 hours a day in protest of Obando's "arbitrary action in removing priests and his silence regard-

---

65. *Barricada,* July 27, 1982.

ing the crimes committed by the Somocistas using the name of God." The visitors from San Francisco joined in the plea for the hierarchy to speak out against the atrocities.[66] (In November Bishop Julian Barni of León was asked his opinion of "those who murder in the name of God." He replied: "No one has the right to murder in the name of God, because God condemns murder. Those who do that are evil.")[67]

At the Dominicans' church of La Merced in León an impressive liturgy was celebrated in memory of the victims, with 22 uniforms in front of the altar representing the dead and kidnapped. Those killed had given their lives "to defend the right of the Nicaraguan people to construct their own destiny," one speaker said. Prayers were offered for the safe return of the kidnapped, who were represented by eight candles, and a small model of a house symbolized the revolution's efforts on behalf of the homeless. Two ears of corn in a sombrero and a machete represented the land reform program and the work and hopes of the peasants.

An encyclopedia symbolized the work of teachers "and their determination to help in the formation of the new person." A nurse represented the right of all Nicaraguans to medical care. The new health centers, hospitals, vaccination campaigns, and the daily labor of all the members of the health profession were offered to the Lord with a prayer that every day they may grow in love for the people. Construction workers were represented by a hammer and saw, and members of the Sandinista Youth offered their work in teaching the illiterate. A map of the world represented international solidarity with Nicaragua.[68] Such liturgical creativity in relation to real-life issues characterizes the celebrations of the Church of the Poor.

On August 3 two Jesuits, Fathers Alvaro Argüello and Napoleón Alvarado of the Central American Historical Institute, issued a public letter to the Christian communities of Honduras, asking them to work for the return of the eight kidnapped. "We are more concerned every day over the situation which has been created between our two countries," they added. "We are determined to defend the dignity we won after so much struggle and the project which is under way in Nicaragua with so much sacrifice.

---

66. *Barricada*, July 30, 1982.

67. *Barricada*, Nov. 9, 1982.

68. *El Nuevo Diario*, Aug. 3, 1982.

We ask for your solidarity and offer you our hope in the God of the poor, knowing that he is on the side of those who work for justice."[69]

In early August the bishops decided to publicize a letter the pope had sent them on Church unity. "Though the letter was dated June 29, the bishops . . . chose not to make it public until early August," *Envío* noted.[70] When the bishops gave the letter to *La Prensa* to be published, the government, "alarmed by the letter's unconditional support for the bishops and its criticism of the 'popular Church,' forbade publication of the letter under the state-of-emergency censorship laws decreed in March 1982. The error in this decision," *Envío* noted, "became clear when the news spread around the world that the Sandinistas had silenced even the voice of the pope. From that time on, the conflict in Nicaragua would be interpreted in terms of 'persecution of the Church' and 'the danger of the popular Church.' The first characterization arises from a one-sided [and highly exaggerated] interpretation of certain errors on the part of the government, while the second was introduced into the discussion by the pope's letter."

On August 10 the government reversed the decision of its communications office, and the pope's letter was published in all three papers. After expressing his desire that the Christians of Nicaragua not be divided over "opposite ideologies," the pope stated that the bishops therefore had a greater responsibility, "since the unity of the faithful must be woven together concretely around the bishop. . . . Thus it is absurd and dangerous for another Church conceived as 'charismatic' and not institutional, 'new' and not traditional, an alternative, 'popular Church' to think of itself as being alongside of, not to say against, the Church built around the bishop."

While the pope recognized that an acceptable meaning can be given to the terms "the Church born of the people" or "popular Church," he noted that the latter expression commonly means "a Church which insists on the autonomy of its so-called *bases* without reference to the legitimate Pastors or Teachers." The term "people," he said, "easily takes on a markedly sociological and political content." Thus the term "popular Church" means a Church "incarnated in the popular organizations, marked by ide-

---

69. *El Nuevo Diario*, Aug. 4, 1982.

70. December, 1983.

ologies put at the service of their demands." [The reader should know that in Spanish the term "popular" is the adjectival form of "people" and thus could be translated as "people's." The word "popular" conjures up images of popular music or even pop-theology and in that sense has very little if any application to the Church of the Poor.]

"It is easy to see," the pope continued, "as the Puebla document explicitly indicated, that the concept of 'popular Church' has a difficult time escaping being infiltrated by strongly ideological connotations. These connotations move in the direction of a certain political radicalization, of class struggle, of the acceptance of violence to achieve certain ends, etc. . . . A 'popular Church' opposed to the Church presided over by its legitimate Pastors is . . . a serious deviation from the will and the plan of salvation of Jesus Christ." The pope gave the bishops "the duty and task of making that known to your faithful with patience and firmness."

The progressive sectors of the Church said that the pope's description of the "popular Church" (a term which is not commonly used among the CBCs in Nicaragua) did not apply to them. They insisted that their differences with the bishops were not doctrinal but matters of political opinion and commitment.

When Archbishop Obando was asked whether he felt that some within the Church had a true intention to divide it, he answered in the affirmative and went on to charge that certain organizations which promote liberation theology have "exclusive access to the state-run mass media which include all television, 90 percent of radio, and two of the three newspapers." Their message contains the following points, according to Obando: "The first duty of the Christian is to support the revolution; loyalty to the revolution must be absolute and must come before any other consideration; Christianity and Marxism are not only compatible, but Marxism is the only way to incarnate Christianity and put it into effect." The over-simplifications and distortions in Obando's description were obvious to informed readers.

The "revolutionary Church," Obando went on, "continually accuses the hierarchy of being identified with the rich and of being counter-revolutionary, and its public protests receive ample publicity in the state media. . . . It has developed vast campaigns of international propaganda to broadcast the supposed novelties and niceties of the regime."[71]

---

71. *La Prensa*, Aug. 14, 1982.

On August 11 a priest in charge of archdiocesan communications was videotaped and shown on the Sandinista TV system running out of a house clad only in his birthday vestments. "The crudity with which the alleged scandal was handled by the press and TV . . . had negative implications for the government."[72]

On August 16, as an expression of solidarity with the priest, five religious-run high schools in Managua were occupied by young anti-Sandinistas. In Masaya a demonstration of young Sandinistas was fired upon "by snipers positioned inside the Salesian high school," according to Envío.[73] One young Sandinista, Eddy Guzmán, was killed by sniper fire from the school. As a result of these events, a Spanish priest, accused of complicity, was deported from the country.

On August 18 the FSLN leadership reiterated its principle of respect for religion, noted that recent problems "do not represent a confrontation between religion and the revolution," and called for maturity in dialogue. "The media should avoid exacerbating tensions," the communiqué added.

In a December 8 pastoral letter on education, the bishops recognized the government's achievements in this area, mentioning the national literacy crusade, adult education, and the efforts to "completely democratize" education. In the latter category the bishops noted pre-school programs, "which have grown more than 60%"; an increase in the number of primary and secondary school students; the construction of many educational centers; the manifest attention given to special education; and the subsidies given by the state to private schools, including religious institutions, "making it possible that private education gradually cease being the privilege of a few."

The bishops went on to express concern about a number of aspects of education. They claimed to see a tendency to treat some aspects of the formation of the youth "from a purely materialistic perspective, without taking into account the religious and transcendent dimension of the human being." They also complained of a "gradual loss of a critical spirit in education" as well as a "marked tendency to favor, under the

---

72. *Envío*, December 1983.

73. Ibid.

pretext of being scientific, one vision and interpretation of the social, economic, and political reality of the country."

They were referring to a Marxist interpretation, and Nicaraguan educators did not deny that they found some elements of Marxist theory useful in analyzing society. As for the first "tendency," defenders of the new educational system stated that the public schools did not have the duty to teach religion but that the Church and its schools had every right and opportunity to do so.

Over the years some very misleading statements have been made about Nicaraguan education. Trying to show that "control is the obsession of sandinismo," Edward R. F. Sheehan quoted "a nun in Estelí," for instance, as saying: "This is a religious school, but we can teach religion only two hours a week. The rest of the curriculum is controlled by the state, the books are provided by the state, the salaries of teachers, lay and religious, are paid by the state."[74]

The fact is that the state, as in the United States, established certain curricular requirements. Religious schools can add as many hours of religious education as they want; as in the United States, most schools find it feasible to have about two hours a week. In private schools which chose to accept government subsidies, those funds helped to pay salaries. As the bishops stated in their 1982 letter, such aid made it possible "that private education gradually cease being the privilege of a few."

The bishops also claimed that certain texts and programs were "sharpening the class struggle and generating and feeding hatred among brothers. This makes it impossible to build the unity and peace which we all long for." They cited a distinction in their November 17, 1979 pastoral letter between "the dynamic fact of class struggle which should lead to a just transformation of structures" and "class hatred which is directed against persons and radically conflicts with the Christian duty to be ruled by love." (This issue of unity is taken up at length in Chapter 11.)

During 1982 two progressive organizations were reined in. The Association of Nicaraguan Clergy (ACLEN) was brought under the hierarchy's control, and the Nicaraguan Conference of Religious (CONFER) had to accept new restrictions on election of officers.

---

74. Op. cit., p. 127.

René Mendoza summarized developments particularly in the Masatepe area from the late 1970s through the early 1980s:

> During the guerrilla period, the religious factor was fundamental in the *comarcas* of Masatepe for developing consciousness and the liberation of the country. In the struggle a Delegate of the Word movement was born. But with the triumph, many of these Delegates ceased that work and took up revolutionary leadership functions. Obando y Bravo and the hierarchy designed a religious structure that completely subsumed the original movement, replacing it with new Delegates expressly obedient to Obando. And at the national level, under his baton, some progressive priests were relocated and various missionary priests and nuns were expelled, sanctioned or prohibited from coming.[75]

Summary to Present

By the close of 1982, most of the important issues in the conflict between the hierarchy and the government and between the hierarchy and the Church of the Poor had been raised. These issues will be analyzed in the next two chapters.

From 1983 to the middle of 1986, the hierarchy's relations with the government steadily worsened. In March 1983 the pope's visit to Nicaragua brought out his own negative attitude toward the revolution (due largely to the information he had received from anti-Sandinista sectors) and the people's strong reaction against his stance.[76] Toward the end of 1983, when the government found it necessary to begin compulsory military service in its war against the invading contras, the bishops came out against the policy, claiming that the army served the interests of one party rather than those of the nation.[77]

In 1984 the bishops proposed that the contras be included in negotiations with the government. It was a very unpopular suggestion, since the

---

75. Op. cit.

76. See *Envío* (March 1983) and Conor Cruise O'Brien, "God and Man in Nicaragua," op. cit..

77. See *Envío* (December 1983).

contras were commonly seen as largely stemming from Somoza's National Guard, depending mainly on U.S. sustenance, with very little support in Nicaragua and with no territory under their control, and guilty of heinous atrocities against civilian targets. Church groups as well as the government roundly attacked the bishops' proposal.[78]

Later that year, the government told Obando that it had evidence (including videotapes) that an archdiocesan priest was collaborating with the contras. When the archdiocese responded by organizing a demonstration (without a permit) in support of the accused priest, the government revoked the residency visas of ten foreign priests, most of whom had participated in the demonstration.[79]

In 1985, just after becoming a cardinal, Obando made a stop in Miami to celebrate Mass before returning home. Among those of the Nicaraguan exile community in attendance were some prominent contra leaders. Many Nicaraguans were outraged at the cardinal's open association with their enemies.[80] Throughout the month of July, Father Miguel D'Escoto, M.M., Nicaragua's Foreign Minister, fasted and prayed for peace in a Managua church, thus launching what he called the "evangelical insurrection."[81]

Later that year the archdiocese went into print with a new publication entitled *Iglesia* without having obtained the authorization for new publications required by Nicaraguan law. The first issue, which had some articles which could be considered anti-draft, was confiscated and the press shut down.

The year 1986 was marked by escalation by both sides. Cardinal Obando and Bishop Pablo Antonio Vega made public statements seriously questioning the legitimacy of the government and serving to justify U.S.

---

78. See *Envío* (August 1984).

79. Ibid.

80. See *Envío* (August 1985).

81. Ibid. See also Father Teófilo Cabestrero's book about the fast, op. cit., and Pablo Richard, "Church of the Poor in Nicaragua," *The Vatican and the Reagan Administration,* by Ana Maria Ezcurra (N.Y.: New York Circus Publications, 1986). See preface of same book for a description of the Way of the Cross for Peace and Life led by Fr. D'Escoto in Lent, 1986. The book also gives a detailed analysis of the anti-Sandinista activities of Cardinal Obando and Bishop Vega.

aid to the contras. In this way they helped President Reagan in his campaign to get $100 million from Congress for his "freedom fighters."

In a May 12 article in the *Washington Post*, Obando developed the thesis that "the insurgent dissidents are now in the same position that the Sandinistas themselves once occupied and, consequently, that they have the same right that the Sandinistas had to seek aid from other nations. . . . The only possible argument against this is that . . . this is a democratic government, legitimately constituted." But the cardinal concluded: "Unfortunately, this is not true either."

He went on to present a number of criticisms of the Nicaraguan government and supported the contras' right "to seek aid from other nations."

It was around this time, recalled COSEP Vice-President Ramiro Gurdián, that Cardinal Obando, in a meeting at the Camino Real hotel, expressed his view that insurrection could be justified if, he said, the government continued its repressive actions.[82] In late 1985 an unnamed "personage" visiting *La Prensa* had opined: "I think that in private Cardinal Obando approves of the contras."[83] In 1986 Obando said: "We're against all violence. In Nicaragua, however, we have no objective information because all information is manipulated by the Sandinistas. We should denounce all injustice, but if we spoke against the contras our words would be twisted."[84] In a later interview Obando again "declined my invitation to condemn the contras," Sheehan reported (p. 291).

Shortly after the United States Congress approved aid to the contras, Bishop Vega was exiled by the government in a move which many considered defensible since Vega had been seeking to justify the violent overthrow of the government.[85]

Just a few weeks after Vega was given a ride over the border to Honduras, a new papal nuncio, Paolo Giglio, arrived in Managua and stated that he hoped to contribute to an improvement in government-hierarchy relations. Rhetoric simmered down, and later that year a much-touted

---

82. My interview of Gurdián, May 1989.

83. Edward R. F. Sheehan, op. cit., p. 107.

84. Ibid., p. 229.

85. See my article on my 1987 debate with Bishop Vega, *National Catholic Reporter* August 14, 1987..

Eucharistic Congress was celebrated without any fireworks between Church and state.

In 1987 the peace process made dramatic gains with the Esquipulas (Guatemala) accords signed by the five Central American presidents in August. One result of the agreement was the formation of the National Reconciliation Commission, of which Obando became president. At the government's request the cardinal shortly began to serve as mediator with the contras in cease-fire talks.

In March 1988 these talks produced a cease-fire agreement. In spite of many contra violations, the war diminished substantially; and in 1989, with Nicaragua moving toward internationally scrutinized elections, the region's five presidents called for the dismantling of the contras. In 1990 the Nicaraguan bishops urged the people to take part fully in the electoral process. (That process is discussed in this book's introduction.)

On March 23, 1990 Cardinal Obando added his signature as witness to an agreement signed in Honduras by representatives of the government-elect and the contras. The latter agreed to "begin the process of general demobilization of our forces, beginning with those in Honduras." These troops were to be demobilized by April 20, five days before the inauguration of Violeta Chamorro. This was carried out, but by April 20 there were only several hundred contras left in Honduras, and most of these were war-disabled with obsolete weapons. Thousands of troops had entered Nicaragua in the meantime.

The agreement also stated, without setting a date, that contras in Nicaragua would move into "security zones" with a view toward demobilization. The president-elect's delegation expressed its appreciation for this decision by the contras, adding: "As an expression of due recognition of the patriotic labor of the Nicaraguan Resistance, there must be assistance for the disabled, orphans, and widows—the innocents who bear the scars of the armed struggle." Many Nicaraguans were outraged and scandalized that Cardinal Obando subscribed to this recognition of the "patriotic labor" of the contras, who have been known as terrorists in the service of a foreign superpower. Probably the cardinal had always agreed with Ronald Reagan's designation of the contras as "freedom fighters."

At 1 a.m. on May 5, after marathon discussions, two contra commanders signed an agreement with the government to begin the process of disarming. Cardinal Obando and President Chamorro had participated in the meeting. The May 6 edition of the *Miami Herald* featured an Agence

France-Presse photo of the two contra commanders arms-over-shoulders with Obando and Chamorro, all smiling broadly. (The cardinal is not noted for his jubilant facial expressions. Here his ear-to-ear smile revealed a personal joy which he never showed in the company of Sandinistas.)

On May 8 eighty-four contras began the process of disarming by turning in their weapons, said to be in very bad condition, to the United Nations peace-keeping force, in the presence of delegates of Chamorro and Obando. Roberto Rivas, according to *Barricada* (May 9), speaking in the name of Obando, described the contras as "brave men who have taken up arms for the country."

Part Five

Roots of the Conflict

*The government and the revolution have no problems whatso-
ever with the Church. There have been problems with some
members of the Catholic hierarchy, and these problems have
to do with political differences.*
—President Daniel Ortega, *Barricada*, December 31, 1988.

Introduction

A certificate of honor from the Permanent Commission for Human
Rights hangs on the wall of Cardinal Obando's outer office; dated April
20, 1986, the award from the fiercely anti-Sandinista organization was
bestowed during the height of the conflict between the hierarchy and the
government over the proposed $100 million in U.S. aid for the contras.
Also displayed is a February 1987 award from the Nicaraguan Chamber
of Commerce.[1] Along with other awards for Obando and pictures of him
with John Paul II, the office also features a framed copy of a New York
Times article (Dec. 30, 1974) about the Sandinista takeover of the home
of Chema Castillo and Obando's work as mediator in that event, with a
picture of Obando.

Citing his position as president of the National Reconciliation Commission, the cardinal declined to answer most of my questions about
Church relations with the Sandinistas.[2] He urged me to talk to auxiliary
bishop Bosco Vivas.

"The present situation is the most critical that we have been in, in the
sense that it remains to be seen whether the government will comply with
the El Salvador accords or not," said Bishop Vivas, referring to the
February 1989 agreement by the Nicaraguan government to advance the
date of the 1990 elections and to carry out reforms in electoral legislation
and media laws so as to assure free and fair elections.[3] The presidents
had agreed to draw up a plan for the demobilization and repatriation or
relocation in third countries of the contra forces and their families in
Honduras, and they had urged an end of aid to irregular forces or insurrectional movements in the area with the exception of humanitarian aid

---

1. The director of Caritas (the Church's official charity organization) in Nicaragua is a
former president of the Chamber of Commerce.

2. My interview of Cardinal Obando, April 1989.

3. See *Envío*, March 1989.

that contributes to the goals of the agreement. Nicaragua moved election day up to February 25, 1990, proceeded to reform the electoral and media laws, and ultimately released all the ex-National Guardsmen.

"I don't believe the government will comply voluntarily," Bishop Vivas judged, implying that aid to the contras as a fighting force should continue in order to keep the pressure on.[4] The bishop's theological views are as clear-cut as his political opinions. "Liberation theology, as we in the Church interpret it, has nothing to contribute," he stated plainly (*Pensamiento Propio*, June-July 1989).

An official of another diocese told me that some of the bishops supported aid for the contras in order to "keep the pressure on" the Sandinistas so that they would "democratize" and respect the Church. The same official said that the political opposition used Cardinal Obando, rallying around him as a public figure who could draw crowds, "like rallying around the flag."

There is some evidence that not all the other bishops in Nicaragua shared the hard political line of Obando and Bosco Vivas. Betsy Cohn and Patricia Hynds pointed out that "although Obando frequently spoke in the name of Nicaragua's bishops, some of the latter made it clear on occasion that they did not completely share his ideas."[5] For instance, now-retired Bishop Rubén López Ardón of Estelí said in November 1985 that "all peoples have the right to free self-determination. As a sovereign and independent country, Nicaragua has this right, and everyone must respect it."[6] In 1984 Bishop Paul Schmitz, auxiliary bishop in Bluefields, said that "in my view any direct aggression would be a disaster for the Nicaraguan people. As a priest, as a Capuchin, as a Christian, I cannot be in favor of U.S. intervention."[7] In a discussion of Ronald Reagan's policies, Bishop Carlos Santi of Matagalpa said: "I am really not in agreement with any government which intervenes in the affairs of another government."[8] The paucity of such laudable statements is strik-

---

4.   My interview of Bishop Bosco Vivas, April 1989. In April 1991 Bosco Vivas was named to succeed Bishop Julian Barni as bishop of León.

5.   Op. cit., p. 100.

6.   *El Nuevo Diario*, November 6, 1985, as cited by Cohn, Hynds, op. cit., p. 100.

7.   *Barricada*, December 20, 1984, as cited by Cohn, Hynds. op. cit., p. 100. On January 1, 1990 Bishop Schmitz was seriously wounded in a contra attack on his vehicle which left one U.S. sister (Maureen Courtney) and a Nicaraguan sister (Teresa Rosales) dead.

ing. (Bishop Pedro Vilchez of Jinotega made news in 1989 by denouncing a contra kidnapping of two people in his diocese.)[9]

As for the clergy, a 1983 survey showed that of the 220 priests who responded (almost all those in Nicaragua) 46 percent supported the revolutionary process and the rest opposed it, "with support and opposition occurring to different degrees. Diocesan and native-born priests [who are more closely tied to the bishops] tend to be more opposed to the process than religious and foreign priests."[10]

Father Omar Aragon Cardenas, pastor of St. Paul the Apostle parish,[11] noted that it was not correct to speak of "persecution of the Church" in Nicaragua. In his view, certain sectors of the Church became intransigent opponents of the government, and in response some Sandinistas engaged in "political harassment" of some priests and lay persons, particularly in the media.

In a similar vein Bishop Sturdie Downs of the Nicaraguan Episcopal Church stated clearly in May 1986 that "there is no religious persecution." He described tension between the Catholic hierarchy and the government as a struggle over power: "If I am a religious leader and I say 'so-so-so' about the government, and the government gets up and says 'so-so-so' about me, I think what we are doing is playing politics. I can't say 'they are persecuting me.'"[12]

Looking at the conflict between the Nicaraguan hierarchy (especially Cardinal Obando and Bishop Vega) and the Sandinista government, one naturally asks: "What was at the bottom of all this?" Discussions in Nicaragua include at least *five* factors, which should be taken in combination to explain the complex problem; these factors will be discussed in Chapter 10. Underlying this problem are *three basic theological questions* about the relationship between the Church and religious freedom, the Church and the Kingdom, and Church unity; these questions will be discussed in Chapter 11.[13]

---

8.   *Barricada*, December 18, 1984, as cited by Cohn, Hynds, op. cit., p. 100.

9.   *El Nuevo Diario*, June 2, 1989.

10. *Envío*, December 1983, p. 9b.

11. See Chapter 5 on this parish as the birthplace of the Christian base communities.

12. Interchange 15, no. 5 (May 1986), p. 4, as cited by Cohn, Hynds, op. cit., p. 102.

13. Some of these points were touched upon briefly in my article in *Latinamerica Press,* June 19, 1986.

10

Five Essential Factors

1. The Economic Factor

The most frequently suggested reason for the conflict is that many bishops and priests, even those who may be from humble origins themselves, tend to identify with the upper-middle and upper classes, depending on them for their livelihood and for the support of Church institutions. Bishops and pastors move comfortably in business and professional circles and receive favors and special cooperation, often for the sake of the smooth functioning of their apostolic institutions, from people with money and power. Thus they usually defend a system which protects established interests against a revolutionary movement putting a radical priority on the needs of the poor majority. Indeed, poor peasants and laborers do not figure prominently in the social world of most ecclesiastical officials.

Bishop Pedro Casaldáliga of São Felix, Brazil has explained: "The Church has not gotten along with any revolution, largely because the Church as institution, and more specifically the hierarchy, has almost always gotten along quite well with the established power of the privileged. If we also take the fear of socialism into account, we can understand the ecclesiastical situation in Nicaragua."[1]

At a July 1989 conference in Managua of Christian solidarity groups from 25 countries, the hierarchy's "lack of real insertion in the life of the people" was cited as an obstacle to the Church's effective participation in the liberation of Latin America.

I asked Bishop Julian Barni of León what he thought of this as a hypothesis to help explain the government-hierarchy conflict. "Is it true,"

---

1. *Prophets in Combat* (Oak Park, IL: Meyer Stone Books, 1987), p. 33.

I asked, "that some bishops and priests identify with the upper classes or at least are very sensitive to their complaints and therefore can't accept social revolution?" The bishop, clad in his Franciscan habit, stated simply and honestly: "Yes, I believe that's true in some cases. Some are guilty of what St. James criticized in his letter."

The bishop explained that he was referring to this passage: "Suppose a rich man wearing a gold ring and fine clothes comes to your meeting, and a poor man in ragged clothes also comes. If you show more respect to the well-dressed man and say to him, 'Have this best seat here,' but say to the poor man, 'Stand over there, or sit here on the floor by my feet,' then you are guilty of creating distinctions among yourselves and of making judgments based on evil motives" (James 2:2-4).[2]

The bishop of another Nicaraguan diocese suggested that in Managua the rich have more influence on the Church, through organizations such as COSEP (Higher Council for Private Enterprise), than they do in other dioceses.

Father Omar, who teaches theology at the Central American University in addition to his pastoral duties, told me that many Nicaraguan priests are from poor families and that after ordination they find themselves advancing socially and economically. "That was not necessarily their intention in becoming priests," Father Omar explained, "but they gradually get used to a comfortable life-style including cars, travel, invitations to dinners, etc." In order to preserve that life-style they have to maintain friendly relations with the rich and above all with the bishop, who controls their income and property.

This interpretation is widely held. Parish priests, who make their living from their priestly work, must require a certain stipend for every service rendered, and so they need a public with some buying power. The poor simply cannot afford the price, and it is a fact that most priests serving the Church of the Poor have other sources of income (a part-time job, their religious order, foreign funders, occasional speaking tours in the United States or Europe, etc.).

A religious who lives and works with the poor said confidently that they will never let a priest (or anyone else who really identifies with and

---

2. My interview of Bishop Barni, June 1989.

serves the community) go hungry. That is true, but most priests get accustomed to a life style a cut above bare survival. The prospect of casting their lot with CBCs, which are rather small groups of poor people, does not seem economically feasible to many priests.

When I asked a bishop of a Nicaraguan diocese (not Managua) whether he saw the hierarchy-Sandinista conflict in terms of class loyalties, he explained that "there are good and bad in every group" and that "some landowners have been very good, very Christian to their peasants." He recalled that Somoza settled many thousands of people in colonies in Nueva Guinea and that the FSLN got nowhere among them in promoting revolution. The bishop said that he and other bishops have traditionally spoken of "evolution, not revolution," trying to provide educational opportunities for individual advancement. The day of our interview, he reported, he had just given a little donation to someone who had come to the city for a thyroid operation.[3]

When I asked two other bishops (separately) how the Church was handling the option for the poor, both emphasized that it was a *preferential* option for the poor and did not mean rejection of the others. The Church of the Poor would respond by noting that it does not reject the rich as persons but does reject their role in committing or perpetuating injustice.

"Let's not be afraid of the word *revolution*," Bishop Casaldáliga stated in 1988, almost as if he were offering some fraternal advice to the bishops of Nicaragua. "We must have a more radical commitment to the transformation of society," he continued. "Reforms, Christian Democracy, Social Democracy, and various kinds of liberalism are not going to resolve the problems of Central America and the rest of the Third World."[4] With regard to Christian Democracy, which seems to be the model of social change favored by many Church officials, Casaldáliga wrote in a poem after a visit to Guatemala: "We will return when democracy in Guatemala makes room for justice, when it is Christian in truth and not just in name."[5]

---

3. In some interviews with bishops and clergy, I stated that I did not need to identify them individually; thus, in these cases, unless the interviewee told me explicitly that I could identify him, I refer to him in general terms.

4. *El Vuelo del Quetzal*, p. 130.

5. Ibid., p. 144.

In my interview with Cardinal Obando, he expressed discomfort with the word *revolution*, saying that the Church wanted to see concrete improvements in education, medical care, and other areas. While Catholic participants in and supporters of the Sandinista government certainly shared the cardinal's desire to see better conditions, they believed that the revolutionary process under the Sandinista government was the way to bring about meaningful structural change. They attributed the hard times largely to the U.S. strategy of low-intensity warfare, without overlooking official limitations in competency and in some cases in ethics. (The cardinal acknowledged that the social and economic problems were due in some degree to the war.)

In Peter Davis' interview of Obando in 1986, the cardinal also expressed uneasiness with the revolution, which he caricatured as absolutized, idolatrous, hateful, and fanatical.

"We don't want to see the revolution raised to the category of idolatry, and we don't want hatred between classes. We encouraged the revolution, but now I think the people of Nicaragua find themselves in a complicated situation where they are asked to become fanatics. One should try to coexist, right? And the church does try to coexist. But we cannot identify the teachings of Christ with the way the government is acting here. Christ does not preach hatred."[6]

In a 1989 interview the cardinal returned to this theme. After saying that he accepted a theology of liberation which would free the oppressed, he expressed his rejection of such theology if it calls for a "re-reading of the bible along Marxist lines" and if it "gets married to the system." This kind of theology, Obando said, leads to "class hatred, even to the point of destroying the adversary if necessary."[7]

Christians with a more radical option for the poor certainly agree that Christ did not preach hatred, although they also point out that he did get angry with the cold-hearted pharisees and with the exploitative money-changers and that his identification with the poor was one of the things that cost him his life. Hatred is not a significant motivation or emotion in the Nicaraguan revolution; commitment to radical social change and to national self-determination is.

---

6. Op. cit., pp. 325-326.

7. Interview of Obando in *La Crónica*, May 24-30, 1989.

Moreover, Christians in the base communities have been aware of the danger of absolutizing the revolution and "getting married to the system." That temptation (which became less seductive in recent years as the "low-intensity warfare" took its toll) is fought by keeping a posture of critical support while maintaining a critical distance between the Church of the Poor and the Sandinista revolution of the poor.

What the cardinal really seems to be against is socialist revolution, not merely his frequent caricatures of it. Jaime Chamorro (brother-in-law of President Violeta Barrios de Chamorro, executive vice-president of *La Prensa*, and a member of the City of God charismatic community) said that most Church officials would be comfortable with a political philosophy safeguarding free enterprise while seeking to avoid the extremes of unrestrained exploitation and unrelieved misery. That is how he described his own option as well.

Chamorro also claimed that the "popular Church" works against the unity of the Church. When I observed that for many Christians the top priority in the short term is not unity in itself but faithfulness to the Church's preferential option for the poor and that there can be authentic unity only on the basis of that option, he responded by saying that the rich are poor in many ways.[8]

This is a frequent comeback to any reference to the Church's "preferential option for the poor." Many, like Father Luis Amado Peña (pastor in Diriamba), immediately ask: "Who are the poor?" and point out that in addition to the economically poor "some are culturally poor, psychologically poor, or spiritually poor." Notions like "equality," he declared, must be deferred "until the Second Coming," not bothering to make any distinctions about degrees of social equality but clearly expressing his disdain for the concept.[9]

"In the eyes of the Church, we are all equal, rich and poor alike," said Jaime Chamorro's colleague at *La Prensa*, César Vivas, the father of Bishop Bosco Vivas. When he asserted that "the Church does not have

---

8. My interview of Jaime Chamorro, May 1989. He also expressed his opinion and concern that the "popular Church" substitutes love of humanity for love of God. Acknowledging the complexity of the mystery and the inadequacy of language, he said that love of God must always include love of humanity but must always take precedence. Most members of the Church of the Poor do not discuss this matter theoretically; they simply pray to God and work for the good of others, pointing to the last judgment in Matthew 25.

9. My interview of Father Peña, May 1989.

any preference for one group or another," I reminded him of the Latin American Church's official "preferential option for the poor." Of course, he said, the Church "must help the poor through charity, but not through promoting communism." He declared that the Church could never accept socialism. "Expropriation is just another word for robbery," he explained, "and that goes against one of the Ten Commandments."[10] (The Catholic pastor in Masatepe has labelled members of agricultural cooperatives who are on expropriated land as "thieves.")

Dr. Myriam Argüello, a leader in the UNO coalition which emerged victorious in the 1990 elections, promising to have "respectful relations" with the Catholic Church if her party were in power, claimed that the "popular Church manipulates the option for the poor into a Marxist-Leninist model for society." She favors a society where there is "equilibrium" and opportunity for all.[11]

In describing Cardinal Obando's political position, Penny Lernoux identified him as being "associated with a Nicaraguan version of" the Christian Democrats.[12] Christian Democracy, which Lernoux described as Cardinal López Trujillo's "third way" between capitalism and socialism, "holds out the best hope for business interests in European countries with a strong left, such as Italy, and in Latin America, where it is hoped that the Christian Democrats can keep the lid on rising nationalism and popular discontent."[13]

If Obando is indeed a Christian Democrat at heart, he is in safe ecclesiastical company. While the Italian Church has been distancing itself from the Christian Democrat party, Pope John Paul II "showed no hesitation in identifying the church with the party and demanding that the Italian bishops follow suit."[14] (Ex-contra leader Edgar Chamorro cited Obando's close ties to the pope and to the United States as the chief factors in his opposition to the Sandinista revolution.)[15]

---

10. My interview of César Vivas, May 1989.

11. My interview of Dr. Myriam Argüello, August 1989.

12. *People of God*, p. 147. Later she described Obando as a "Christian Democratic sympathizer" (p. 331).

13. Ibid., p. 332.

14. Ibid., p. 334.

15. My interview of Edgar Chamorro, July 1989.

José Espinoza of the CUS (Confederation for Labor Unity), an organization which works closely with the AFL-CIO's American Institute for Free Labor Development and which has close ties to the Chamorro government, described the hierarchy-Sandinista conflict as "ideological," tracing the Church's anti-socialist position back to Pope Leo XIII's *Rerum Novarum.* Espinoza, who said he is a friend of Obando, told me that the cardinal and other Church officials have close ties to the Social Christian Party, the Christian Democrat affiliate in Nicaragua.[16]

Founded in 1957, the Nicaraguan Social Christian Party proclaimed itself to be "the response of an essentially Christian social and economic doctrine." The founding charter named some basic principles of the party, including this: "the right to private property with regard to consumer goods and the goods of production is of the nature of the human person." The document cautioned: "the private ownership of such goods is not the prerogative of a few, as is the case in society today where the vast majority, because of their miserable condition, find it impossible to obtain what they should have."

The charter ends with an affirmation of the party's anti-communism: "the only way to defeat international communism in our country is by implanting Republican Democracy and Social Christian Justice." (At the bottom of the document appears the name of Silvio Mayorga as a member of the consultative body; four years later he would be one of the founders of the FSLN.)

Some believe that Obando and other bishops and priests may be Christian Democrats in their general political thinking without opting specifically for the Social Christian Party. Luís Humberto Guzmán, editor of the weekly *La Cronica,* said that Obando would be "expressing support for the opposition in various ways, but not necessarily for one party."[17] During the campaign leading up to the electoral defeat of the Sandinistas, Obando expressed his support in various ways for the UNO coalition, not for the independent Social Christian Party.

In the early years of the Sandinista government, David Chavarria Rocha, who was active in the CBC in the Riguero neighborhood of Ma-

---

16. My interview of José Espinoza, June 1989. As another aspect of the conflict he mentioned that the Sandinista government was "a lay government" not promoting any particular religion.

17. My interview of Luís Humberto Guzmán, May 1989.

nagua, pointed to the Church's tendency to defend "class privileges and attitudes. Even now, after the victory, the bishop has not been able to go to the poor sectors. Our leaders have gone there," he noted, "and have solved problems and have heard the concerns of our people. Obando has not been able to do that. He has divorced himself from the . . . poor, from the Christians who live and suffer every day. For me, he has lost credibility."[18]

A priest in Managua claimed that Obando really is in contact with the poor, but as examples he mentioned sacramental visits to parishes and traditional seasonal processions. These appearances do draw many of the poor and allow the cardinal to catch a glimpse of their misery, but they do not necessarily constitute the kind of "contact" which leads to personal identification and active solidarity with the poor.

It may be true, as Luís Humberto Guzmán opined, that "the bishops believe they represent the interests of the people."[19] But if they remain distant from the poor masses and resistant to revolutionary approaches, they will be obstacles to the needed radical change.

There are priests in Nicaragua, as everywhere else, who have indeed spent their lives among the poor. As they share their experiences and their compassion and concerns, the interviewer can only recognize their sacrificial hard work and their genuine love for the poor.

But the problem in a revolutionary situation is that many of them have little or no preparation for political and economic analysis; they can't see the structural forest for the individual trees. Some are imbued with the same kind of anti-communism and skepticism about radical change which coexisted with real compassion for the workers in the hearts of the labor priests decades ago in the United States.

Perhaps Casaldáliga had this sector of the clergy in mind when he commented on how "the Church is so fearful of the class problem that it refuses to look at it, because it leads to class struggle." But he tells those who want to stick to charity: "charity, if it is correctly understood, must always be liberating. But in fact it often remains paternalistic and even works against liberation."[20]

---

18. Margaret Randall, op. cit, pp. 198-99. David continued: "There cannot be a church of the rich. Christ was the first to accuse the rich, telling them that it was easier for a camel to go through the eye of a needle than for a rich man to enter the kingdom of heaven."

19. My interview of Guzmán, May 1989.

In Nicaragua in 1990, many of these priests who have excelled in practicing an interpersonal form of charity were convinced that the poor, at least those they serve, were in worse shape economically than before 1979. (They readily granted that there was no comparison between the murderous National Guard, which many of them denounced, and the Sandinista security forces.)

Thus these priests began to turn against the revolution, claiming that the government was failing the people and that it had "not fulfilled its promises or kept up its laudable programs," as one bishop told me. While many of their empirical observations may be accurate, they failed to see the larger factors at work in the deterioration of conditions for their people, and they did not seem to notice that all of Central America had experienced a decline in living conditions as a result of the contemporary economic crisis.

Edward R. F. Sheehan "marveled" about an experience which he considered "perfectly Nicaraguan": "you meet a cardinal and discuss vegetables. The next day, you meet a Jesuit and discuss utopia."[21] In Sheehan's interview of Obando in 1986, the cardinal had complained of the rising cost of vegetables and had also complained about the Jesuits of Managua, whom he described as "almost all Marxists" who propose socialism as the solution for poor countries. The Jesuit who discussed utopia was a "Father R," who explained that "the Kingdom of God is utopian" and who went on to speak of revolution and social justice. Sheehan's sympathies lie with Obando and other priests who lament specific problems like the high price of food but who shun structural analysis and revolutionary solutions.

Such priests also tended to react abruptly and strongly against any statements or actions by bureaucrats who, in their youth and their newfound power, may have exceeded the bounds of prudence or propriety. On the other hand, priests with a more developed political analysis and philosophy, who considered the thrust and goals of the revolution to be in the best interests of the poor, tended to say "let's not make a mountain out of a molehill" when they came into minor conflicts with Sandinista officials. (On the other hand, they did not take real violations of human rights lightly.)

---

20. *El Vuelo del Quetzal*, p. 168.

21. Op. cit., p. 230.

Obando's turn against the revolution coincided with the growing hostility of the bourgeois groups against the Sandinistas. "The revolution's commitment to place a priority on the needs of the majority inevitably conflicted with the aspirations of certain minorities. Although these latter groups had also opposed Somoza, they did not want a profound transformation of society which would prevent them from developing the social hegemony that they had hoped to achieve with the departure of Somoza.

"On April 22, 1980, businessman Alfonso Robelo quit the government junta, expressing his disagreement with its plans for social transformation. (Violeta Chamorro had quit the junta days earlier, stating that her health was not good.)"[22] Robelo became one of the civilian leaders of the contras.

"Less than a month after Robelo's resignation," the article continued, "the bishops' conference unexpectedly issued a communiqúe calling for the resignation of those priests holding public office. The announcement seemed to express the same disagreement with the direction of the process that had led to Robelo's resignation."

Looking back on this event years later, Father Juan Hernández Pico, S.J., noted that the hierarchy's turn against the government "coincided with" the bourgeoisie's decision "to break its anti-Somoza alliance with the Sandinistas." The bourgeois sectors recognized their political weakness and saw in the bishops' lack of confidence in the revolution a chance to improve their own political fortunes. The Reagan administration would soon follow suit in its efforts to find Church support for its aggression against the Sandinistas.[23]

Rodolfo Cardenal, S.J., explained that the fears felt by Christians with regard to the revolution "have had their origin to a great extent in the bourgeoisie" which is naturally opposed to the revolutionary process. This bourgeoisie "is manipulating the sacred to justify its social reformism," identifying the latter with the faith. "The right-wing opposition is trying to stop the revolutionary process by trying to change it into a nonradical reformism."[24]

---

22. *Envío*, Dec., 1983.

23. "Religión y Revolución en Nicaragua," op. cit., p. 81.

24. *Historia General de la Iglesia en America Latina*, p. 567.

These reformist sectors "have raised the flags of private property, political pluralism, and the inter-class nationalism of Sandino. At the same time they proudly profess their Catholicism and proclaim their decision to struggle to the very end for religious freedom. This represents a dangerous manipulation of religion, lending a sacred aura to the demands of the bourgeoisie and leading the people to the conclusion that one cannot be a Christian without defending private property, political pluralism, and national conciliation."[25] (It should be noted that the Sandinistas are not fundamentally opposed to the last three notions, although it is true that their interpretation of these principles is colored by their basic option for the poor.)

Luís Serra identified "unlimited individual freedom" and an "idealistic view of social reality" as well as "private ownership of the means of production" as key elements of the bourgeois ideology which have been assimilated by the Christian churches as essential constituents of their religious tradition and thought. The majority of the Nicaraguan clergy have been formed in this way of thinking, Serra also noted, as distinct from a liberation theology approach. "This kind of education, abstract and impervious to the advances in the social sciences, has prepared the clergy for ritualistic duties and for a moralizing kind of preaching as a remedy to individual and social evils. A Church which emphasized the afterlife, relegating people to a passive role in history and seeking to bring harmony to the class struggle, became an essential ally of the dominating bourgeoisie."[26]

Archdiocesan seminarians in Managua are still being trained to think dualistically. At a mini-course at the Central American University in April 1989, a seminarian in third-year theology objected to the formulation of a question as to whether the values of the faith were in conflict with the values of the revolution. He said the question did not make any sense to him, since the values of the faith were the dogmas of the Trinity, the Eucharist, the incarnation, etc., which were in a totally different category from revolutionary values. When I suggested that love, sharing, community, the search for justice, and the building of a new society were gospel values, he dismissed them as merely "sociological" values.

---

25. Ibid., p. 568.

26. "Ideologia, Religión y Lucha de Clases en la Revolución," in *La Revolución en Nicaragua,* eds. Richard Harris y Carlos M. Vilas (Mexico: Ediciones Era, 1985), p. 274.

Continuing his class analysis of the hierarchy's opposition to the revolution, Serra mentioned that the Vatican and certain Protestant churches have stock in transnational corporations, and he also noted the "third-way" social doctrine of the Vatican "which proposes certain reforms to capitalism."[27]

Another important factor in Serra's estimation has been the "pro-imperialist bourgeoisie's skillful recruiting of the Church hierarchs. Through personal relationships, visits, testimonial banquets, family ties, participation in public liturgies, and the personality cult offered especially to Obando, the bourgeoisie has been able to gain an important ally."[28]

A call for the Nicaraguan Church to embrace the option for the poor was expressed in poetry by Father Arnaldo Zenteno, a Mexican Jesuit who worked for many years with the CBCs in his own country and has worked with the communities in Nicaragua since 1982. Zenteno's poetry arises from the people he loves and serves. In a poem entitled "This is Our Church," he wrote: "Our Church / Will it become light and hope for the poor in Nicaragua? / Or will it continue to be the security and strength of the rich?"[29]

In "A Little Remnant" Zenteno wrote: "They slander us and accuse us of dividing the Church / And they divide it by their commitment to the rich. / They say we betray the gospel and are allied with the Sandinistas. / They don't see that we are defending the very heart of the gospel: justice for the poor. / With the Sandinistas, we maintain our freedom and our prophetic word / And if we join with them, it is in the project of the poor."[30]

In another poem Zenteno described the sinfulness of the Church: "The sin of the Church today in Nicaragua / Is not to believe in the poor but in the powerful . . . to see the process as all bad and not to find anything good. / The sin of my Church today in Nicaragua / Is to 'demand its rights' and not respect the cause of the poor."[31]

---

27. Ibid.
28. Ibid., pp. 274-275.
29. *Nicaragua: Grito y Ternura Indomable* (Mexico, 1986), p. 66.
30. Ibid., pp. 69-70.
31. Ibid., p. 72.

Visitors to the parish of St. Dominic in Las Sierritas, where Cardinal Obando usually celebrates Mass, are struck by the number of cars in the parking lot and by the well-to-do appearance of most of the faithful. "The congregation was lighter skinned than others I had seen," reported Peter Davis, "and the sanctuary seemed to hold the last contingent of those who can dress nicely in Nicaragua."[32] Davis also noted that Obando's sermon on the second Sunday after Easter 1986 included a thinly veiled bit of political advice. Homilizing on the risen Lord's appearance to the apostles (John 21:1-14) at Lake Tiberias, Obando reportedly emphasized that Jesus told the dejected fishermen to cast their net "on the *right* [Davis's emphasis] side of the ship." According to Davis, the cardinal said: "Look in your Bibles, that's exactly what He said. The *right* side. So the disciples did cast their net over to the right, and they were rewarded. . . . It's utterly clear, isn't it? Christ told them to go to the right and they would find what they were looking for. Being on the *right*, my friends, implies faith, dignity and abundance." Davis noted that the congregation "murmured in appreciation."[33] Later, when Davis brought this up in an interview with Obando, the cardinal "earnestly denied any ideological intentions."[34]

An indication of the Nicaraguan bishops' class identification may be seen in their constantly reiterated charge that the revolution seeks to foment class hatred and conflict. They stress the unity of the Church and of the Nicaraguan family, urging the government not to favor any particular sector of society. In dedicating the nation to the Immaculate Heart of Mary in 1982, Obando solemnly promised: "We will strive to love one another as brothers, forgiving injuries past or present, and overcoming ideological and class differences, since we all have You as our Mother."[35]

In their desire for a reformist government, the bishops have found their political options severely reduced. A "serious problem" for the hierarchy, according to Father Xabier Gorostiaga, S.J., director of the Managua-based Regional Coordinating Center for Economic and Social Research (CRIES), is the disappearance of "the political center" as a viable option

---

32. Op. cit., p. 308.

33. Ibid., p. 309.

34. Ibid., p. 325.

35. Hoja Dominical, Arquidiocesis de Managua, Nov. 28, 1982.

(and valid alternative to revolutionary groups) in Central America. Thus the Central American bishops "who have not made the option for the poor" cannot find a political platform to support. Without this, the bishops are "drafted by the oligarchies to legitimize the old power structure which is crumbling or to pull together the political center under construction."

In the case of Nicaragua, Archbishop Obando's position is clear, according to Gorostiaga: "Whether unconsciously or consciously, he serves to legitimize and pull together the political opponents of the [Sandinista] revolution, and in this he is in line with the policy of the United States."[36]

The view of society expressed by Paolo Giglio, the papal nuncio to Nicaragua, is probably shared by the Nicaraguan hierarchy to some extent. The nuncio was interviewed by *Barricada* in December 1986. His remarks seemed so unguarded and unadorned that I thought perhaps he was the victim of some anti-clerical journalist.

But I have interviewed the nuncio twice; he begins his discussion of society with the words of Jesus: "The poor you will always have with you." And his view of society, expressed spontaneously and clearly, is indeed that which he described in *Barricada*.

In that interview he said: "It is necessary to have the rich and the poor, because the rich are destined to provide employment for the poor. If everyone were rich, no one would want to work. It's not possible for all of us to be at the same level. In any country not everyone can be president."

He did add: "The poor must live in conditions that are decent and human, and have a minimum of comfort, but not luxury, because luxury is not necessary for life."[37]

The foregoing remarks, whether one agrees with them or not, show that the speaker holds a world-view which would predispose him to oppose revolutionary change, especially any movement which would seek to diminish or eliminate class differences. Giglio ended our conversation by calling into question the legitimacy of the Nicaraguan government.

---

36. Cited by Cabestrero, op. cit., pp. 205-6.

37. Text cited and translated in *Envío* (December 1987).

Bishop Casaldáliga also respects the words of Jesus: "the poor you will always have with you." The kind deed will always be necessary, Casaldáliga says, "since the structures will not solve everything." However, he warns against both paternalism and developmentalism. "We are not against progress, but we are against developmentalism and reformism. That should be a specific contribution of Christian revolutionaries in Central America: to say no to the various kinds of reformism. Let's not fall into a Christian Democracy or a Social Democracy or some kind of watered-down revolution. We should be clear about our radicalism." (He acknowledged that there may be a need at certain times for tactics which may seem reformist, but the overall strategy must remain clear.)[38]

Since 1986 I have been asking people in the CBCs why some priests and bishops are against the revolutionary process. Most often, the response has to do with this first reason—the clerics' social class affiliation—as perceived by the people at the base. Priests, religious, theologians, sociologists, and others who have analyzed and written about the hierarchy-revolution conflict tend to accept the ordinary person's explanation but add the other factors to be discussed in this chapter.

2. Fear of Marxists

When asked to analyze the reasons for the Sandinista-hierarchy conflict, some clerics answer simply that the revolution is "Marxist." When I asked a top Church official (not of Managua) what it is about Marxism that bothers the bishops, he said it is partly the socialist view of property. "Some bishops and priests are close to the wealthy families who fear that their property may be confiscated," he said.

But another reason that he and others have given to help explain the conflict is that some bishops simply cannot believe that a government which includes Marxists of some shape or form could allow religion to exist and flourish. According to this view, some bishops felt that the Sandinista government would abolish religion whenever such a move might be seen as feasible.

---

38. *El Vuelo del Quetzal*, p. 170.

"The hierarchy's fears were reinforced by a position paper that circulated within the Sandinista party during the fall of 1979," Dodson and O'Shaughnessy noted. "This paper, which was obtained and published by *La Prensa*, was prepared by a Sandinista militant for discussion at a party conference. It assumed a dogmatic Marxist view of religion, arguing that spiritual faith was anachronistic in a revolutionary society. Consequently, organized religion should be discouraged, and gradually abolished." Religious holidays like Christmas would become secular celebrations. "Publication of this document in *La Prensa* gave the impression that it was soon to be Sandinista Policy." When Catholic Church officials responded angrily, Sandinista leaders explained that the document was only a working paper and never had the approval of the FSLN. The bishops and conservative Catholics were not convinced by the Sandinista explanation.

In November 1980 Father Edgard Parrales, the minister of social welfare, announced that the government "would take part in Christmas celebrations by seeing to it that every Nicaraguan child received some sort of gift." *La Prensa* sharply criticized the Sandinistas' involvement in the religious celebration.[39] René Mendoza has noted that in some places Sandinistas themselves "contributed to the hierarchy's strategy [to present the government as an enemy of religion] by calling the peasants to meetings at the very hour of the Sunday Mass or other religious celebrations" (op. cit.).

A personal experience by Archbishop Obando not long after the triumph of the revolution probably colored his thinking about the new government. On a visit to young Nicaraguans studying on the Isle of Youth in Cuba, Obando was told that he would not be permitted to celebrate Mass with the group. He reportedly vowed never to allow such a system to be implemented in Nicaragua. Instead of distinguishing between the Cuban reality, with its stark opposition between Church and revolution, and the Nicaraguan historical experience of Christian participation in the revolution and Sandinista assurances of full respect for religion, Obando seemed to view his experience in Cuba as tending to confirm prejudices about Sandinista intentions.

Obando was also upset by what he felt were threats on his life. In a conversation with a priest in 1983, Obando said that the Sandinistas were going to kill him.[40] Some conservatives reportedly had adopted the tactic

---

39. Dodson and O'Shaughnessy, *Nicaragua's Other Revolution: Religious Faith and Political Struggle*, op. cit., pp. 149-152.

of going to Obando and pledging to defend him against supposedly oncoming Sandinistas. There is no evidence of any such plot on his life.

Father Juan Hernández Pico, S.J., has explained that "the history of confrontation between Marxist revolutions and the Christian Churches has been so constant (e.g., in the Soviet Union, Eastern Europe, People's China, Vietnam, Cuba) that it has been impossible to calm the fears of a certain notable part of the Nicaraguan Church. They are not convinced by the argument that Nicaraguan Marxists—nationalist, Sandinista—are different from their historical predecessors" or that many Nicaraguan revolutionaries are fully respectful of religion or indeed are Christians themselves. Some bishops believe that history must repeat itself and are highly skeptical about the possibility that human beings can transform history, especially if their efforts do not have an explicitly religious identity.[41]

Bishop Bosco Vivas, auxiliary bishop of Managua, did not believe that the Sandinista government would try to abolish religion entirely. "It is in their interests," he told me, "that religion and the Church exist in Nicaragua." That way, according to the bishop, the government could display freedom of religion. "But the Sandinistas will continue to try to diminish the influence of the Church," he asserted.

Many Christians would say that the Sandinista government had a right to try to diminish the influence of the Church to the extent that such influence was used by certain bishops and priests to assist the violent overthrow of the government—e.g., by promoting draft resistance in time of war, by trying to delegitimize the government and by recognizing the contras as a legitimate force, and by helping them to get aid from foreign sources.

The fearful predictions of Bosco Vivas and the even more dire ones of others flew in the face not only of the Sandinista track record of respect for religious freedom but also in the face of a new empirical reality in Latin America—the active participation of Christians in revolutionary movements.

It is true that in Nicaragua some lower-level government officials may have delivered some militantly atheistic statements. However, the official

---

40. My interview of the priest, June 1990.

41. "Religión y Revolución en Nicaragua," op. cit., p. 82.

position of the government on religious freedom was clear, and there was no evidence to suggest that the crystal ball of doom was anything but paranoid. In an interview published in *Christianity and Crisis* (April 1, 1985), I asked James E. Goff, a Presbyterian lay missioner who had worked in various parts of Latin American for 36 years and who was then on the staff of the Antonio Valdivieso Ecumenical Center in Managua: "What is really at the root of the Roman Catholic hierarchy's opposition to the Sandinistas?"

"I believe the bishops think that every revolution ends sooner or later in the persecution of the church," he said. "They really haven't gotten over the French Revolution yet, and now they have one in their own dioceses." (Chilean theologian Pablo Richard points to the Spanish civil war as the key experience which has instilled fear of communists in many of the clergy in Latin America.[42] Others commonly cite the Russian and Cuban revolutions in this regard.)

"But," Goff continued, "the government has gone on record very clearly that it intends to respect the religious traditions and beliefs of the Nicaraguan people." The bishops were convinced that the government's official position was "just a tactic to give the revolution time to gain enough strength to take on the church and eliminate it and drive it underground.

"I see that as a serious misreading, a blunder every bit as monumental as the blunder the bishops made at the time of the Wars of Independence in Latin America at the beginning of the last century, when they told the faithful that they should not fight against the king of Spain because he was God's agent in ruling over these lands. The effects of that blunder are still with us."

In a conversation in 1989 Jacinto García, Delegate of the Word in El Arenal, put the issue succinctly: "Some people in the Church think this government is atheistic just because our leaders do not go around making the sign of the cross on themselves and talking about God all the time. But I consider them basically Christian because of the good they have done for the people."

Sandinista leaders have spoken positively and respectfully of the role religion can play in social change. Sandino himself said that "social injustice comes from disregard of the divine laws; injustice has no reason to

---

42. My interview of Pablo Richard, May 1989.

exist." While rejecting the Christian churches as tools of the national bourgeoisie and of U.S. imperialism, he included Jesus among those who have had the mission to "destroy injustice" and to "struggle for the freedom of people."[43]

Sandino also explained the final judgment as "the destruction of injustice on earth and the reign of the Spirit of Light and Truth, or Love." He said that the oppressed peoples will break the imperialists' chains and that Nicaraguans had "the honor of being chosen by Divine justice to begin the judgment against injustice on earth."[44]

FSLN founder Carlos Fonseca said that "unity between true revolutionaries and true Christians is fundamental in the Frente Sandinista," calling to mind Ernesto Che Guevara and Father Camilo Torres (Colombian priest-sociologist who joined a revolutionary organization in armed struggle and was killed in 1966).[45]

Large numbers of Nicaraguans joined the Sandinista revolution because of their Christian commitment, thus contributing to "breaking down the atheistic dogmatism of one sector of Sandinista revolutionaries."[46] In its official 1980 statement on religion the FSLN recognized religious freedom and affirmed that there is no conflict between being a revolutionary and being a Christian. Daniel Ortega and Tomás Borge have reiterated this position frequently, as have other top FSLN leaders. Comandante Victor Tirado stated in 1983 that the gospel, Sandinismo, and Marxism found in Nicaragua that they "came together in their central goals and that they agreed on the need to raise up the poor and the marginal classes." Comandante Luís Carrión has said: "I came to the revolution through a religious experience," i.e. his involvement in the Christian student community in the Riguero barrio of Managua.[47]

43. Sergio Ramírez, *El Pensamiento Vivo de Sandino,* EDUCA, 5a ed., Costa Rica, 1980, p. 205, as cited by Luis Serra, op. cit., p. 275.

44. Sergio Ramírez, ibid., p. 213, as cited by Serra, p. 275.

45. Carlos Fonseca, *Bajo las Banderas del Sandinismo,* ed. Nueva Nicaragua, Managua, 1981, p. 199, as cited by Luis Serra, op. cit., p. 276.

46. Luis Serra, op. cit., p. 276.

47. Ibid., p. 277.

In spite of all these positive signs, there is no doubt that there have been conflicts between Christianity and Marxism in Nicaragua. Serra and others attribute these conflicts to extremists and dogmatists on both sides. "A traditional religious sector," he wrote, "carrying the banner of a ritualistic, idealistic, and charismatic Christianity, has refueled the conflict with a Marxist sector which is militantly atheist and which emphasizes economic determinism and metaphysical materialism. This polemic has objectively fulfilled the goals of imperialism," Serra added, "by identifying Sandinismo with Marxism in order to later on identify Sandinismo with atheism and set it against the Christianity of the Nicaraguan people."[48] And also against the Christianity of the Vatican and the U.S. people, we might add.

Representatives of that dogmatic Marxist sector have been in the minority, according to Father César Jerez, S.J., president of the Central American University, who identified five positions within the FSLN regarding religion:

1) Christians who do not participate in liturgical practices except for the baptism of their children.

2) Christians who actively practice their faith without denying their Marxism.

3) Those who are indifferent or who have not defined their position regarding religion.

4) Those with a pragmatic atheist position who see no political benefit in confronting religion at this stage.

5) Those with a militant atheist position against religion.[49]

The last two groups have not been dominant, Serra noted, but "their attitudes have been an irritant" in relations between the FSLN and some religious institutions. These attitudes do not carry much weight among the top leaders of the FSLN, who have assimilated Marxism in connection with their involvement in the revolutionary struggle; but they are found in those who have emerged as leaders more recently and who have learned Marxism in a theoretical way and in courses stressing memory work and using Soviet manuals. "In these texts a scientific, materialistic,

---

48. Ibid., p. 278.

49. Jerez, *Diakonia*, March 1984, Managua, as cited by Serra, ibid. See César Jerez, S.J., *The Church and the Nicaraguan Revolution* (London: Catholic Institute for International Relations, 1984).

revolutionary, and proletarian way of seeing things is set against an idealistic, religious, reactionary, and bourgeois way of viewing reality," Serra continued.[50]

With support from the upper echelons of the Sandinista government, efforts had gotten under way in 1989 especially at the university level to revamp the presentation of Marxism precisely to get away from the dogmatic simplifications of the manuals.

The small minority of Sandinistas who "take a militant atheist position" would be the agents of "indoctrination" mentioned by Penny Lernoux: "The urban young increasingly rejected religion, partly because the traditional church opposed the revolution, but also because of indoctrination by the Sandinista army and police."[51] If there was some indoctrination, it was not very extensive or effective, since in a 1988 survey by the Jesuits' Central American University it was discovered that only 9% of the students interviewed said that they did not believe in God.[52] Lernoux may have been right in saying that the urban young are *increasingly* rejecting religion, but the magnitude of that rejection should not be overestimated.

Father José Alvarez Lobo, O.P., who worked with the Ministry of the Interior's educational programs for its personnel, told me that the main problem is not "Sandinista indoctrination in atheism." Rather, young people in Nicaragua are experiencing the same crisis of faith that is found in other modern or modernizing societies. Many were taught by parents and grandparents to make the sign of the cross, to recite the Our Father and Hail Mary, and to spend some time adoring the Blessed Sacrament on Thursdays (a strong Nicaraguan custom). Given that degree of theological development, they are prime candidates for a crisis of faith when they come into contact with a scientific view of the universe and of society. (Hernández Pico, S.J., speaks of the "secularizing tendency" of revolutionary movements.)

"They learn to see the natural, not divine, causes of problems," Father José explained, "and they search for effective human responses. As their world becomes more demythologized and demystified, they have increasing trouble relating to a traditional religiosity based on prayers for mira-

---

50. Serra, p. 279. See also Hernández Pico, "Religión y Revolución en Nicaragua," p. 83.

51. *People of God,* p. 405.

52. *Envío,* March 1989.

cles and resignation to fate." What they need is a theological approach which puts the accent on human responsibility.

Serra also noted that the media sometimes played up the conflicts, that religious personages sometimes received gross treatment in the media, and that the mass organizations sometimes mobilized people to protest certain political decisions by the hierarchy. Such behavior, "which must be seen in the context of an intense ideological struggle, stems from the fact that the reactionaries have taken advantage of the pulpit and of liturgical celebrations to make political propaganda." But the sharpening of the public conflict played into the hands of the counterrevolution, which wanted to make the Frente appear to be against the Church.[53]

The conflict was greatly exacerbated by the U.S.-sponsored contra war. Reactionary activity by some clergy confirmed some Marxists in their belief that religion really is the opiate of the people and, as in Sandino's time, a tool of imperialism. Easy to formulate but difficult to apply correctly, the Sandinista principle has been that "in Nicaragua there is religious freedom but there is no freedom to use religion to make counterrevolution."[54]

The Sandinistas had the good fortune to struggle against a dictatorship in a country where the majority Christian population was becoming more aware of its social and political responsibilities, but they had the bad luck to come to power as social revolutionaries in a country where the hierarchy was one of the most conservative politically and theologically in Latin America. The traditional formation of the priests and bishops had not prepared them to deal with the nuances of Christian-Marxist dialogue. "They fear what they do not know, and they are not even interested in learning more about this thing called Marxism," noted Luís Rocha, who edited *Testimonio* in 1969-1970 and who is now an editor at *El Nuevo Diario*.[55]

A theology professor in Managua's major seminary said that St. Thomas Aquinas has been the only theologian in the history of the

---

53. Op. cit., p. 280.

54. Ibid., p. 282.

55. My interview of Luís Rocha, May 1989.

Church. Some witnesses claim that he added: "St. Thomas was never wrong; he could never have been wrong."

These first two aspects of the hierarchy-government conflict were noted in the anthology, *Nicaragua: The First Five Years.* The conflict was "rooted in several causes, including the Sandinista leadership's clear embrace of some aspects of Marxism, their propensity to use rhetoric of class conflict, and their pursuit of public policies intended to favor the poor, sometimes at the expense of the privileged."[56]

3. The Authority Structure of the Church

In the third place, some Church officials felt that the Sandinistas in government were aiding and abetting a revolution within the Church which challenged the old pyramidal notion of authority. One of the breezes let in by the Second Vatican Council was the empowerment and maturation of the laity. Clodovis Boff has pointed out that in the Third World "it is basically the poor who are becoming a force within the church, making it a church of the poor majorities. We can say that this church is essentially democratic, while the church of the North is an aristocratic church, a church marked by the clergy and by middle class movements."[57]

Boff's brother, Leonardo, put it succinctly: "The cause of Christ and the People of God is too important to leave to the hierarchy." While the Church of the Poor in Nicaragua certainly did not identify the cause of Christ with the Sandinista revolution, the people did see a significant convergence of the two, and they could not allow the hierarchy to be the exclusive voice of the Church on such an important political issue as revolution.[58]

Leonardo Boff recalled the distance the Church has traversed over the last century, citing Gregory XVI (1831-46): "No one can deny that the Church is an unequal society in which God destined some to be gov-

56. Michael Dodson and Laura N. O'Shaughnessy, "Religion and Politics," in *Nicaragua: The First Five Years,* ed. Thomas W. Walker (New York: Praeger Publishers, 1985), p. 119.

57. Latin America Press, March 13, 1986.

58. *Church: Charism and Power,* p. 58.

emors and others to be servants. The latter are the laity; the former, the clergy." He also cited the "even more rigid" Pius X: "Only the college of pastors have the right and authority to lead and govern. The masses have no right or authority except that of being governed, like an obedient flock that follows its Shepherd."[59] *La Prensa* editor César Vivas, who described the Church as "vertical, dictatorial, and not democratic," must have been schooled in these pre-Vatican II papal doctrines.

A Nicaraguan Church official pointed to the selection of Father Juan Abelardo Mata to be one of the new auxiliary bishops of Managua (now bishop of Estelí) as evidence that the Church is not a democracy: Father Mata, a Salesian, had lived outside Nicaragua for 22 years prior to his consecration, and so the people did not even know him much less have any say in his nomination.[60]

Boff described the progress made in recent times: "Happily, Vatican II brought things back into perspective, recovering its theologically threatened health. The Church is fundamentally the People of God. All share in the magisterial role of Christ, even the laity (*Lumen Gentium*, 35). The hierarchy, as a part of this people, enjoys an official role but always in service to the entire Christian community (*Lumen Gentium*, 25)."[61]

In July 1989 Christians from seven Third World countries (Nicaragua, El Salvador, Guatemala, South Korea, the Philippines, South Africa, and Namibia) issued a theological proclamation called "The Road to Damascus," which dealt with the problem of Christians being on both sides of the struggle between rich and poor. Some Church leaders "profess commitment to democracy, but do not wish the people to exercise power effectively," the document stated. What follows seems especially pertinent to the Nicaraguan situation: "They accuse progressive Christians of dividing the Church, but in some countries they use their position to force a split between the institutional and the popular Church, even denying that some base communities are part of the Church" (Paragraph 78).

Dodson and O'Shaughnessy also included this aspect in their analysis of the hierarchy-revolution conflict in Nicaragua. Even at the time of the triumph, the bishops "were concerned about the participation of Catholics in

---

59. Ibid., p. 142.

60. My interview of Church official, June 1989.

61. Op. cit., p. 142.

the mass organizations and in the CEBs [CBCs]. In Catholic tradition, lay activity is supervised by priests who are loyal to the bishops. Therefore, the CEBs were a problem for the institutional church, as was Catholic participation in the mass organizations, because it was difficult to control the spontaneity and autonomy of Catholics in these organizations. The bishops were fearful that if these revolutionary Christians continued to unite grass-roots religious commitment to the poor with loyalty to the Revolution the government's authority would supersede that of the Church."[62]

Protectors of the old ecclesiastical order heard the Sandinista government talking officially about the power of the people, the dignity of the poor, the need for participation, the servant role of authority, and other such democratic notions which could easily spread from the political to the Church sphere. Furthermore, when the formerly timid experience their own power and freedom in civil society (as they began to do in Nicaragua), they may feel that they also have a right to be heard in the Church.[63]

When Father Antonio Caballo, pastor in Ocotal, was asked whether the revolution is reflected in the Church, he said: "I would say that the presence of the poor has been strengthened."[64]

A resident of the small town of Villanueva criticized the bishops' attitude: "The hierarchy could have played a historic role by placing itself alongside the poor of Nicaragua. But what they are doing is seeking their own interests, not wanting to lose their power over all of us even though this means allying themselves with the counterrevolution."[65]

The people's desire to participate intelligently could be seen in other spheres of life as well. Joel Kovel has described the post-triumph experience of many in the medical profession. More trying, perhaps, than the relative leveling of wages has been "the change in power and the whole shift in priorities and values." He recalled a conference at the hospital in León: "the representatives of the health workers' union had as much authority and respect as the medical staff. Nothing of the sort would have

---

62. "Religion and Politics," in *Nicaragua: The First Five Years,* op. cit., p. 131.

63. Serra, op. cit., pp. 283-284.

64. *Barricada,* Nov. 17, 1982.

65. O. Rolando Sierra Pop, *Informe Sobre el Bloque Intercomunitario Pro-Bienestar Cristiano,* 1983, p. 80.

ever taken place before the revolution, any more than it would take place in the United States."[66] No doubt this opening up of the decision-making structures in various professions brought its share of difficulties, but the democratizing thrust was undeniable.

When a well-known, fiercely anti-Sandinista big businessman was asked what really bothered him about the Sandinista revolution, he explained that the peasants used to tip their hat to him and address him with a deferential lowering of their glance; now they look him straight in the eye and speak as equals.

Members of the CBCs of Estelí, in an open letter concerning the decision by the Vatican (instigated by Obando) to ban Bishop Pedro Casaldáliga from visiting Nicaragua, expressed a strong sense of their own dignity: "We have participated in a revolution where we all have something to contribute to making the changes we consider necessary. It is clear that after this experience we cannot accept the tendency in our Church to reduce the laity to a truly infantile condition in which we simply receive what is already decided and are not even listened to."[67]

They certainly have not been able to accept the bishops' political likes and dislikes as gospel truth, especially when some bishops disparaged and rejected a revolution which the poor considered to be for them. "We are among the thousands of Christians who feel abandoned by the hierarchy," they wrote. "It is true that we are Christians and revolutionaries. But is this any reason for neglecting our pastoral needs? This revolution is ours, because as Christians starting out from our gospel commitment we have made and set out on a road which seeks to give life to the needy. . . .

"It is true," they acknowledged, "that the revolution has its faults and mistakes, but why is there such intransigent opposition to this search which we Nicaraguans have begun and such tolerance for those who have made us suffer for many years and still are making us suffer? Can the pope or the bishops tell us that we can only be Christians within the capitalist system? Is the gospel of Jesus Christ really incompatible with this search we have undertaken?"[68]

---

66. *In Nicaragua* (London: Free Association Books, 1988), p. 21. U.S. distributor: Columbia University Press.

67. El Tísey (*Boletín de INSFOP*), November, 1988, p. 37.

68. Ibid., p. 35.

While many Nicaraguans have grown in a critical historical and scientific consciousness, many of the clergy and hierarchy want to continue to promote a kind of religiosity which is almost magical in its emphasis on miracles and in its devotion to sacred objects. (Serra and others see the interests of the bourgeoisie being served conveniently by the latter kind of alienating religion.)[69]

Christian revolutionaries naturally want to help their coreligionists develop a biblical faith perspective which sees God at work in the process of human love and liberation and which promotes personal responsibility rather than passivity and fatalism; but many reactionary Christians view this kind of "modernizing" catechesis as an assault on Church dogma and authority, casting part of the blame for it on the Sandinista revolution.

4. Losing Some Power and Privilege in Society

A fourth reason for Church leaders' displeasure with the revolution was their feeling that they did not enjoy a sufficiently privileged or important position in the new system. The bishops felt that "both the revolution and the grass roots movement within the church might threaten their hierarchical influence and control."[70]

Father Fernando Cardenal put the spotlight on this factor in a challenge to his fellow clergy less than two months after the triumph. After citing the words of Jesus as to the servant nature of discipleship, Cardenal noted: "Often we priests have wanted to be the first among the people, understanding our authority as domination and not as service. In practice we have considered the Holy Spirit as our private property and have not known how to listen to the Spirit who is the collective patrimony of the people of God.

"Our religious authority," he continued in his article in *La Prensa* (September 10, 1979), "has often been part of a combination of authorities—that of the state, of the big landowners, of the business people—seeking to subjugate the people either paternalistically or by despotism and repression."

---

69. Op. cit., p. 284.

70. Cohn, Hynds, op. cit., p. 100.

Cardenal called upon the priests to help in the formation of "true structures of Church community, in which the poor make their voice heard and forge their character as the principal protagonists of the new history opening up in Nicaragua." Priests should help in the "coming of age of our people—a people responsible and aware, builders of their own destiny, architects of their liberation."

Over the years observers have pointed out that Obando likes to be treated deferentially by all, including government leaders, and is resentful when he is not. The very fact that Obando played a significant role in the movement against Somoza perhaps led him to feel "that he should be one of the top leaders in the new society."[71] After all, the Somoza regime had tagged Obando as "Comandante Miguel." According to ex-contra leader Edgar Chamorro, Cardinal Obando does not feel that he must earn the people's respect but wants to exercise power and influence in society "by virtue of his office itself."[72]

One priest in Managua recounted, with a certain amount of satisfaction, an anecdote told by Obando which "says a lot," in the priest's estimation. Not long after the triumph of the revolution Comandante Tomás Borge called Obando, said that he had something important to discuss with him, and urged the archbishop to come right away. Obando's reported response: "It's the same distance from my office to yours as from yours to mine. I'll go to see you this time, but next time you come to me."

The same priest told a story from his own experience which he also considered significant in terms of clergy-state conflict at a lower level. When Daniel Ortega and other government leaders were going to come to the neighborhood for a special event, the organizers requested and were granted the use of the parish hall. Just before the event started, the local officials discovered that a Mass was going to be celebrated at the same time in another building of the parish. When they told the priest that he could not celebrate the Mass, he told them plainly that they had requested the use of only one facility, that the Mass would involve a small number of people and would not create any problems for the official event, and that they could not tell him whether or not he could celebrate Mass in the parish.

---

71. My interview of Luís Rocha, May 1989.

72. My interview of Edgar Chamorro, July 1989.

This priest feels that a series of such brushes between authority figures added up to "harassment" of the Church and that this was the key factor in the hierarchy-Sandinista conflict. "During the Somoza era," he said, "there were wholesale abuses and violations of the people's human rights, which we denounced, but Somoza did not lock horns with the hierarchy to the same extent the Sandinista government did."

This observation was echoed by La Prensa's César Vivas, who noted that "Somoza, although he committed abuses and atrocities, respected the Church." Vivas added that "the harsh treatment and disrespect shown to the pope in his visit to Nicaragua would never have happened under Somoza."[73]

According to Luís Humberto Guzmán, the hierarchy "feared that they might lose their influence in society under the Sandinista government." He also characterized the early years of hierarchy-Sandinista relations as a time of "reciprocal intolerance," with both institutions being "jealous of their power."[74]

Some point out that Obando and other high churchmen did not enjoy positions of sufficient honor at major government events. These hurt feelings were soothed somewhat in 1987 when the cardinal was asked to be president of the National Reconciliation Commission in the wake of the Central American Peace Accord and then was asked to be mediator in the talks between the government and the contras.

Why, in Sandinista Nicaragua, did the bishops not enjoy the same kind of alliance (with accompanying privileges) which Latin American hierarchies have traditionally had with government? Jesuit theologian Juan Luís Segundo (writing before the Nicaraguan triumph) shed light on the nature of such alliances: "They are offered and maintained so long as no clear-cut popular support exists for the government in question. The alliance with the Church compensates for the lack or the loss of popularity."[75] Thus the Church is "needed" to bestow legitimacy on an unpopular government or at least to convince the oppressed to remain subject.

Such governments "maintain that their countries are officially or unofficially 'Catholic,'" Jon Sobrino pointed out, "even when other kinds of

---

73. My interview of César Vivas, May 1989.

74. My interview of Guzmán, May 1989.

75. The Hidden Motives of Pastoral Action (Maryknoll, New York: Orbis, 1978), p. 42.

Christian communities are allowed. It is often in the interest of people in government to put in an appearance at religious events in order to give public, symbolic expression to this 'Catholicism.' A great deal of emphasis is placed on strictly religious terms such as 'God,' 'the Almighty,' 'the Supreme Maker,' etc."[76]

Such a state "values the use of religious symbols of the absolute which it can manipulate," Sobrino continued. Chaplains to the armed forces also play a role in this arrangement, "including a military Ordinary with the rank of colonel or even general. The purpose of all this is to defend special interests under the cloak of a defense of 'Western Christian civilization.'"

In this scheme of things the Catholic religion provides "religious justification for political institutions, while an appeal to the complete incompatibility of communism and religion makes it possible to defend any and every attack on real or supposed communists as a defense of religion."[77]

But in Nicaragua after the revolutionary triumph, the political institutions did not "need" religious justification: "in Nicaragua the legitimacy of the revolutionary process and of its institutions is determined by the extent to which the revolution provides jobs, food, shelter, health, education, participation, liberty, and dignity to ordinary working people," one Latin American theologian pointed out. He noted that it was not the function of the hierarchy or of the "popular church" to legitimize the revolution "since the revolution will legitimize itself with or without the Church."

The same kind of analysis was made by Brazilian theologian Frei Betto in an interview in *El Nuevo Diario*: "Since the bourgeois state is by its very nature anti-people and anti-democratic, it needs the Church to legitimize and sacralize it in the eyes of the people."[78] In exchange for this help, the government gives the Church a series of privileges which "make it feel like a power face to face with another power."

---

76. *The True Church and the Poor*, trans. Matthew J. O'Connell (Maryknoll, N.Y.: Orbis, 1984), p. 232.

77. Ibid., p. 233. When the Church breaks out of such servitude and takes up the cause of the poor, persecution ensues. "This persecution has been directed not against the Church as an institution but against the mission of the Church, its agents of evangelization, and the addressees of evangelization" (p. 300).

78. March 24, 1986.

Betto noted that this situation of interdependency had been broken in Nicaragua, where the revolution did not "need" the Church to legitimize it. "Some bishops," however, "cannot accept this reality of a poor, servant Church like that of the first centuries, and they feel uncomfortable because the state now does not deal with the Church as a 'power.'"

Penny Lernoux also mentioned this factor: "Fear that [religious] approval [of the revolution] would not be needed in the future was at the root of the conflict between the government and the churches. Convinced that Nicaragua was headed toward a Marxist dictatorship," she added, "the Sandinistas' religious opponents, led by . . . Obando y Bravo, fought the government and its religious supporters at every turn, even to the point of supporting the contras."[79]

François Houtart also emphasized the concern on the part of many Church officials for institutional power. "The institutional concern, which of course the Church does not state officially and which some Church people may not even be conscious of, is more important than economic interests. This is tied in with a certain kind of ecclesiology and theory of evangelization in which the Church feels that it must have, if not hegemony, at least a great space in civic society—in education, health, mass media, etc."

Applying this to Nicaragua, Houtart observed that the Church had "hegemony" in the educational system before the revolution. "The revolution did not close a single Catholic school, but it organized the whole educational system, so all at once the Church finds itself a minority in the system. This gives it the impression that it is losing social space, and then it quickly starts talking about persecution!"[80]

Marina Castillo, who began teaching history in 1972, gave Peter Davis her personal testimony on Church hegemony in education during Somoza's time: "Although this is a state school and not a parochial one, my problem as a teacher before was less Somoza than the church. The priests were very powerful, and religion was inserted everywhere. If you didn't teach that the New World was discovered because of divine intervention, someone would tell a priest, and the priest would tell his bishop, and the bishop would tell your administrator. The administrator would

---

79. *People of God*, p. 367.

80. My interview of Houtart, *Monthly Review*, January 1988.

have to talk to you about this whether he wanted to or not. So you would always have to say that God willed the voyages of Columbus."

After the 1979 victory, the teacher could explain to her students the political, economic, and social reasons for the age of European exploration. "You will see we have some emphasis on the existence of classes and class interests," she told Davis, "but it is hardly fanatic Marxism." (In her lecture to her students she explained that by the end of the 15th century Spain and Portugal "were losing the important Far Eastern markets to Venice and other Italian cities that were in league with Arab traders." Spain and Portugal needed "a new route to the East and new markets for trade to free themselves from the Italian and Arabian monopoly." Looking for a "new commercial route for trading with India," Columbus arrived "by accident" in the New World.)[81]

Since the Church's "social space" and worldly status in pre-revolutionary situations are bought by entering into a contradictory and evangelically debilitating partnership with the rich and powerful, the Church "should lose status more and more," said Casaldáliga. "It must move out of certain structures and go more and more to the margin, the periphery— be marginalized, lose status and consideration. That loss of status also brings us more freedom and greater communication." As for the Vatican and the diocesan chanceries, he feels that their critics are right. "There is no doubt that if the Vatican lost status it would gain gospel authenticity, witness, and possibilities for ecumenism."[82]

5. Competing for Moral Leadership

A fifth cause of hierarchy-Sandinista friction was a certain rivalry between the Sandinista revolution and the hierarchy for moral leadership, especially with the young. Some clerics seem to have been afraid they were losing their presumed monopoly on the promotion of morality and values in society. Father Omar Aragon Cardenas said that many of the clergy do not really know how to appeal to young people today. "In the early years after the triumph," he recalled, "the Sandinistas had great appeal for the youth and the Church felt it was losing out." One bishop in the Nicaraguan Church echoed the same view, while another felt that the

---

81. Davis, op. cit., pp. 316-317.

82. *El Vuelo del Quetzal*, p. 173.

Church in 1989 was pulling ahead in the "struggle for leadership," showing its capacity to draw crowds.[83]

This concern about the attractive power of the gospel, which of course can be found in many countries, was analyzed by Segundo in the 1970's. "What impact can the gospel message have today," he asked, "when everybody displays love to some extent and Christians do not seem to love more or better than anyone else? Marxism itself, now the official doctrine of countries that contain more than half the world's population, proclaims the implementation of real and effective love as Christianity once did." Marxism promotes equal opportunity and fulfillment for all but disclaims all ties with religion. And it "directly opposes the profit motive as a basis for social relations, associating that motive with the Western capitalist world where most Christians live.

"In short," Segundo concluded, "some evangelical values have become so generally known and accepted that the gospel message itself no longer has the peculiar attractiveness it once had. But dismay over the fact can only be justified if one assumes that the gospel is preached only to win adherents to the church. One can hardly be dismayed if one assumes that the proclamation of the gospel was meant to bring about such widespread recognition and acceptance of its basic values."[84]

In 1980 Frei Betto saw a "political thought-world emerging in Nicaragua which does not have religious connotations, and this is a little jarring to our ears since we are accustomed to having some religious reference." Not only is our pastoral thought-world absent from the new political thought-world, he said, but often "our Christian activists find a better explanation of history in the Marxist thought-world emerging today in Nicaragua than in the pastoral thinking in our Christian communities."

According to Betto, in this sense there will always be competition between the CBCs and the people's organizations. "Why? Because they are two foci for organizing the people. It is necessary to define yourself: will you go to the CDS [Sandinista Defense Committee—neighborhood organization], to the ATC [Farmworkers' Association], to the union, or to the Christian base community?"

---

83. My interviews of two bishops, July 1989.

84. Op. cit., p. 80.

This institutional competition led the Church to entrench itself ideologically in a campaign to fight the Marxist danger. But in fact, Betto pointed out, what this kind of crusading Christian mentality seeks to do is to preserve the "ideology of bourgeois liberalism."[85]

Irene Selser described the "problem" for the Catholic hierarchy in similar terms: "The Sandinistas' arrival in power meant, without their wishing it, a reduction of the political, religious, ideological, and social space occupied traditionally by the Catholic Church." The revolutionary government "generated new motivation and a different dynamic in the life of the masses, in their organization, education, and democratic forms." Many social services which the Church had previously assumed as part of its mission to the people "began to be absorbed and surpassed by the health, housing, and educational programs promoted by the revolution." Selser also noted the internal conflict in the Church "due to the active participation of representatives of the progressive clergy in the new structures of power."[86]

Deeper analysis revealed that the conflict between revolutionary organizations and Christian institutions could be resolved if the Church underwent a *metanoia*: in many Latin American countries the Church serves as a kind of party of the poor, but "when a society emerges whose structures and institutions are of the poor, as is the case in Nicaragua [in the 1980s], the Church is called to a conversion and to a change in its mission," Betto observed. "We should thank God that now the people have their own mass organizations of a political and class nature. What is left for the Church to do? To be a religious organization running parallel to these new organizations?"

Betto considered that option a "pharisaical" one, noting that Jesus went against the pharisees' notion of the religious body as being separate and cut off from society. Jesus did not intend to create a Church "where the people would come to it but rather an apostolic missionary community which would go to the people." This kind of Church does not see neighborhood organizations or labor unions or political parties as "parallel or competing spheres fighting over areas of influence. Rather, this apostolic Church wants its faithful, its Christian militants, to be present in

---

85. *Apuntes para una Teología Nicaraguense* (Managua: Centro Antonio Valdivieso y Instituto Histórico Centroamericano, 1981), pp. 88-90.

86. Selser, op. cit., p. 47.

all these organizations, since religion is not to be separate in its own sphere but to be present and announce Jesus in the life and organizations of the people.

"The Church in Nicaragua should be happy now that the people have their own organizations. The Church can once again take up its ecclesial function in a more peaceful situation; that is, it can be a community of faith which comes together to nourish, celebrate, and reaffirm its commitment in faith, hope, and love." Militants in the people's organizations will come to this community to nourish their praxis.[87]

In its final report the theological assembly in which Betto was participating came up with a brief statement about the nature of the Christian communities: "The Church's task is not to establish organizations running parallel to the people's organizations of the revolution; rather, the Christian community should be the privileged place where the faith sheds light on our people's commitment to take part in the tasks and organizations of our revolution."[88]

Betto did not see this Christian community sacrificing its critical function: "Our criticism of the Frente should be made through our Christian militants who are inside the Frente" rather than through a frontal attack by the Church as a power organization.[89]

"The ideological hegemony that Obando has as a person and as an institution has for the first time met a challenge in Sandinismo," noted Roberto Gutierrez, who was a member of the university community in the Riguero barrio. "The ideological hegemony of Sandinismo does not necessarily imply a decline in the religiosity of the people. But it gives a different content to it. In any case, this shouldn't be seen as a competition, but unfortunately that's how Obando sees it."[90]

The revolutionary "symbol system is secular in origin and thus has no kind of confessional religious identity," in the words of Rosa Maria Pochet and Abelino Martínez.[91] It draws upon the struggle and example

87. *Apuntes*, pp. 88-90.

88. *Apuntes*, p. 194

89. Ibid., p. 90.

90. Randall, op. cit., p. 199.

91. *Nicaragua—Iglesia: manipulación o profecía* (San José, Costa Rica: Editorial DEI, 1987), p. 157.

of Sandino and his heirs. "Given the moral capital which the long years of Sandinista struggle give to the newer generations, the new symbol system does not need to look for religious inspiration in order to legitimate the new society."[92] The authors noted that a "revolutionary and humanistic symbol system gives full sense and meaning to the changes which begin to happen. The religious institution feels a nervous chill when it discovers that the new articulation of meaning is eminently non-sacral."[93]

An example of the moral competition offered to the bishops by the Sandinistas can be found in the challenging words of Orlando Nuñez, former director of Nicaragua's Center for Research and Study of Agrarian Reform (CIERA): "In the class struggle, morality is part of the ideological struggle. If the concept of morality has been used more in religions than by revolutions, this should not prejudice revolutionaries against waging struggle in this area. . . . Nor should we hesitate to build a revolutionary morality, thinking that we are trespassing on territory reserved for religion. . . ."[94]

Nuñez laid down the moral gauntlet: "Revolutionary practice has a moral content, and a plethora of moral standards exist within it. . . . Ideological struggle means invoking the principles and values of the most revolutionary *compañeros*, competing with the traditions and religions of the moment, picking up on the workers' revolutionary values. . . ."

In this revolutionary's view, Christian morality was a morality "for the poor which favored exploitation, a morality of consolation and resignation of the weakest which favored the maintenance of all those factors that caused weakness for some and power for others, . . . a morality that Nietzsche denounced as fitting only for sheep, one increasingly submissive and responsible for the alienating relations between master

---

92. Ibid.

93. Ibid., p. 164.

94. "Morality and Revolution in Daily Life," *Annual Review of Nicaraguan Sociology* (Vol. 1, Nos. 1 & 2, 1988), pp. 90-104. This journal, a joint project of Loyola University (New Orleans) and the Central American University (Managua), is published by the Institute of Human Relations, Loyola University, New Orleans, LA 70118.

and slave. . . ." Given his view of Christianity as an inherently reactionary force, he is compelled to do ideological battle against it.[95]

This dehumanizing morality must be replaced by a revolutionary one which emphasizes "heroic actions and the very human values of fraternity, solidarity, the willingness to risk one's life, altruism in combat, boldness, companionship, sympathy, etc."

Nuñez quoted "one in a position of high moral authority within the FSLN," Commander Dora Maria Téllez, Sandinista Minister of Health: Life in the revolutionary struggle "was a tough school in the sense of being demanding. A school in which there were no aspirations for moral or material remuneration. There was a rule: if you are doing things well, you are barely fulfilling your duty.

"If you had to carry out a mission," Téllez continued, "you carried it out, period. You went on foot, by bus, in a car, on a star, you swung on a vine, or whatever, but you fulfilled your mission. The demands were extremely hard. Before you joined the Frente you made a pledge and received initial training. You had to read and discuss the statutes which were very demanding." (Téllez went on to acknowledge the difficulty of maintaining such a high moral level since the triumph of the revolution in 1979.)[96]

Nuñez's article was followed by a response by Father Peter Marchetti, S.J., director of the Office of Research and Graduate Studies of the Central American University in Managua. Marchetti traced the involvement of Nicaraguan Christians in the revolutionary process, arguing forcefully against the thesis that revolutionary morality must be opposed to Christianity. He recognized, however, the ideological struggle which has been played out between the Church hierarchy and the revolution and analyzed the conflict in terms of competition for moral power.

"The logic of power is terrible," Marchetti noted, "be it economic, political, or ideological. The logic of ideological power is maybe the

---

95. Belgian priest-sociologist François Houtart considers it "almost too late" for a real rapprochement between revolutionaries and Christians. In my interview of Houtart (*Monthly Review*, January, 1988) he stated: "The Church has almost lost credibility among revolutionaries, although they will accept Christians. But they will never trust the Church as an institution."

96. "El mito era la realidad," in *Nuevo Amanecer Cultural*, July 19, 1986, as cited by Nuñez.

most rigid of all, as we can judge from the behavior of the inquisitions carried out over history. . . . When the ideological apparatus loses prestige and status, it loses everything, because without credibility it is unable to forge either legitimacy or consensus within society."[97]

The Church is part of the "ideological apparatus" in society. "In Nicaragua," Marchetti continued, "the basic symbol that is generated and manipulated by the conservative hierarchy is the image of the priest as the exclusive channel between God and the people." Before the revolution, the voice of the Church (as the channel of God's message) and the voice of the dictatorship were the only ones to be heard in public, and the Somozas certainly presented no challenge to the Church in terms of moral leadership.

"But with the revolution," Marchetti explained, "the people, the peasants, everyone lost their fear of talking. The priest was not listened to as before, because there were now several voices." These voices, including those criticizing the government, were even broadcast on a couple of radio talk shows. "As a result of this explosion, those who had lived on the basis of their prestige and control over symbols began to react against the process. The voice of the bishop was no longer the only voice that could be heard. The message of justice, of love, of God arose from all sides. In the opinion of some bishops, the revolution must be diabolical if it blocks the Church hierarchy's monopoly control of the channel between God [truth and goodness] and the people."

This question of moral control is crucial: "This is the only way to understand the religious phenomenon of a certain portion of the hierarchy who refuse to pray for the dead if they gave their lives for the revolution. Only in this way can we understand how some of the members of the hierarchy have opted so clearly for the imperial project or have remained silent during moments of great historical importance for this hemisphere."

An early experience of episcopal resentment over Sandinista moralizing came in 1978 with the rebels' takeover of the National Palace. When Obando and two other bishops arrived on the scene as mediators, Commander Zero (Edén Pastora) told them that they would have to talk with Commander Two (Dora María Téllez). "To our surprise," Obando recalled twelve years later, "she began to talk to us about the work which

---

97. "Revolution and Religion in Nicaragua," *Annual Review of Nicaraguan Sociology,* op. cit., pp. 105-116.

the Church must do for the people. She kept telling us how life had to be improved" and how hospitals needed more medicines.

"She continued with a long sermon," Obando noted, "trying to teach us how the Church should behave. The dialogue had become a monologue. She was trying to give us a lecture on ecclesiology. After listening without interruption for a half hour, we said: 'Look, we know something about theology, since that is one of our obligations as bishops. Frankly, we have not come here to discuss this with you. I think it is better that you tell us right away what are the demands and suggestions that you have to make to President Somoza. That is why we are all here.'"[98]

In a July 1989 seminar at the Antonio Valdivieso Ecumenical Center, Nuñez accused the churches of taking over and monopolizing the best humanistic values. "Now the people's movements are taking back, expropriating their morality," he declared. In the same seminar Father Xabier Gorostiaga, S.J., put the issue differently, noting that the people of God can now read the bible themselves and do not have to depend totally and unthinkingly on interpretations handed down by Church officials. As one Nicaraguan bishop told me, the CBCs are "coming up with their own interpretations of Scripture."[99] In either Nuñez's or Gorostiaga's way of putting the issue, the "challenge" to the traditional role of religious authority is clear, if that authority insists on being the sole arbiter of morality in society.

Many Christians have become active in the Sandinista programs, finding in them a concrete expression of Christian values of solidarity, service to the poor, and building a better world. These Christians do not perceive any rivalry between the gospel and the values and goals of the revolution. But Church officials with a narrow view of the moral influence of their institutions may be upset when they see the Sandinista Youth or the Sandinista health crusades or coffee-picking brigades getting a more enthusiastic response than the parish or school youth club.

These different attitudes toward the revolution spring from lived personal experience. Christians and Marxists who struggled shoulder to shoulder in the insurrection and who continue working together for a new Nicaragua are close friends with a deep respect for one another's moral

98. Obando, *Agonía en el bunker*, p. 96.

99. My interview of the bishop, August 1989.

values. In the September 1979 seminar on "Christian Faith and Sandinista Revolution," the majority of the participants in the dialogue emphasized strongly that for them the relationship between non-believing revolutionaries and Christian revolutionaries was very different from a mere object of rational discussion; rather, it was a question of a lived experience.

"In their concrete practice," the introduction continued, "non-believing revolutionaries and Christian revolutionaries had come together in an embrace of total solidarity." Luís Carrión, one of the Comandantes of the Revolution, expressed his surprise at some of the questions prepared for the dialogue, "questions which could insinuate that there was some kind of confrontation."[100]

Christians in the revolution frequently had the experience of finding God in their brothers and sisters who "had embraced the cause of the oppressed, putting aside their own self-interest." Christians saw their partners in struggle dying for others without proclaiming that they were doing this because of their faith in God. This experience freed these Christians from the prejudice of thinking that true love can be found only among believers. At the same time they were liberated from the "temptation of thinking that a revolutionary process is not authentic if it does not call itself Christian."[101] Christians were challenged by the revolutionary commitment of many non-believers who were "filled with love for the oppressed classes." These Christians became ashamed of a "perverted version of Christianity which emphasized doctrine, sacraments, and almsgiving but neglected the weightier matters of justice and love. They were also ashamed of the fact that it was the Sandinistas and not 'the Christians' who had begun to bind up the wounds of the Nicaraguan people who had been assaulted, robbed, and left to die."[102]

In conversation during the seminar Luis Carrión said: "People define who they are by their commitment, by their position for or against the interests of our people."[103] Thus between Christian revolutionaries and non-believing revolutionaries "it is not a question now of establishing a strategic alliance, because if we are revolutionaries we are already to-

---

100. *Fe Cristiana y Revolución Sandinista en Nicaragua*, p. 10.

101. Ibid., p. 12.

102. Ibid., p. 17.

103. Ibid., p. 13.

gether in one group, we are brothers and sisters and compañeros, which means much more than allies."[104]

Father Benjamin Forcano, a Spanish theologian, summarized the question of competition for moral leadership in an article in *El Nuevo Diario* (November 30, 1985). The Nicaraguan hierarchy saw its position of moral leadership "become shaky," he said. Somoza's government had no legal legitimacy or popular support, and so it offered no moral competition to the bishops. "But the Sandinistas offer the people a project which has meaning as a response to human problems, and this tends to compete with the Church on moral grounds."

---

104. Ibid., p. 20.

11

Three Underlying Theological Questions

Three basic theological questions run through this discussion of the conflict between the hierarchy and the Sandinistas. The first has to do with the very notion of religious freedom and freedom of conscience; the second question concerns the relation between the Church and the Kingdom; and the third question deals with the theme of unity.

1. First Basic Theological Question: Can the Hierarchy Accept Religious Freedom?

The Church's affirmation of freedom of conscience is a recent development which required a long struggle. And its assimilation of that affirmation, which implies "the Church's independence from governments and cultures and thus a loss of privilege in civil society, has been a slow and painful process."[1]

In Nicaragua and other Latin American countries, the Catholic Church under the Spanish crown was the official state religion, enjoying all the exclusive "benefits" entailed in that relationship. After independence, Conservative governments continued to give Catholicism a privileged position, showing various kinds and degrees of discrimination against non-Catholics and any atheists who may have wanted to promote their beliefs. With the Somoza dynasty, the Church had to accept the traditional Liberal policy on religion but still enjoyed a certain amount of official support.

---

1. Hernández Pico, S.J., "Religión y Revolución en Nicaragua," op. cit., p. 80.

245

The Sandinista government was charged with persecuting the Church. But in reality the government's position on religion was one of strict neutrality—not favoring belief over non-belief or one church over another. Some analysts suggest that some Church leaders, unaccustomed to and uncomfortable with the very notion of religious freedom, were confusing official government neutrality with hostility.

People in the CBCs would qualify the statement that the revolutionary government was neutral. They feel that the government was promoting true Christian values in its option for the poor majority, and they also point out that the government subsidized many private schools (most of which are Catholic) so that the poor would not be excluded.

But the main lines of official policy were clear, as enunciated in the Sandinistas' official communiqúe on religion in 1980: "For the FSLN, the freedom to profess a religious faith is an inalienable right of persons which the revolutionary government fully guarantees. No one can be discriminated against in the New Nicaragua for publicly professing or disseminating his/her religious beliefs. Those who profess no religious faith also have this same right."

The statement continued: "The revolutionary state, like any modern state, is a lay state and can adopt no religion because it represents the whole people, both believers and non-believers." The communiqúe also expressed real appreciation for the contributions which Christians made first to the overthrow of Somoza and later to the development of the new society. The Nicaraguan constitution promulgated in 1987 has the same affirmation of religious freedom and a similar expression of appreciation for Christian participation in the revolution.

Several elements should be highlighted in the declaration. First, the government recognized the inalienable right to have and profess a religious faith and barred discrimination against anyone for *disseminating* his/her religious beliefs or non-belief. Here was the rub for many Church leaders. In the Sandinistas' *Barricada* or in the independent (but pro-revolutionary) *Nuevo Diario,* page one might highlight an article on the 190-mile Way of the Cross for Peace, Life, and an End to the Aggression led in 1986 by Father Miguel D'Escoto, then Minister of Foreign Relations who remained a member in good standing of Maryknoll though suspended as a priest. D'Escoto had invited the bishops to take part in the procession and to have a change of heart which would lead them to speak out against the atrocities committed by the U.S.-supported contras. But there was also a strong prophetic tone in D'Escoto's words as he criticized the bishops for their silence on this issue and for their support of U.S. aid to the contras.

In 1985, when D'Escoto entered into a one-month fast for peace and for respect for his country's right to self-determination, he issued a public call to Christians to join him in some way in this first phase of an "evangelical insurrection." Church officials challenged his right to call the Christian people to do anything, asserting their own authority as the leaders who alone can call the people to religious activity.[2]

Another issue of one of the dailies might carry a declaration by a CBC about the Church's preferential option for the poor or about its responsibility for liberation. The statement might very well criticize the official Church for falling short on both counts. "We would ask his sublime eminence, Cardinal Obando, to be more open to the liberation of this oppressed people," said Adán Aráuz, Delegate of the Word in Jinotega, who along with his wife Adilia was featured in a full-page interview in *El Nuevo Diario* (May 13, 1989). "We would ask the cardinal to study perhaps the book of Exodus a little more," Adán suggested. In revolutionary Nicaragua such advice could appear in the media, whether the bishops liked it or not.

Four days later the same newspaper carried an editorial entitled "Yes, the People Have Lost Their Fear of the Bourgeoisie and its Taboos." Before discussing liberation from religious fear the editorial dealt with the people's new attitude toward the bourgeoisie and the security forces. "The people now do not see the bourgeoisie as the untouchables of society, who previously were treated with fawning reverence, but rather as the people's historical class adversaries." The people also lost their fear of demanding their rights as workers, because "they know that now there is no army like the National Guard which the bourgeois bosses can call out to brutally repress the workers."

Moving on to the religious sector, the editorial stated that the people had lost their fear "of religious taboos, realizing that heaven, hell, and purgatory were ideological weapons of the ruling class to perpetuate itself in power with the blessing and assistance of the most reactionary Church. Thus, while keeping their religious faith which the revolution has respected, the people now do not believe in the virgins of Cuapa, much less

---

2.   Teófilo Cabestrero, op. cit., p. 30.

in the sweating ones,[3] nor do they believe that religious are beings endowed with supernatural powers but rather men and women like any others."

The people had also lost the fear of "questioning the political conduct of their spiritual leaders, recognizing that a good number of them may be in favor of the integral (complete) salvation of the person, that is, they support the liberation of the poor, while others are married to the exploiters and oppressors. To sum up, the people are no longer afraid of their own power, and they have shown that by participating . . . in the exercise of a new democracy which is not only representative but also participatory" (*El Nuevo Diario*, May 17, 1989).

While Obando had convinced the Vatican to ban Bishop Pedro Casaldáliga from visiting Nicaragua, *El Nuevo Diario* gave the bishop a public forum for his revolutionary views by carrying daily installments of his book, *El Vuelo del Quetzal*. The newspaper also features regular religious columns, including liberation-oriented commentaries on the Sunday scripture readings, by the Antonio Valdivieso Ecumenical Center (which the bishops have tried to discredit) and other progressive theological centers.

Atheists, too, who still think that religion must be the opiate of the people found the freedom to present their views publicly. In fact, they did not get much coverage in the mass media, perhaps because of the very limited acceptance of their message. The Sandinista government neither promoted their opinions nor discriminated against them for expressing them.

Did the bishops ever express their distaste for freedom of the press? Some years ago Obando, on a visit to St. Paul the Apostle parish, complained that the CBC had never defended him against the "attacks" he was suffering in the mass media. Community members point out that the "attacks" consisted of criticism of Obando's political positions. Since they agreed with that criticism, they could not simply fall in line to defend him.[4]

More officially, in their April 6, 1986 pastoral letter the bishops, insisting on their own authority, denounced "a belligerent group of priests,

---

3. A statue of Mary which was touted as sweating.

4. My interviews with members of the community, May 1989.

religious men and women, and lay people of various nationalities who are working actively to undermine the unity of the Church . . . by challenging the constituted authorities of the Church." The bishops complained that this "people's Church" issues its "calumnies and accusations" through media "which the State itself puts at their disposal." Thus the bishops expressed their annoyance at the fact that the government made it possible for *all* religious sectors to have access to the mass media.

On May 8, 1987 Church officials promoted a message supposedly from the Virgin Mary urging Nicaraguans to burn certain books. In a concelebrated Mass in a village near Managua, auxiliary bishop Bosco Vivas announced that Mary had appeared once again to Bernardo Martínez. (The first apparition was said to have occurred in 1980 in the town of Cuapa.) This time, according to Bernardo in his statement during the Mass, Mary wanted people "to burn bad books, evil books, atheistic books." When Bernardo asked whether it was bad to burn books, he heard this response: "It is bad to burn the sinner, but it is all right to burn the sin."

Bosco Vivas told the faithful at the Mass: "Mary has said that all homes should burn bad books, books which deny God and teach sin. Last night in this parish we burned some bad books. We should act in accord with what she told Bernardo." Among the books devoured by the flames were works of Marx, Lenin, and Engels. On other occasions Cardinal Obando affirmed the authenticity of the revelation.

In 1989, when asked by the Nicaraguan weekly *La Crónica* (May 24-30) how the last ten years had affected his work as pastor, Obando complained of the expulsion of some priests and added: "We have also suffered attacks in the newspapers."

Nicaraguan television belonged to Somoza and, along with his other holdings, became state property in 1979. As Obando adopted a more stringent tone in expressing his political opinion of the new government, the Sandinista TV system decided to restrict his monopoly on the televised Sunday Mass. The archbishop refused to accept an arrangement by which the Mass would have stayed on TV but with a variety of featured celebrants. In 1986 Miguel D'Escoto and several other religious figures were guests on a Sandinista TV program. Cardinal Obando had been invited but had turned it down.

Another combat zone was the area of education. In a 1981 letter on education, as we have seen in Chapter 9, the bishops asserted: "Our people, deeply religious and Christian for centuries, want for their children an education inspired by the gospel and attentive to the orientations of the Church." Such a statement, especially the last phrase, was fraught with potential conflicts not only between Church and state but between believers and non-believers and among religious bodies. The government was not about to promote Catholicism or any other religion in the public schools.

In 1985 Obando got a bit more specific about his problems with the national educational system. In an interview with Congressman Robert Dornan (R-CA), the archbishop complained that the Sandinistas "disregard God and emphasize evolution. Likewise they also emphasize biology, economics, and politics and insist on teaching about the martyrs and heroes of the revolution."[5]

It was clear that some Church officials would undoubtedly be happier with a conservative government in power. Dr. Myriam Argüello, secretary general of the "Popular Conservative Alliance" (one of the factions of the Conservative Party in Nicaragua), told me that if her party were in power "it would have respectful relations with the Church, since the vast majority of the people have great respect for the Church and its leaders." Dr. Argüello, whose office features paintings of Popes John XXIII and John Paul II, got more specific, stating that under her party it would be possible to teach religion in the public schools on a non-obligatory basis.[6] Argüello, who ran on the UNO coalition ticket, became president of the National Assembly.

In its Easter message the bishops' conference lamented the "painful reality" which had been Nicaragua's plight "for some time," without even mentioning the external causes of the pain.

On April 9, 1989, amidst growing preparations for the February 1990 elections, Cardinal Obando used part of his Sunday sermon to give advice on what to look for in candidates for public office. "What is important is to look for true shepherds," he said, "not mercenaries who want to enrich themselves. The good shepherd must seek the common good." As the

---

5.   Update (Central American Historical Institute), June 12, 1985. This bulletin notes that Dornan read Obando's remarks into the Congressional Record.

6.   My interview of Dr. Argüello, August 1989.

people look for their political leader, they must ask whether a particular candidate "loves God, because charity has a vertical dimension of love of God and a horizontal one of love of neighbor," Obando said (*La Prensa,* April 10, 1989). Again, in an interview in *La Prensa* (April 24), the cardinal said that he would encourage Christians "to vote for the candidate who gives testimony of being the best Christian."

Obando spelled out this criterion further in an interview in *La Crónica* (May 30, 1989), where he said he would support a candidate who looked to the common good and who believed in God. "I feel that the believer, because he believes in God, tries to look to the good of his neighbor," Obando said. "If he really believes, if he truly has faith in God, and if this faith is not just in words but is shown in deeds, then this person doesn't do evil to anyone."

No one quarreled with the cardinal's criticism of political "mercenaries" and their self-enrichment. What was problematic was his insistence on the presumably explicit religious faith of a candidate. Theologically the cardinal seemed to feel that a non-believer cannot love others and serve the common good. Perhaps he also believed that, with a president who would be more public about his Christianity than Daniel Ortega was, the Church as institution, and even the gospel itself, would be in a more powerful position in society. In this connection, Ramiro Gurdián of COSEP, the big-business council, noted that the Sandinista *comandantes* do not attend Mass and that the FSLN does not project a Catholic image.[7]

A diocesan priest commented that Somoza met the criterion of being very explicit about his Christianity, "but the bishops and everyone else turned against him since he obviously fell short in terms of seeking the common good. What the cardinal is saying here is that he wants a government which will support the institutional Church." (Bishop Casaldáliga, on the other hand, has expressed a different set of priorities with regard to electoral criteria: "I would rather vote for an honest atheist than for a corrupt Christian.")

Those who have analyzed Obando's religious discourses over the years have pointed to the only partially disguised political messages imbedded in his language. One of the clearest examples of this was found in the cardinal's homily in the Church of St. Dominic on April 23, 1989, preaching to a congregation which was generally considered to be anti-

---

7. My interview of Gurdián, May 1989.

Sandinista: "As St. John says, the old has passed away, we are going to bring in something new. You have to consider carefully how you are going to put an end to the old in order to build something new in our society. When the old comes to an end here in Nicaragua, will you be able to make everything new? What will be the tactics or policies you will follow to make everything new?"[8]

In May the bishops' conference issued a pastoral letter ostensibly on education but with a strong political message for the pre-election period. Identifying themselves as the bishops of "this Church suffering," they recognized the efforts which had been made to expand education but claimed that the government was promoting a "materialistic and atheistic education, imposing on the youth the ideology of certain minorities against the wishes and faith of parents." Moreover, the schools are of poor quality and education is still not available to all, the bishops complain, and cutbacks in state subsidies are jeopardizing the future of Catholic schools. The Catholic school is in danger of becoming "extinct." And they suggest that Nicaragua is a country where "anti-religious legislation seeks to impede education in the faith" and where disbelief and secularism have reached dangerous levels.

Shortly after being named by the right-wing UNO coalition as its presidential candidate, *La Prensa* publisher Violeta Chamorro made a rather ostentatious display of Catholic piety. Asked if she felt prepared to be president, she replied, "Of course I am. I have enormous faith in God. He will illuminate me and show me how to do what my conscience dictates."[9]

At a rally in a Managua movie theater, "her remarks conveyed her deep Roman Catholic convictions," according to the *Miami Herald*. The widow of anti-Somoza leader Pedro Joaquin Chamorro who was slain in 1978, Mrs. Chamorro assured the crowd: "I have asked the advice of Pedro Joaquin and of God whether I should serve as a link of love with all of you. And they said, 'Yes.'"[10]

The religious aspect gathered steam along with the campaign. "Every night I pray to God and to Pedro to give me strength," she said. After that quote, the *Miami Herald* (International Edition, Sept. 16, 1989) said

---

8.   Quoted by Irene Selser, op. cit., p. 25.

9.   *The New York Times* (International), September 4, 1989.

10. *Miami Herald* (International), Sept. 5, 1989.

that "it will be a campaign of contrasts: the grandmother vs. the guerrilla, the devoutly Roman Catholic widow squaring off with the olive-green clad, Yankee-baiting revolutionary." The reporter noted that Mrs. Chamorro's speeches are kept short and hinted that they are rather contentless. But her lack of a politician's skills reportedly did not worry her supporters. "She is an icon like the Virgin of Fatima," said one opposition leader. "She doesn't need to talk, she can just lead the procession."

In October Mrs. Chamorro's campaign managers began to use the cardinal in their TV spots, showing him blessing the candidate. And shortly before election day *La Prensa* featured a photo of the cardinal blessing Mrs. Chamorro. (Candidate Ortega was also shown in the Sandinista press with the cardinal but could never make a strong case for being Obando's favorite.)

Priests, Delegates of the Word, and "charismatic" leaders subservient to Obando's political wishes reportedly played a much more explicit and direct role in supporting the UNO coalition than did their "spiritual" guide. René Mendoza noted that in one village near Masatepe "the day after the elections, the charismatics gave thanks to God for having 'won.' They had always said they weren't 'political,' that you 'shouldn't get mixed up in politics,' but here they were, giving thanks for 'their' political victory. That same day one of the charismatic Delegates of the Word, upon seeing a campesino wearing a Frente cap, told him, 'We're going to take that hat off, head and all.'" (Op. cit.)

With the election of Mrs. Chamorro, Obando could enjoy the fruits of a victory he had helped to bring about. He was soon basking in the political limelight. At the inauguration of the new president on April 25, Obando felt entitled to turn an "invocation" into a 25-minute speech, rivaling (at least in duration) the addresses by the outgoing and incoming presidents. The cardinal's tone was characteristically tough as he laid down Catholic social and political doctrine to the attending foreign presidents, ambassadors, and Nicaraguan officials and public. He seemed an angry and hurt schoolteacher scolding his pupils who have to sit respectfully but without paying much attention.

"What constitutes the nation as such is essentially its culture," he insisted. "And the culture of the Nicaraguan people contains a nucleus of values which are fundamentally gospel values. We have no doubts about affirming that the soul of Nicaragua is Christian." In case any atheists or non-Christian believers were listening, the cardinal added: "And for that very reason the soul of Nicaragua, in genuine respect for freedom of conscience, is open in a pluralistic sense to other conceptions."

Obando made it clear, however, that tolerance has its limits. "In the present circumstances we cannot help but express our concern about currents which seek to introduce a culture which goes against our very being as a nation." He indicated that government should use its power to defend Nicaragua against unwanted cultural influences: "We trust that those who must guard the common good of the nation [patria] will fulfill their duty to defend the cultural identity of our people, sometimes subjected to pressures which are foreign to it."

In this context, he said, the area of education is of special importance. The family has the primary responsibility for education, "in keeping with the teachings of the Second Vatican Council." Not the slightest indication by the cardinal that perhaps a few of his listeners might not know what the Second Vatican Council was or might not feel especially bound to obey its teachings. For Obando, Nicaragua is not only a Christian nation but a very Catholic one as well; non-Catholics have already expressed concern that the new government may share and even cater to Obando's way of thinking.

(In 1987 Obando, after expressing his satisfaction at finding many Nicaraguans outside the country who prayed frequently to Mary, had said that "those are the true Nicaraguans. I wish that all Nicaraguans did likewise. Those who do not pray should not be considered Nicaraguans.")[11]

Continuing his lecture at the inauguration of Mrs. Chamorro, Obando noted: "Education is not only for all men," perhaps in a reference to the Sandinistas' emphasis on equal opportunity, "but also for the whole man—a rational creature with a transcendent destiny. An education which limits itself to being a school without God and without morality falls short of being a complete education." The new Ministry of Education, whose minister and vice-minister were considered to have been anointed by Obando for their jobs, may seek to bring explicitly religious content into public education. Whether the morality they teach will be more Christian than that promoted by the Sandinista educational system remains to be seen. (Shortly after leaving the Ministry of Education,

---

11. Homily by Obando in Niquinohomo, July 26, 1987, quoted by Irene Selser, op. cit., p. 229.

Father Fernando Cardenal wrote about the kind of young person the schools have sought to form during the last ten years. Father Cardenal borrowed from Scripture in observing that "a tree is known by its fruits" and noted that "a good majority of students have shown that they are capable of giving themselves in loving service of their neighbor. They have learned that we should bring together our individual interests with social and national interests. They have gladly sacrificed their vacations to go off to pick coffee or cotton; they have given up free days to join in the vaccination campaigns; and they have abandoned their favorite TV shows to teach reading and writing in the barrio. There is a broad new appreciation of the country's independence, sovereignty, and dignity, along with a thorough rejection of injustice, exploitation, racism, discrimination, and above all a rejection of imperialism." He ended by noting that there is no serious drug problem among Nicaraguan youth.)[12]

"Society must watch very closely to prevent the entry of anti-values which would contaminate it," Obando went on. The last minute of his long discourse was devoted to an invocation: "May Jesus Christ always be the light of Nicaragua, and may the world recognize us as his disciples because we remain in his Word and we know the truth which will make us free with the freedom of the children of God."

In her inaugural discourse the new president, a devout Catholic, made it clear that Obando would enjoy a special place of honor during her administration. Mrs. Chamorro began by including the cardinal among the dignitaries mentioned by name: "my dear friend and esteemed Cardinal Miguel Obando y Bravo."

In one of her more memorable lines, she rendered the nation's tribute to all who had died in the war but noted that "more honor still is due to those who have understood that reconciliation is more beautiful than victory." In this regard, she continued, the whole nation and her government had the duty to give homage and express its deepest gratitude "to the highest spiritual authority, his Eminence Cardinal Miguel Obando y Bravo, our Archbishop, tireless in his struggle for reconciliation as mediator and witness of the peace agreements."

For the fifteen to twenty percent of the population who are Protestant and for other non-Catholics, Obando is not the highest spiritual authority; these Nicaraguan citizens fear that President Chamorro may be inclined

---

12. *Barricada*, May 8, 1990.

to make policy decisions on the basis of her personal piety, thus ushering in a new era of an unsigned Concordat.

Obando, she said, has been "a blessing for our country." He has "incarnated the Gospel of Christ in a humble, generous, and always firm way. . . ."[13]

Obando had always seemed to have a difficult time with the ideological pluralism and religious freedom rampant under the Sandinistas. But the Nicaraguan hierarchy was not the first one to use the charge of "religious persecution" against a government which would not cater to the bishops' wishes. As Segundo has pointed out, when Juan Perón brought about separation of church and state in Argentina, laicized the public schools, and promulgated a law permitting divorce, "most of the Argentinian bishops attacked him as a persecutor of the Church, going so far as to welcome the military revolt that overthrew him."[14]

The charge of religious persecution can be used whenever the Church begins to lose some of its control over public policies. Segundo added that the Church "is used to speaking in a context where it exerts pressure and finds itself quite defenseless when there is no possibility of controlling its audience in some way."[15] In Segundo's view, this control can be exercised through a political alliance with the government, as in the case of colonial Christendom, or with Conservative governments, where Catholicism is taught in the public schools, Catholic moral teaching is enforced by law, and at the very least presidents and generals give lip service to Catholic practice.

Emilio F. Mignone, in his bitter denunciation of "the complicity of Church and dictatorship in Argentina," argued that Church officials accepted and justified the Argentinian military coup and the horrors that followed because they felt that the generals intended to defend "Western Christian civilization" and would bolster the privileges of the Church.[16] The author's analysis of the Argentinian bishops' attitude toward the mili-

---

13. *La Prensa,* April 25, 1990.

14. Op.cit., p. 42.

15. Ibid., p. 66.

16. *Witness to the Truth* (Maryknoll, N.Y: Orbis, 1988), p. 19.

tary dictatorship sheds some light on the Nicaraguan bishops' mentality regarding the U.S.-supported contras.

Mignone had the impression "that some bishops were pleased to see bothersome elements eliminated and even gave their approval for it to take place." The author recalled how an auxiliary bishop of Paris told him: "What astonishes me is that the Argentine military junta should kill in the name of God and the bishops do not point out what a scandal this is."[17]

The Nicaraguan bishops also claimed that it was exceedingly difficult to prove torture, attacks on civilians, and other human rights violations by the contras, who killed "in the name of God." A dirty war seems tolerable if it is to defend God and the institutional interests of the Church.

For many Argentinian bishops the continuation of the military regime was "reassuring," in Mignone's words, "for it enabled them to keep up the fiction of living in a nominally Catholic country and allowed them to use the power of the state to exert their influence. . . . Integralism and national Catholicism are opposed to pluralism and democracy, which the bishops have a hard time getting along with, for they regard both of them as stepping stones on the way to communism."[18]

The desire on the part of Church leaders to exercise religious control over people can be fulfilled in other ways besides the direct alliance of throne and altar. Control can be exercised through Christian institutions which meet some material needs of the population and when necessary can be used as carrots (in the modern absence of the official stick) to draw people into at least being physically present at sermons, rituals, classes, and other religious activities. Students in Catholic schools can be required to listen to theology lectures; patients in Catholic hospitals are not eager to close the door on the chaplain; the poor at the kitchen door of the rectory may see a certain practical wisdom in attending Mass.[19]

All of this, according to Segundo, is based on pastoral agents' lack of faith in the power of the gospel itself to draw people. But the problem he sees is twofold: such recruiting does not, at least in itself, lead to real

---

17. Ibid, p. 137.

18. Ibid., p. 95.

19. Segundo, op. cit., pp. 66-68.

personal Christian commitment, and the maintenance of Christian institutions as carrots requires a "visible alliance of the church with the centers of economic power." Especially in Latin America, money comes from those whose "wealth usually derives, directly or indirectly, from the exploitation of other human beings." Such an alliance, like the political one with governments whose lack of popular support pushes them to the chancery door, is a counter-sign working against the real proclamation of the gospel.[20]

Segundo's analysis is important in that it sheds light on the motivation of Church leaders with their penchant for making alliances with the powerful and/or the rich. They are not necessarily lusting for power or gold for its own sake; indeed, while most would not want to embrace radical poverty, they are content with middle-class comforts and conveniences. The alliances, then, are part of their pastoral strategy: since they do not believe the gospel itself is sufficiently effective in winning masses of people, they want to add to its luster with a touch of legal or economic coercion. Or at least they want a government which will speak of itself as "Christian" or as the protector of "Christian values," thus promoting the Church in the eyes of the public. The brutal Argentinian military regime "proclaimed its Catholicism to the four winds."[21] But as Segundo noted this strategy is seriously flawed because the public, especially the poor masses and the socially conscious among the other sectors, see the Church's alliance with many governments and with the economic elites as a kiss of death.

Chilean theologian Pablo Richard described the Church alliance with the powerful as a form of "Christendom." In this model of Christianity, the Church finds support for its intention to evangelize the whole society "in the political, civil, and social power of the ruling classes." Why did the Church open private schools for the children of the oligarchy? Because those children were going to be the generals, judges, senators, and even presidents, "and so with the support of these alumni the Church could have power in society."

Richard noted that the Church's intention in this is not bad, but "it is mistaken in its choice of means—the ruling power." The Church be-

---

20. Ibid., pp. 43-44.

21. Mignone, op. cit., p. 47.

lieves that it can christianize society "by christianizing the state, having it as a friend and getting it to pass 'Catholic' laws, to allow the Church to teach in the public schools, to affirm Christian family morality, etc." Richard calls upon the Church to break free of this smothering embrace, to be the Church of the people, and to proclaim the gospel with only the power of faith, hope, and love.[22]

"In terms of power," Leonardo Boff wrote, "the Church fears all transformations that jeopardize the security of its acquired power. And power itself will never abdicate. It is only shared when it is in jeopardy. The institution always seeks to be on top, with the winners."[23] Preoccupation with its own rights leads the Church to accept unjust systems: "Because of its centralized and authoritarian structure, the Church has no qualms of conscience in accepting authoritarian and even totalitarian regimes as long as its own rights are not attacked."

Boff shares Segundo's explanation of the Church's purpose: the Church seeks "to strengthen the survival of the institution so that the Gospel may be made present in the world," Boff noted.[24] "Institutional Christianity," he explained further, "means a particular relationship between the Church and civil society, carried on through the state and the ruling social and cultural structures of a given nation; the Church sides with the dominant classes in order to be able to exercise its power within civil society."[25]

He also raised the same question Segundo raised: "Is it true that the Gospel needs power, prudence, concessions, the typical tricks of pagan power, all criticized by Jesus (Matt 10:42), or does its strength lie precisely in weakness, renunciation of all security, prophetic courage, as practiced in the Church of the first three centuries? Such practices of power in the Church," he said, "generating ecclesial marginality, tenuous and lifeless communication between its members, as well as religious and evangelical underdevelopment, result in the image of a Church almost neurotically preoccupied with itself and, as such, lacking a real interest in the major problems facing humanity."[26]

---

22. *Fe Cristiana y Revolución Sandinista en Nicaragua*, pp. 337-8.

23. *Church: Charism and Power*, p. 54.

24. Ibid., p. 55.

25. Ibid, p. 119.

The Church in Nicaragua traditionally accepted the power structure, since it had a pre-eminent place in it. It is true that during the 1970's the Church began to criticize the National Guard for its abuses, and six weeks before the triumph the bishops enunciated the Church teaching on the justification of insurrection. But the bishops never embraced the goal of revolutionary change in the political system and much less in the economic structures.

2. Second Basic Theological Question: Is the Kingdom Bigger than the Church?

A second theological question involved in the relationship which some clerics had with the revolutionary government is: Does the Church exist mainly for its own institutional growth and advancement, or does it exist as a seed or leaven for the growth of the Kingdom in history?

It is apparently a key issue for Cardinal Obando. In a 1986 interview he criticized the Jesuits of Managua as being "mostly Marxists" and added: "Religion is not their first priority. Their first priority is politico-sociological; religion comes later."[27] Obando also complained that the Jesuits "think they can Christianize the Sandinistas, but . . . the Sandinistas go on ridiculing religion . . . and their goal is to eliminate religion." In what follows, Jesuits and others of the Church of the Poor explain their priorities.

In the September 1980 theological conference in Managua, Jon Sobrino, S.J., of the Central American University in San Salvador, posed the basic theological question with regard to a revolution: does this process enhance or diminish life for the poor majority? "In Nicaragua today," he asked, "is the life of the poor majority held more sacred than during the time of Somoza or not?" The Church should judge a revolutionary process "not according to how it affects the Church as an institution but according to how it affects the poor majority. The Church's problem in a revolution is to learn to rejoice or to weep with the people. It would be sad to rejoice over the difficulties of the process when those

---

26. Ibid., p. 55.
27. Sheehan, op. cit., p. 228.

difficulties would point to a counterrevolution in favor of the perennial minority.

"In no way does this remove the need for criticism of a revolutionary process," Sobrino added. "Revolutions are also tempted to absolutize their power, and this inexorably leads to a diminishment of life in the people. Nor does this take anything away from the need for the Church's religious mission."[28]

In March 1981 a large group of priests, men and women religious, and representatives of grass-roots Christian communities published a message entitled "Christian Fidelity in the Nicaraguan Revolutionary Process." "There is a clear criterion with which we should formulate a Christian judgment on the revolutionary process," they said. "That criterion is not first and foremost the well-being of our Churches and institutions. The decisive thing should be, not how the Church feels in the process, but what does the process mean in terms of the hopes of the poor?

"This is not to say that the Church is separate from the people," they explained, "but we are saying that the Church's priorities, like those of Jesus, lie in the good news announced to the poor. This means there is an emphasis on the Church as serving the Kingdom of God, which means serving the people. This Church has its true authority, according to the gospel, when it is in the midst of people 'as one who serves.'

"The Church is not a center unto itself. Its center is the glory of God shown in Jesus, and Jesus is found in the poor and in their struggle." The document quoted the martyred Archbishop Oscar Romero of San Salvador: "Everyone who struggles for justice, everyone who makes just claims in unjust surroundings, is working for God's reign, even though not a Christian." Romero continued: "The church does not comprise all of God's reign; God's reign goes beyond the church's boundaries. The church values everything that is in tune with its struggle to set up God's reign. . . . The authentic church is one that does not mind conversing with prostitutes and publicans and sinners, as Christ did—and with Marxists and those of various political movements—in order to bring them salvation's true message."[29]

---

28. *Apuntes,* p. 113.

29. Statement of December 3, 1978, cited in *The Violence of Love: The Pastoral Wisdom of Archbishop Oscar Romero,* compiled and translated by James R. Brockman, S.J. (San Francisco, Harper & Row, 1988), p. 123.

On December 17 Romero spoke again to the same theme: "How shameful to think that perhaps pagans, people with no faith in Christ, may be better than we and nearer to God's reign." Nicaraguan Father Luis Amado Peña and many other traditionalists in theology would not share Romero's sense of shame. "Someone who does not love God [professedly] cannot love people," Peña told me in an affirmative response to my question as to whether the next president of Nicaragua should be a believer. After recalling the faith of the pagan centurion in the gospel (Matthew 8:5-13), Romero continued: "Christ will also say of this church: outside the limits of Catholicism perhaps is more faith, more holiness. So we must not extinguish the Spirit. The Spirit is not the monopoly of a movement, even of a Christian movement, of a hierarchy, or priesthood, or religious congregation. . . .

"I know that some people come to the cathedral," Romero continued, "who have even lost the faith or are non-Christians. Let them be welcome."[30]

If Romero had been able to visit the new Nicaragua, as he intended, he might have helped the Nicaraguan bishops and clergy to be more open to recognizing the work of the Spirit in society. But an assassin's bullet on March 24, 1980 prevented that potentially fruitful dialogue.

A very similar perspective was expressed by Bishop Casaldáliga in his talk to the CBCs of Managua in 1988: "The Church does not exist to serve itself, just as Christ did not come to serve himself nor even to be served, but to serve. The reign of God is not to be built within the Church but within the world. Those of us who comprise the Church are strengthened by our faith, by the sacraments, and by the Word of God to go forth into the world to build the reign of God. That is mission."

Noting that some fundamentalist Christians interpret Scripture in such a way that everything from dancing to getting involved in politics is sinful, Casaldáliga said that in his view even prayer can be sinful. "It depends, doesn't it? If I spend the whole day praying, without taking care of my commitments, obligations, and responsibilities, is that not a sin? We are in mission when we proclaim and build the reign of God in life, in society, in the family, in the revolution, in health care, in education, in

---

30. Ibid.

the mountains, and in the barrios. We are to be a seed, the yeast in the dough—not the yeast in the yeast."

For Casaldáliga "the kingdom, which judges both the Church and the revolution, is always the ultimate" concern.[31] The Church "is not *the* kingdom of God" but is rather "a sign, an instrument to serve that kingdom."[32]

The bishop recounted a statement of Fidel Castro: "In the final analysis it will not be important whether one is a communist or a Christian but whether one is a revolutionary." Casaldáliga put this in Christian terms: "It will not be important whether one calls oneself Christian or communist but whether one really is building the kingdom of God and people."[33]

He believes that it is quite possible, even certain, that "many who believe they are part of the Church may not be of the People of God, that many who call themselves Christians may not be followers of Jesus in fact, and that many who do not call themselves Christians may really be followers of Jesus."[34]

He later explained: "It would be a frightening heresy to want to make the people of God identical with the Church. The Church is a small portion of the people of God. It is the people of God consciously and explicitly called together in Jesus Christ." But a great part of the people of God is scattered all around, some having lived before Christ, others after but without contact with him. Many are members of the people of God without contact with the Church and even "in spite of the Church."[35]

Likewise, many who call themselves revolutionaries may be just opportunists taking advantage of something already established, Casaldáliga said, noting the need for constant revolution of individuals and society. For him as a Christian, the true revolution is that of the kingdom: "It never ends."

The bishop considered it important to tell a story about his visit to a group of Marxist political prisoners in Brazil during the military dictator-

---

31. *El Vuelo del Quetzal*, p. 69.

32. Ibid., p. 93.

33. Ibid.

34. Ibid., p. 94.

35. Ibid., p. 167.

ship. After several hours the question arose: "If we agree so much, in what do we differ?" He said he agreed with them in practically everything but added: "As a Christian I make explicit what we Christians call transcendence. . . ." What is this transcendence? "It means affirming that God really does exist," he said, and that "after death the personal life of each one of us, not only the collective history of humanity, continues. We believe in the living God and in the resurrection and eternal life."[36]

The Church of the Poor does not simply give lip service to the dimension of transcendence. A popular hymn sung frequently at Masses, meetings, and assemblies of the CBCs is "Let Us Be Honest," printed in the Tayacán hymn book. "Let us be honest," it begins, "there is no love in the whole world which fills our soul; there is no passion which fulfills our desire. We are like travelers, running the paths of life, always seeking peace of heart. We are born with a thirst for eternity; and this thirst for eternity, which nothing can change, has grown. I can only aspire to live the immensity of being, filled with happiness."

A similar perspective is brought out and celebrated in another popular hymn, "Pilgrim Church": "United we all form one body, members of Christ redeemed in blood, the pilgrim Church of God. In us lives the power of the Spirit, sent by the Son; he pushes us, guides us, and nourishes us as the pilgrim Church of God. We are the seed on earth of another kingdom, giving testimony to love. Storms gather, and sometimes our boat seems to have lost its rudder; you look with fear, without trust, pilgrim Church of God. A hope fills us with joy, the presence which the Lord promised; we move on, singing, he comes with us. We are the body and Christ the head."

Critics who allege that the Church of the Poor has abandoned the vertical for the horizontal should attend the communities' celebrations, where in addition to the above they will also frequently hear "A People Walking": "We are a people walking, and walking together we will be able to reach that other city which has no end, the eternal city without suffering or sadness."

But this kingdom, which is transcendent, also approaches in justice and dignity, as Leonardo Boff has noted: "Justice is so crucial that without its advent there is no coming of the Kingdom of God. The sign that the Kingdom of God approaches and begins to abide in our cities is that

---

36. Ibid., pp. 94-95.

the poor have justice done to them, that they participate and share in the goods of life as well as in the life of the community, and that they are raised in terms of their dignity and defended against the violence they suffer at the hands of the current economic and political system."[37]

This vision of the Kingdom characterizes the spirituality of the CBCs in Nicaragua. Father Arnaldo Zenteno, S.J., gave voice to this perspective in "The Kingdom of God": "The Kingdom is the prostitute who becomes a woman again / the oppressed who frees himself / all that is inhuman, when it becomes human again / the person who recognizes himself as a son of God and brother of his brother."[38]

Sobrino explained that "it is the poor, the oppressed majorities, who make the non-equivalence [between the Church and the kingdom] clear. As long as these majorities exist in the world, the kingdom of God has obviously not come, and no Church can be presumptuous enough to identify itself with the kingdom. Moreover, as long as the poor have not regained their dignity, even in the Church, then no Church will ever be a sacrament of the kingdom of God, much less the reality of the kingdom."[39]

If the Nicaraguan bishops had a broader vision of the Church as serving the Kingdom of God and if they put a real priority and urgency on meeting the desperate needs of the poor, perhaps they would have been able to rejoice in the gains and goals of the revolution. They would have welcomed the spread of moral leadership in society, whether explicitly Christian or not, seeing that as a victory for the values of the gospel and for the poor, and they might even have been glad to see some of their leaders going off to serve in the construction of a new social order. They would have been critical of the Sandinista government, as the Church must always be, but in a constructive way and perhaps within the context of "critical support"[40] for the revolutionary process instead of being associated with those inside and outside Nicaragua who did not recognize the legitimacy of the government and sought to destroy the revolution.

---

37. *Church: Charism and Power,* p. 25.

38. Op. cit., p. 85.

39. *The True Church and the Poor,* op. cit., pp. 118-119.

40. This is the expression the Jesuits used to characterize their relationship to the revolutionary process.

Hernández Pico has noted that religious authorities frequently "consider themselves the principal historical manifestation of God, the principal theophany, thus identifying the rights of God and religious values with the good of the religious corporation." Official religion seems to believe that man is made for the sabbath. On the other hand, the Church of the Poor as a prophetic movement which sees itself humbly as a yeast in society associates the rights of God and religious values "with the good of the majority, since the poor are seen as the principal manifestation of God."

The Nicaraguan hierarchy's conception of itself as having the mission to create "sacred culture" and its fear of losing some of its privileged status affected its view of the revolution. "This is seen most clearly with regard to the war," Hernández Pico continued. "They have not identified sufficiently with the poor in order to denounce the crime of aggression. Also, the bishops have given more weight to their fear of atheism (what they call 'ideological intervention') than to the bloodshed of the people." Some made the unbiblical dichotomy between body and soul, claiming that the contras' murdering and torturing bodies was not as grave as killing the soul, which they presented as the insidious aim of the revolution. "With regard to imperialism, they have favored prudence over protest." But this is only an extreme manifestation of a fear which prevented them from encouraging Christians to be the yeast in a very promising revolutionary process.[41]

In 1986 Peter Davis asked Cardinal Obando "why, since he was so critical of the Sandinistas, he had never spoken out against the activities of the contras when so many human rights organizations, including those sponsored by Roman Catholic groups, had done so." The cardinal's response showed that he was light years away from understanding Sobrino's notion that the Church should judge a revolutionary process "not according to how it affects the Church as an institution but according to how it affects the poor majority."

The cardinal said: "If someone slaps you, you're going to say that he slapped you. It is not the contras who have closed down our radio station and our magazine. It is not the contras who insult the church in their newspapers. They didn't surround my car and damage it, or block my

---

41. "Religión y Revolución en Nicaragua," op. cit., pp. 85-86.

path when I was attempting to enter a church once. They have not taken priests into custody and fingerprinted them. It is not the contras who censor my pastoral letters and search the social service office of the diocese. I'm not saying I'm in agreement with the contras," he claimed, "but it's logical that if someone steps on you, you will protest against the person who has done this."[42]

We could argue about Obando's charges, but that is not the point. What is clear in this statement is that the cardinal judged the government not on the basis of its struggle on behalf of the poor, but primarily on the basis of its treatment of the institutions and officials of the Church. Similarly, his main criterion concerning the contras was not their treatment of the population or where their money came from and for what purpose, but rather their hands-off policy with regard to the cardinal. (In fact, they praised him as their champion.)

At a July 1989 conference in Managua of Christian solidarity groups, "the Church seen as an end in itself" was cited as a serious obstacle to the Church's participation in the struggle for Latin American liberation.

3. Third Basic Theological Question: What Price Unity?

Cardinal Obando has said that bishops and priests must speak out against violations of human rights, "but they should not be active in party politics because they would run the risk of dividing the faithful more and more."[43] Clearly Church unity is the primary value. "But in a broad sense," Obando added, "I believe that we must all take an active part in politics when it is a question of seeking the common good." Here he seemed to be proposing some general way of being involved in politics without taking sides. Many progressive Christians, while agreeing that clerics ordinarily should not become party professionals, do not see how any Christian can be involved in politics without taking sides for the oppressed even if that means offending Catholic oppressors.

The cardinal also spoke positively of liberation theology in so far as it seeks to free the oppressed, but he rejected any kind of liberation theol-

---

42. Op. cit., pp. 326-327.

43. Interview, *La Crónica*, May 30, 1989.

ogy which promotes "class hatred" as part of a Marxist re-reading of the bible. "There is no doubt," he said, that Nicaraguan society "has become full of hatred" in the last ten years.[44]

The Nicaraguan bishops accused the Sandinista revolution of fomenting class conflict and hatred and also accused "a belligerent group" within the Church (those who basically supported the revolution) of undermining Church unity. Many Nicaraguans would agree that revolution involves class struggle but would not grant that the alleged hatred plays a significant part in motivating that struggle. In any event, a movement which brings out the disunity and conflict in society has the same effect within the Church, since the Church is a broad mass institution in countries like Nicaragua. Thus the bishops felt that the Sandinistas were stirring up rich-poor conflicts within the Church as well as within society as a whole.

The right-wing big-business sector had the same point of view. "The FSLN has promoted class struggle but has not been able to bring it about," said Ramiro Gurdián. "The Church can never accept class struggle," he added, "since its message is one of unity."[45]

The issue of unity was posed dramatically in January 1982 when the CBCs of Managua protested the archbishop's decision to remove Father Mauro Jacomelli from the helm of Our Lady of Fatima parish. This was part of a series of such moves interpreted as a campaign against progressive priests and sisters. (See Chapter 9.) The communities asked to dialogue with Obando about the matter. A member of one community said that the communities were not against the archbishop but "wanted to come to some understanding with him, because the Church is one but must always be faithful to its option for the poor."[46] Another member stated: "As long as there is no dialogue, there will not be unity in the Church."[47]

While Obando and other bishops and priests extolled unity and insisted that the Church must not take sides, in reality Church leaders and institutions did take sides—expressing in various ways their hostility

44. Ibid.

45. My interview of Gurdián, May 1989.

46. El Nuevo Diario, Jan. 19, 1982.

47. Barricada, Jan. 21, 1982.

against the Sandinistas and their support for the opposition, including the armed contras. Perhaps this is seen most clearly in the programming of Radio Católica, the archdiocesan radio station.

Just before the government suspended the station's license in July 1988, I had tuned in to Radio Católica rather frequently and had been surprised to discover that the station devoted an inordinate amount of time to the political proselytizing of the right-wing coalition, the Democratic Coordinator. This led me to agree with *Barricada's* characterization of the station as one "where the reactionary political message predominates over ecclesiastical information" (July 12). Papal nuncio Paolo Giglio later expressed his opinion that Radio Católica should concentrate more on hymns and religious news and not always be attacking the government.[48]

I myself would not insist that a church radio station should stick to "ecclesiastical information." Nor was the government promoting such a restricted use of the media. The key issue in Nicaragua in July 1988 was the ongoing war and the Democratic Coordinator's more and more open support for the violent overthrow of the government by the U.S.-supported contras.[49] It was clear to me that any radio station which promoted the campaigns and tactics of such an organization was subjecting itself to legal action.

In August the government office of communications presented an analysis of Radio Católica's news programming (Noticiero Iglesia) from January 1 to July 8, 1988. The report noted that on the national and regional stations run by the government or by the Frente Sandinista 52 religious programs were heard every week (80% Catholic and 20% Protestant).

In the period studied, Radio Católica news carried 221 interviews. The report stated that 124 of these interviews were with "opposition political personalities," while another 34 were with representatives of opposition labor, business, and professional groups. Some may consider the foregoing simply as an expression of a private radio's freedom to program its politics, but the following finding is more troublesome in that it raises serious *legal* questions in a country at war: 35 interviews were

---

48. Interview by author, September 8, 1988.

49. Tomás Borge said on August 13: "The counter-revolution does the dirty work; the ultra-right does the clean work. Both bloody jobs have the same end in view."

with "members of the counterrevolution" living outside Nicaragua. Of these interviews with contras, 28 were with political leaders and 7 with military chiefs.

In its interpretation of the data, the report pointed out that the Church had a special social function in relation to the broad opposition. "It appears as an entity above all political parties, bearing the torch of reconciliation and of the defense of justice and human rights; but in reality it is ready to legitimize by its moral approval any form of opposition to Sandinismo."

As the electoral campaign got under way in late 1989, Radio Católica continued showing its lop-sided favoritism to the opposition, especially to the right-wing UNO coalition and its candidate, Violeta Chamorro. After the UNO victory, Radio Católica shocked many listeners by broadcasting the hard anti-Sandinista, non-conciliatory line represented by Virgilio Godoy, the Vice-president elect.

Whether or not Church leaders do or should take sides, a more fundamental question needs attention: Is unity to be prized above all other values? If so, is it to be seen and striven for as an immediate goal or an ultimate one? Jon Sobrino cited Jürgen Moltmann as seeking the source of Church unity in the Church's mission: unity within the Church requires it to be "a fellowship of believers with the poor, a fellowship of the hopeful with the sick, and a fellowship of the loving with the oppressed."[50]

Sobrino argued that the true Church must always be the Church of the Poor, never sacrificing that identity for the sake of a fictitious unity. "Unity in faith does not come solely from the apex of the Church nor does it derive solely from the imposed formulas of faith." When the Church decides to listen to the poor, then the "miracle" of unity will happen.[51]

Two months after the triumph of the Nicaraguan revolution, Father Alvaro Argüello, S.J., emphasized this dynamic concept of unity: "A revolutionary praxis for the good of the poor is what can make all Christians

---

50. *The Church in the Power of the Spirit: a Contribution to Messianic Eschatology*, trans. M. Kohl (New York: Harper & Row, 1977), p. 345, as cited by Sobrino, *The True Church and the Poor*, op. cit., p. 101.

51. *The True Church and the Poor*, pp. 102-103.

one, in an option of the Church for liberation. This was decided at Puebla when the bishops spoke of the preferential option for the poor as the attitude of the *whole* Latin American Church. This is the hub which will unite all of us in the one Church of Jesus Christ."[52]

"Rare in Latin America," Sobrino observed, "is the country or diocese in which there is no conflict between the hierarchy and Christians at the base and—this is even more striking—among the bishops."[53] Archbishop Oscar Romero's disputes with his fellow bishops and with the papal nuncio in El Salvador were well known, and his successor's differences with the CBCs over political options are becoming more pronounced.

In some retreat notes made shortly before he was assassinated, Romero mentioned that he was analyzing "my conflictive situation with the other bishops." He was convinced that "the only thing that counts is the radicalness of the gospel which not everyone can understand. It is possible to give in on some accidental aspects but not when it comes to following the gospel radically. This radicalness must always bring conflicts and even painful divisions."[54]

In Nicaragua there may have been some differences of opinion among the bishops concerning the Sandinistas, but Cardinal Obando's forceful manner and his primacy as the spokesperson with Rome managed to prevent any differences from surfacing.

González Faus has pointed out that the differences in the early Church as described in Acts of the Apostles "often led to a separation, which was not a break-down of communion; each went his way respecting the freedom of the other. In the midst of these differences, the apostles (especially Peter) acted in a mediating and coordinating way, maintaining unity, not letting one position devour the other or become an absolute and thus get off the Christian path. Authority was a ministry of unity and communion among diversity rather than a ministry of uniformity and absorption. And the principle of the council of Jerusalem of 'not imposing more bur-

---

52. *Fe Cristiana y Revolución Sandinista en Nicaragua*, p. 102.

53. *The True Church and the Poor*, p. 194.

54. Cited by José Ignacio González Faus, "Iglesia popular, iglesia del pueblo," *Diakonía* (Boletín del Centro Ignaciano de Centro America), Septiembre 1989, p. 303. Other relevant articles in this issue are: "La Iglesia que Jesus quería" and "Como era la comunidad que Jesus quería?".

dens than those that are strictly indispensable' (Acts 15:28) is a model for the exercise of authority which saved the unity of the Church."[55]

Many Catholics today feel that certain Church leaders like Cardinal Obando would do well to seek guidance in their apostolic predecessors concerning this distinction between fostering unity and forcing uniformity, especially since the latter militates against the former.

When Bishop Casaldáliga made his first visit to Nicaragua, in the summer of 1985, during Father Miguel D'Escoto's long fast for peace, he knew that his presence would be "conflictual." "Love for the Church itself," he said, "puts one in a conflictual situation. I want to help the Church in Central America. This is part of the responsibility to the universal Church which I and every bishop have, within the context of respect for the local bishops and within the pastoral unity which the pope presides over.

"But this cannot always be lived out in joyful harmony," he added. "It is the conflictual nature of co-responsibility. I have discovered in the bible and in theological writings that the conflictual dimension is an underlying current in the spirituality of Jesus. He not only died on the cross, he always lived on the cross.

"And I think that this conflictual aspect must be a permanent and universal current in the Church of Jesus. Wherever the Church is not living in conflict, it is unlikely that it is being faithful to the gospel. The very unity of the Church will only be legitimate if it is the fruit of conflict lived out in the peace of charity. There are places and moments, like Central America and Nicaragua, where the conflictual comes to the fore as a sign of the prophetic."

The bishop ended his remarks with an expression of humility: "Believe me, I am not in Nicaragua to give anyone any lesson. I assure you that I am the one learning a great lesson, and after Nicaragua I will have to be a changed person."[56]

A few years later Casaldáliga returned to the theme of evangelical conflict: "What divides us now are not the dogmas like the Trinity or the Eucharist but rather ideology, the stance taken, the political and social

55. "Iglesia Popular, Iglesia del Pueblo," op. cit., p. 295.

56. Cabestrero, *Un Grito a Dios y al Mundo*, p. 188.

option, and the means we use. If we want the God of Jesus to enter into politics and transform the economy and the structures of society and put an end to empire and all forms of exploitation and slavery, then we will not agree with those who want to keep that God of Jesus out of these areas, reserving them for the gods of power, money, and domination."[57] To the latter group Casaldáliga and many others would say: Your god is too small!

As a bishop of the universal Church, Casaldáliga felt a certain responsibility for the Church in Nicaragua; and he saw that the Church, especially in its structural, hierarchical aspects, was losing credibility. He visited Nicaragua "to give a little help to the credibility of the Church as an instrument of the kingdom of God and, even more importantly, the credibility of the gospel itself which we bear in our structures." His concern is also for the credibility of Jesus Christ and ultimately of the living God.[58]

In Nicaragua, members of the CBCs, convinced that bishops are not the only ones in the Church with a sense of "co-responsibility," could never accept a unity which would force them to reject or betray a revolutionary process which they consider theirs and which they deem to be a naturally limited but real expression of their Christian commitment to bring good news to the poor. A working paper prepared for use in the CBCs in 1986 summed up the position of the Nicaraguan Church of the Poor: "Within the framework of the preferential option for the poor, which is not exclusive, we understand and work for unity in the Church, and we live through the conflict in the Church."[59]

---

57. *El Vuelo del Quetzal*, p. 82.

58. Ibid., pp. 188-189.

59. "Plan de Trabajo Comun," mimeographed paper.

Postscript

The Political Counter-Revolution and the Catholic Restoration: The First Hundred Days

Francisco Mayorga, the new administration's first minister of the economy and president of the Central Bank, promised that the first hundred days of the Chamorro administration would bring remarkable improvements in the economic situation. While skyrocketing inflation gave the lie to that prediction, the first hundred days demonstrated the counter-revolutionary thrust of the new government and also the privileged place of Catholicism in the new regime. In fact, the developments described in this final section round out the picture presented in previous chapters. Cardinal Obando is now basking in the privileges and power which he sought during the Sandinista years and for which he struggled against the revolutionary government.

On May 4 several hundred Christians held a vigil outside the convention site where the president was meeting with contra commander Israel Galeano ("Franklyn"). The ecumenical group demanded the immediate demobilization and disarming of the contras.

In a May 16 statement the CBCs of Managua expressed concern that "the land which the peasants received is in danger of being lost, and in the cities the powerful are threatening us with eviction. . . . Up to now we are seeing reconciliation only with contra leaders who have caused our people so much pain and death. While they are received with kisses and hugs, there is not even the desire to listen to the working people. We are seeing reconciliation only with the rich—landlords and business owners—while the system turns its back on the poor and tramples over their social gains."

The communities pointed to the signs of the upper-class nature of the new government: "The miserable salary of the workers cannot be increased, but the cabinet ministers pay themselves juicy salaries; and in the midst of the people's poverty, the new leaders celebrate their rise to power with lavish parties in luxury hotels."

"We have good news," announced President Chamorro at the close of a private meeting with Cardinal Obando on May 16. "We are going to build the cathedral." Chamorro's *La Prensa* explained that the president had made a personal visit to the cardinal's office "out of courtesy for the high position of the Head of the Catholic Church." Chamorro told Obando that this was one of the first actions her government would take in favor of the Catholic Church, which is the Church of the majority of Nicaraguans, as *La Prensa* pointed out.[1] It was later reported that the cathedral would cost about 3 million dollars. An architect told me, however, that it will undoubtedly cost much more.

Obando said he was very happy with the government's offer to help with the architectural costs. (The same edition noted that Tom Monaghan, owner of the Detroit Tigers and Domino's Pizza and member of the Knights of Malta, was going to pick up most of the cost of the new cathedral. Obando had been flown back to Nicaragua by Monaghan in his private jet after the prelate's visit with the pope in Curacao.)

Earlier the same day, Daniel Ortega had visited the cardinal to ask him to assist in bringing about dialogue between the government and the Sandinistas. The government's decision to suspend a civil service law and to reject salary demands by state workers had led to a very tense political situation, with government workers not only going on strike but also occupying state buildings.

Just a few days after the government agreed to rescind the suspension of the civil service law, the UNO majority in the National Assembly voted to "reform" the law, allowing the government to fire workers who held "positions of trust" in the former administration.[2] While the govern-

---

1. *La Prensa*, May 17, 1990.

ment agreed to a slight pay raise, it fell far short of keeping up with galloping inflation.

With service workers on edge because of these policies, the government then struck fear into the hearts of the peasant sector by decreeing that expropriations of land by the Sandinista government would come under review. The government also said that former owners who claimed that their property had been unjustly nationalized could rent the land from the state and farm it while their claims were being processed.

These counter-revolutionary moves by an administration known to be dominated by the upper classes (not to mention its U.S. sponsors) were not suprising in themselves, but rather in the rapidity and provocative style in which they were initiated. Many observers, including *Envío* (June 1990), considered this part of a strategy to undermine the political power of the Frente Sandinista as representative of the affected sectors. The new government came in fighting, perhaps in order to test as well as weaken the Sandinistas' power, but learned that the Frente and the mass organizations founded by it could fight back effectively. "The government could not break the strike and win an important battle against the people's movement because the majority which voted for Chamorro is a silent and passive majority," noted *Envío*. "The FSLN, on the other hand, in spite of the weaknesses caused by its verticalism, has a significant capacity to mobilize the people."

Shortly after receiving land and some of the financing for the new cathedral, Obando received another bow from the Chamorro government when the state-run TV station announced that it would begin televising the cardinal's Sunday Mass. *La Prensa* said this decision was in keeping with the wishes of President Chamorro. The director of the TV station added: "In this way we are trying to promote religious values and satisfy the desires of the majority of TV viewers."[3] While recognizing the potential value of a televised Mass for shut-ins, many pastoral workers feel that for a general audience it is highly deficient for several reasons: e.g., it

---

2. *La Prensa*, May 19, 1990.

3. *La Prensa*, May 19, 1990.

does not help to form a local Church community (in fact, it may keep people at home), it cannot relate the Word of God to immediate local issues, and the tube hardly invites participation in the liturgy.

The Ecumenical Committee for Peace and Life called upon Radio Católica "to drop its one-sided and aggressive political campaign which is only creating more polarization and opening the gates to more tension and violence which we all want to avoid." Since the February elections the Catholic radio station continued its aggressive anti-Sandinista campaign, with only one rival for the dubious distinction of being the most extreme right-wing voice on radio.

In the May 21 statement the Ecumenical Committee also called upon religious leaders, "and in particular the most publicized, Cardinal Obando, to put the interests of the people above the Church's institutional interests." The statement noted that President Chamorro goes out of her way "to project her government's close relationship with the Catholic hierarchy, to the extent that it begins to acquire the image of a Catholic government instead of one representing all Nicaraguans."

The interests of the people, especially the poor, are not being served by this "extremely anti-labor and pro-capital government," the Committee said. In the rural areas, "a climate of fear, tension, and violence grows every day." This is caused "by the return of former owners to their farms, with threats to the present owners; by the armed land invasions promoted by local UNO leaders; and by the denial and delay of credit to peasants who benefited from the land reform" of the previous government. The Committee, whose statement was presented at a press conference by members of farm cooperatives, said it would hold the government responsible "for the violence unleashed by its policy of confrontation."

On May 30 Obando joined President Chamorro and contra commander "Franklin" (Israel Galeano) in signing a protocol calling for the establishment of "development poles" for demobilized contras who wish to settle in them. According to the document, the contras would have their own police force (under the Ministry of Government) in these areas, as well as representation in the local political structures and in all government ministries involved in the project. The accord also assured the sick and war-disabled among the contras and their families that they would be treated in the nation's hospitals, and their orphans and widows would receive public pensions.[4] Contra soldiers, including those who choose to return home rather than enter the development poles, were promised economic assistance from the government.

This turn of events is the most troublesome for Sandinistas and supporters of the Nicaraguan revolutionary process, since it allows the contras to remain armed (as police) and to control territory (a victory they were never able to achieve militarily). Members of farming cooperatives and other supporters of the Sandinista revolution have cause to feel seriously threatened. Indeed, violent land struggles have ensued.

The war-disabled among those who served in the Sandinista army and the widows and children of those who died in service resent the fact that their benefits are in jeopardy while the contras are being treated as the favorite sons of the Chamorro government.

A June 3 pastoral letter by Bishop John F. Wilson and Superintendent Ofreciano Julias addressed to the Nicaraguan Moravian Church and the international community expressed "deep concern" over the government's "excessive attention to just one sector of the religious community of Nicaragua, a country which until now has enjoyed religious pluralism without any declared state church. All denominations have equal rights according to the constitution."[5]

On the same day the Moravian letter was released, Obando told reporters that the new government had taken many positive steps, particularly in ending obligatory military service, which he characterized as a form of martyrdom for mothers and youth, according to *La Prensa*. He also expressed agreement with the formation of a rural police force in the development poles.

Obando's favorable view of the government was reflected in a June 4 public statement by the bishops' conference, reported in *La Prensa* under the title "Church Supports Government." "We hope that the new

---

4. *La Prensa*, May 30, 1990.

5. *Amanecer*, Mayo-Junio 1990.

government's promise to establish and guarantee an authentic democracy in Nicaragua will be fulfilled completely," the bishops began, thus implying their agreement with those who felt that the previous government was not a true democracy. "We also believe that those who were designated by popular vote to govern should do so effectively. By the same token, those laws which prevent the new government from working for the common good should be abolished through the legal channels." Here the bishops were alluding to legislation passed by the Sandinista majority in the previous national assembly, such as the civil service law, the university autonomy statute, and one guaranteeing people who had received land the right to remain on it. The new government had expressed its hostility toward these laws.

The accords between the government and the "Resistance" (in keeping with Obando's preferred term for the contras) were deemed a "positive step," and the bishops added that "civilians throughout the country who were imprudently armed should be disarmed immediately for the tranquility of all." Thus the bishops came out in support of government policy and against those peasants and others who felt that without weapons they would be easy prey for vengeful contras, especially in the zones under contra control. They also called for progress in reducing the army and "restructuring" it "so that it would become in fact a National Army," thus echoing their contention over the years that the Sandinista People's Army was the army of one party rather than the armed forces of the nation.

Christian reconciliation, the bishops stressed, is not possible "without conversion of hearts, a conversion which must manifest itself in making reparation for the harm caused to others and in returning goods unjustly held." This was a clear reference to the Sandinista government's policy of expropriating the land of Somocistas and some other owners (especially those who were not using their land) for the sake of land reform to benefit the marginated peasants. Here the bishops showed their preferential option for the rich who were "harmed" by the revolution. Later in June the government began to return large state farms to their former owners.

"The new government must count on the decided support of all, with recognition of the positive steps it has taken," the bishops urged, citing the abolition of the draft and the "attitude of dialogue" as examples of the positive steps. "This support," they noted, "does not deprive citizens of their freedom to point out to the government those situations and attitudes which should be corrected or improved." Government officials are urged to have a spirit of service to the community, "not looking for privileges or personal or family enrichment." The right to organize unions freely chosen by the workers is affirmed; the right to strike must be used responsibly so as not to cause destabilization or harm to the common good. (The latter affirmation lends itself to being used as a tool by the government against the Sandinista unions.)

An article in *Barricada* (June 7) took the bishops to task for dropping all pretense of political neutrality and particularly for "ignoring the fact that the contras are not fulfilling their commitment to disarm totally by June 10." The article also pointed out that civilians who were "imprudently" armed were often members of the militia who defended lives and property against marauding contras.

In early July Father Xabier Gorostiaga, S.J., said that the hierarchy's letter expressed "unrestricted and uncritical support for the Chamorro government." The evangelical churches are offended by "this attitude of returning to a Catholic christendom where the cardinal plays the role almost of a king and Violeta Chamorro becomes a kind of prime minister. Everything must revolve around the figure of the cardinal, from negotiations with the contras to the blessing of the presidential building." In this regard Gorostiaga mentioned the cardinal's lengthy address during the inauguration of the president, which, he said, "bothered the visiting Latin American politicians." (By January 1991 *Barricada* was complaining: "there is practically no official event of any significance which does not include a liturgy and sermon by the Prelate.")

Gorostiaga asserted that the Nicaraguan hierarchy and others were "going against the gospel" by taking up a "political role in support of [economic] adjustment policies which go against the interests of the people." Such policies, he added, "are tied into the rebuilding of right-wing power based on a new wave of neo-liberal capitalism." This new "right-wing technocracy seeks to legitimize itself basically with the support of the official Church when its policies are extraordinarily anti-people."

In relation to this he mentioned the pope's visit to Mexico, where President Carlos Salinas sought legitimation by the Church "to contain the social cost of his policies." As an economist, Gorostiaga granted that adjustments were needed and that deficits had to be cut, but he criticized the tendency to focus on cuts in health and education.[6]

In *La Voz del Campesino* (June 1990), Father Antonio Castro, pastor of a Managua parish, defended the rights of peasants who benefited from the Sandinistas' land reform programs. "God created the earth and gave it to human beings so that they would be the masters of it and make it produce for the benefit of all. The land belongs to humanity, not to just a few." Father Castro attributed the development of large land holdings to "the selfishness and ambition of the strongest."

Asked whether the revolution was justified in suppressing large land holdings and affording peasants the opportunity to form cooperatives, the priest responded: "Of course. During the dictatorship a few owned all the land. What the revolution did was to recover those lands which had been taken from the poor peasants by the landlords and return them to the people in an organized way in the form of cooperatives for the good of all, giving the peasants legal right to use the lands." This "revolutionary and Christian project" is precisely what is being targeted by the decrees calling for the review of expropriations and the provisional renting of land, he pointed out. "With the new government there is a return to the past structure of landlords, capitalists, and exploiters," Castro noted, urging the people to consider themselves owners of their land. "The biblical prophets speak of the people's right to have land," he concluded.

Obando expressed increasing annoyance at being questioned about his efforts to find those who were kidnapped by the contras, accepting the contra leaders' contention that no such individuals are being held. Mothers of the kidnap victims spoke out strongly in June against the cardinal's attitude. "They do not forgive his eminence for his deep concern for the fate of the victimizers of their children," said *El Nuevo Diario* (June 5). "He has never sat down to dialogue with us," noted one mother. Why? "For sure, because we are poor and lower class," she explained.

In the judgment of another mother, Obando does not know what it is to love. "First he must love his neighbor in order to love God," she said.

---

6. *Noticias Aliadas* (Peru), Julio 19, 1990.

On the same page a broadly smiling Obando extended his ring to be kissed by Arnoldo Alemán, the tough-talking right-wing mayor of Managua who, along with President Chamorro and Obando, heads up the special commission in charge of building the new Managua cathedral. (In a move which seemed to symbolize his petty but deep-seated anti-Sandinista feelings, Alemán had ordered Daniel Ortega to demolish a security wall around his home, claiming that it and other such walls in Managua were obstructing free passage. The new mayor threatened to take legal action against the ex-president if he did not comply; President Chamorro reportedly told him to back off. Alemán had also gained infamy in the progressive press when he spent thousands of dollars on his inaugural bash at the Intercontinental Hotel, attended by fellow Somocistas, contra leaders, and standard-bearers of the radical right within UNO. He also provoked the wrath of the sellers in the Eastern Market by trying to abolish their merchants' associations.)

In a June 5 editorial, *La Prensa* said that the new cathedral should be "a truly Metropolitan Cathedral in keeping with the high rank of the cardinal archbishop." Sketching out what they called their "dream-project," the editors of President Chamorro's newspaper proposed that the cathedral setting should follow the traditional Latin American pattern which placed the "House of God alongside the house of government or National Palace, with a great plaza as the heart of the city." City hall would also be part of this "new civil and religious center of the city."

A *Barricada* editorial (May 28) noted a historical precedent for the new government's proposed changes in education: "With the fall of Zelaya, precipitated by the U.S. intervention in 1909, the whole system of lay education which he had introduced in his liberal modernizing project was swept away completely in a frenzy of ideological vengeance. Under the Marines' protection, a regressive and intolerant current of thought changed all the curricula, persecuted and fired the liberal professors, and handed over the national educational system to foreign religious orders."

In June the media focused much attention on the government's educational policy, with special concern for its pro-Catholic bias. Then-Minister of Education Sofonías Cisneros, in a *Barricada* interview (June 4), said that the previous administration's statement of goals and principles was partly acceptable. "That declaration says that education will be patriotic, revolutionary, and committed to the interests of workers and peasants," Cisneros noted. "All of this remains applicable except the revolutionary part, because we believe that the revolution has no validity, not in Nicaragua or in any other country."

Sensitive to the widespread suspicion that the new government wants to impose Catholicism in the public schools, Cisneros stated: "We are not saying that we are going to introduce religious education, but rather the values which characterize a modern, Western citizen. We start out from a Christian vision of man, which promotes the Western values which attract all of us: brotherhood, charity, love, reconciliation." (Later in the year it was reported that Cisneros was opening some staff meetings by having his underlings join hands and recite the Our Father.)

Cisneros then revealed the connection between such values (at least as he interprets them) and socio-political realities: "We are speaking of a Christian education which even serves the communists, because they have to confiscate property in order to make an owner give to the poor, whereas a Christianized man gives with love."

He had made the same point in my 1986 interview with him when he spoke of an "evangelizing education" which would promote the values of the Christian gospel, such as concern for the poor, sharing of goods, and love. As people become converted along these lines and have a change of heart, he asserted, they will see to it that social justice is implemented in society, and thus there will be no need for any governmental confiscation of private property, he concluded.[7]

In that interview Cisneros objected to what he claimed was the promotion of "class hatred" in Nicaraguan education under the Sandinistas and cited an example from a primary school text which devotes a page to showing a variety of shoe styles. One kind of shoe is identified as a worker's shoe, another as a peasant's shoe, another as a soldier's shoe, and finally (to Cisneros's dismay) a bourgeois shoe.

Cisneros, then president of the Nicaraguan Association of Parents of Christian Schools, also expressed concern about the presentation of certain historical events. The examples he cited from textbooks authorized by the Ministry of Education included: "General Sandino was born in 1895," "the anti-imperialist struggle began in 1926," "General Sandino was assassinated in 1934," "the FSLN was founded in 1961," and "the

---

7. *Update* (Central American Historical Institute), May 23, 1986.

Sandinista revolution triumphed in 1979." Other problematic examples for Cisneros included a history lesson which took a critical view of the Spanish conquest of the new world and a sex-education program for teenagers.

These examples, Cisneros charged, showed that "the Sandinista government has excessively influenced Nicaraguan education in favor of its own political interests." Four years later, Cisneros was in a position to influence education in favor of his and his fellow conservatives' political interests. The new Ministry of Education is indeed replacing the textbooks which contain the above-cited offensive examples with new books financed by U.S. government aid. (In his purifying zeal, Cisneros was taking a cue from his president. Since certain words have unbearable Sandinista connotations in the new Nicaragua, one of President Chamorro's first official acts was to forbid the use of "compañero," as well as miniskirts, in the offices of the presidential building.)

The June 5 edition of *La Prensa* carried an article entitled "Parents Happy about Change in Textbooks." Those interviewed supported the Ministry of Education's intention to eliminate what it calls a Marxist-Leninist tendency or revolutionary propaganda from the school books. "In this country we are infested with communist literature," said one parent, "and the elimination of that contagion should not be the sole responsibility of the Ministry of Education. The Ministry of Culture should also contribute to the task by sweeping the bookstores clean of such works which go against our customs and beliefs."

Father Fernando Cardenal, Minister of Education in the Sandinista government, told me, in response to Cisneros' criticisms years ago, that the educational system was not promoting Marxist-Leninist doctrine but that it was fostering the social values of the Sandinista revolution. "Education is never neutral in any society," he emphasized.

Not surprisingly, the June 5 edition of *Barricada* contained comments critical of Cisneros. "It would be very harmful to inculcate in the people a kind of resignation and fatalism," said one teacher. (In October Cisneros, speaking in an event commemorating World Food Day, would say that people should not worry so much about hunger "because we have the nourishment of the Word of God."[8] Many were outraged and

---

8. *Barricada,* October 17.

insulted by this distortion of the role of biblical faith in the people's daily struggle for survival.) The June 6 edition of *Barricada* seemed to be joking in reporting that Ministry of Education officials were inviting all Nicaraguans to a "monumental public book-burning."

The same edition of *Barricada* quoted Cisneros on the topic of sex education in the schools. Regarding birth control he said that "planning is good, but not on the basis of contraceptives and practices not approved by the Church. These kinds of devices will no longer be recommended. The Church approves other methods of family planning, and those are the ones which will be made known."

Rather than holding a nationwide book-burning, within a few months the government simply sold hundreds of thousands of textbooks, including the "Carlitos" readers, for pulp. One education official said the sale was made because some of the books contained objectionable sex-education material (*Barricada*, October 17). *La Prensa* (October 16), however, said the move was made "to take out of circulation those textbooks of a political nature which were used by the extinct Sandinista regime to ideologize education."

The grade-school readers were replaced by the "Blue and White" readers, named after the colors of the Nicaraguan flag. One new 80-page textbook shows in a number of places that education cannot be ideologically neutral. Columbus was the "intrepid" captain who "discovered" America in 1492; the Indians' simple life-style is briefly described, but no indication is given of their ensuing decimation. In the next grade's reader, children are taught that the wind can "help people," and as an example they are reminded that Columbus discovered America in a ship powered by the wind.

In the first reader in a lesson on symbols the cross is said to "symbolize the sacrifice God made for all of us," and the children read that "the white dress for first communion symbolizes purity." The next page asks the children: "What does the Christian cross symbolize?" And "what does the white dress for first communion symbolize?" Such items are at home in a culture of Catholic Christendom.

A little message is also suggested by a sentence a few pages later: "The girl is white, tall, and pretty." Finally, a story is told about a Nicaraguan family "who lived on a farm a long time ago and had a servant." One evening the servant forgot to round up the cattle on a certain hill; when he went for them the next day, he found a gold cow and calf. On hearing this, the incredulous "patrón" went to see but found nothing on the site. So "he gave the servant a beating for being a liar."

In the next year's reader, one lesson teaches that people need one another; we all need the products of the butcher, baker, miner, etc. "Life will be better the more we learn to live with others; we should all do our best possible work." Ideologization by omission: no hint of exploitation of wage labor.

A king asks a poor orphan girl to marry him; she told him she was very poor, but that was no obstacle to his love.

Finally, the "conquistadors" are mentioned, but the only damage they are said to have done to "the country of the Indians" was to the rivers and forests.

(In January 1991, when Vice-minister Humberto Belli replaced Cisneros in the top job, *Barricada* quipped: "one cardinal's man replaces another cardinal's man.")

On June 8 *El Nuevo Diario* asked in its top headline: "Official Religion?" The government is "violating the Constitution and regressing to the past century," the paper added, suggesting that "a tacit concordat is harmful to Protestant churches and to freedom of conscience." The religious community is deeply concerned about "the tacit declaration of Catholicism as the official religion of the new government."

As evidence the paper cited the government's relationship with Obando as its spiritual guide, its decision to foot the bill for the cardinal's Sunday Mass on state TV, and its "enthusiastic offer to finance a very costly and luxurious cathedral." Thus the government is "excluding the rest of the religious institutions," while for its part the Catholic bishops' conference "in a political communiqué declared its loyalty to the new government."

Rev. Roger Zavala, president of the Baptist Convention of Nicaragua, said that the Baptists "have always defended religious freedom precisely because we as a minority church have suffered repression, especially in countries colonized by Spain where the official church was always the Catholic church." Nevertheless, in recent times rivalry has given way to an ecumenical, fraternal spirit, especially among the people of the churches, Rev. Zavala noted.

"In recent months it has become obvious," he continued, "that the religious authorities of the Catholic Church and the civil authorities have been coming together." He also expressed concern about the attempt to move education "toward a certain religion," adding that "the right to a lay system of education is one of the achievements of the Protestants, who have always identified with the struggle for religious freedom." Zavala said that government projects in favor of the Catholic Church point toward the possibility of a "tacit, unofficial marriage between the Catholic Church and the government."

Rev. Roger Velásquez, general secretary of CEPAD (formerly Evangelical Committee for Aid to Development, now Evangelical Church Council for Denominational Alliance), echoed Zavala's concerns and added: "We thought that the problem was solved ever since our government became a lay state in 1893 [with the ascent to power of the Liberal Party's General Zelaya]." Velásquez expressed concern about "the constant statements by Cardinal Obando and the recent letter of the bishops' conference calling for total, absolute, and unconditional support for the government." For its part the government has given evidence of this church-state marriage in the president's "public statement that Obando is the pastor of all Nicaraguans."

Rev. Miguel Angel Casco of CEPRES (Evangelical Committee for Social Responsibility) criticized President Chamorro for being one of the presiding members of the commission to build the new cathedral. "I doubt she would be willing to preside over a commission to build a Protestant church," he said.

Before the revolution, Obando had a great deal of power, Casco explained, and the Protestants were considered third-class citizens. This changed completely with the revolution, with Protestants gaining a level of respect and the right to be heard and seen. "From 1979 on, the Catholic hierarchy felt deprived of its privileges of power and devoted itself to a pastoral project of opposition. Now, with the government of Doña Violeta, they have regained a pastoral position of power," Casco said, citing the recent bishops' letter in support of the government.

In a brief meeting with leaders of CEPRES, the president indicated that it might be possible to give them some TV time to present the Word of God from the Protestant viewpoint. The CEPRES members expressed their concern about the facile use of the name of God by cabinet members who then deny God by their actions.[9]

---

9. *Nuevo Diario*, June 8, 1990.

On June 8 President Chamorro participated in a Mass at the Jesuits' Central American University celebrating Father Alvaro Argüello's 25th anniversary of priestly ordination. The president sat in the first row of the congregation, but near the side door. Until the very last minute of the Mass, no mention was made of Doña Violeta's presence. (In his sermon Argüello did refer to the president's statement in her inaugural address about her concern for the poor, noting that he and other Jesuits would support the new government in so far as it worked for the good of the poor majority.) The president stood in line with others while some of the twenty concelebrating priests (all but two of whom had an attitude of critical support for the Sandinista revolutionary process) distributed communion. At the end of Mass Argüello did express his gratitude for her presence.

Father Arnaldo Zenteno, S.J., announced an upcoming day of prayer for peace in which people would express their demand for the immediate disarming of the contras, the continuation of programs for the war-disabled and other victims, restitution of damages done by the contras, and the revelation of the whereabouts of persons kidnapped by the contras.

Throughout the liturgy the songs of struggle and liberation of the Nicaraguan Peasants' Mass were sung with fervor by choir and people. During the closing song, Daniel Ortega walked in briskly and was embraced by Father Miguel D'Escoto and just about everyone else in the packed auditorium, with loud and sustained applause. The president sat and looked. Many of us were glad that she had come, in spite of the contradictions between her government's policy and the option for the poor which the event was celebrating. I hoped that the experience of a participative liturgy of the Church of the Poor was a positive one for her.

On June 9 Obando blessed the contra troops, still brandishing their guns and grenades, in a Mass celebrating what President Chamorro called the end of the war. She said with satisfaction that 11,000 contras had been demobilized, out of a total of over 13,000. The event, held in the town of El Almendro, where the contras were concentrated, ended with "vivas" to the Virgin Mary.[10]

---

10. *La Prensa*, June 11.

In early June the Ecumenical Committee for Peace and Life, representing progressive sectors of Protestantism and Catholicism in Nicaragua, issued a public statement challenging the laudatory rhetoric about the contras now in vogue in official discourse. "The contras are now called the Resistance," the statement began, "and there is talk of their patriotic work. All of this is being done in the name of peace and reconciliation."

But the search for peace must not minimize or disguise the responsibility of those who have caused so much suffering and injustice for the majority of Nicaraguans, the committee continued. The various types of contra violence and terrorism are enumerated.

"In this whole process of disarming of the Resistance, they have not uttered one word recognizing their faults. Nor have the government or the religious authorities denounced their crimes, abuses, and excesses. Things have even gotten to the point where gratitude is expressed for their worthy service to the nation. The recent letter of the bishops' conference never mentions them by name in condemning death and violence, but does name the 'civilians armed imprudently.'

"We cannot fall into a false reconciliation, nor can we simply erase the past by falsifying what happened. Those who have destroyed the lives of poor peasants . . . cannot continue to present themselves as the builders of peace and democracy. Whom are we referring to?

"First of all, we refer to the U.S. government. No matter how many dollars they give the new government, no matter how much food and medicine they give in trying to present themselves as benefactors, no matter how many crumbs they throw us, they will never be able to erase the crime of having sponsored the cruelest war which has ever been inflicted against a Latin American country in this century."

One of the main "sights" of Managua during the years of the Sandinista government were the huge letters FSLN built into the side of a mountain on the west side of the city. On June 15 a work crew under the orders of Mayor Alemán, who said he was obeying a presidential decree prohibiting political symbols and propaganda in public places, erased the S and changed the L into an I, thus spelling FIN (end). While the official explanation was that this meant an end to the war, *La Prensa* in its photo caption said that it referred to the end of the previous regime.[11]

In his homily on the feast of Corpus Christi (Body of Christ), Cardinal Obando emphasized a favorite theme, the inter-class unity of the Church: "The Holy Eucharist is a banquet to which rich and poor can come. Christ wants all men to be saved." He expressed his gratitude to those who had turned in their weapons. After Mass Obando said he supported the efforts of the president to drastically reduce and even eventually eliminate the army, with the money saved being used to meet social needs.[12]

According to a *New York Times* editorial (June 29), a "monumental moment" occurred on June 27: "the end of the contra war." Top contra leaders turned over their remaining weapons to a UN peace-making force, in the presence of President Chamorro and Cardinal Obando (both featured in a photo above the editorial). The editorial's jubilation was not felt by many in Nicaragua, where people were concerned about galloping inflation, the government's regressive social policies, the widespread conviction that the contras are storing their better weapons in hiding, and the contras' control of "development poles" with their own police.

Many who learned about the momentous event by radio or newspaper were saddened and even scandalized by a public statement by "Ruben," one of the contra commanders. Expressing gratitude to Cardinal Obando, Ruben said: "When the road ahead seemed darkest, there was Cardinal Obando lighting the way and encouraging us to continue to struggle." He added that Obando "always offered a helping hand and gave us advice."[13] Obando let the statement stand.

Some days before Ruben's statement, the Sandinistas had released a major document analyzing the political situation. In a section on religion they said that "the traditional distrust on the part of Church leaders toward revolutionary processes as well as political mistakes made by the government and the FSLN in relation to the Church resulted in a strident confrontation which led the Catholic hierarchy in particular into active opposition against our government. We were unable to eliminate that mutual distrust," the Frente continued; "on the contrary, we found ourselves in situations where some priests involved themselves in armed con-

---

11. *La Prensa,* June 16, 1990.

12. *La Prensa,* June 19, 1990.

13. *Barricada,* June 28.

spiracies, and we took coercive measures against some Church leaders, to the point of expelling a bishop from the country. Without judging at this time the legitimacy of these actions," the Frente said, such actions "distanced the Church from the Revolution."

In the recent elections "priests, pastors, and lay leaders of various Churches worked with the UNO. In recent years religious leaders, above all in rural areas, worked to mobilize the peasant bases in support for the counter-revolution. Now the Catholic Church supports the government and exercises a decisive influence over it, especially in education."[14]

On June 27 some state workers began a strike which eventually involved thousands of government employees, peasants, and neighborhood residents in a militant protest movement bringing the country to the verge of civil war. Church events during July must be seen in this turbulent context.

Among the workers' demands were: wage increases to keep up with inflation, which had averaged over 100% in May and June; job security against not only a threat but a pattern of firings of workers associated with Sandinismo; continued government support for the state-owned companies; more funds for health and education; and abolition of the presidential decrees which called for the renting out of state farms to those who were processing a claim on them and which also proposed a general revision of confiscations.

Many peasants were occupying state farms to prevent their privatization. Cutbacks in subsidies raised bus fares and costs of energy and water. In spite of the obvious economic hardships experienced by the people, the government considered the strike "political"—i.e., a Sandinista tactic to sabotage the government's development plans—and refused to negotiate with the union federation as long as the strike continued. The Sandinistas' TV news program was banned. This hard line, with threats of police force and prosecution of strikers, drew more labor sectors into the strike and occupation of government facilities.

Police obeyed commands to keep order and to assure access to buildings, using some non-lethal force. Some admired the police for doing their job with restraint, while the other side accused them of favoring the

---

14. *Barricada*, June 28.

strikers and not being effective. Greater danger came from the strike-breakers reportedly organized by the extreme right wing of UNO under Vice-president Virgilio Godoy and Managua mayor Arnoldo Alemán. Some bus drivers who were against the strike holed up in the bus depot for some days; heavily armed, they occasionally fired at strike supporters in the street outside. Several were killed and over 100 injured during the 14 days of conflict.

One evening I visited a barrio near the scene of considerable violence. The CBC, at an emergency meeting, decided to donate food to strikers; community members told of rumors to the effect that the UNO people were going to burn down the houses of the pro-Sandinistas that night.

All around Managua, thousands of bricks had been torn up from the streets to make barricades in an expression of support for the strike and as a defensive measure against armed contras or UNO extremists who, it was feared, might attack the focal points of strike support. In addition, some students briefly held the state TV station and the government radio, and eventually the airport workers also joined the strike.

Gunmen identified as contras or ex-contras patrolled and controlled some streets in Ciudad Jardín, a commercial district of Managua, stopping cars and pedestrians, robbing and detaining people. They claimed to be protecting the rabidly anti-Sandinista and anti-strike Radio Corporación; security at the station's antenna outside the city was not beefed up, however, and it was severely damaged by a bomb. The saboteurs in that incident have not been identified.

The most alarming development, and one with serious repercussions for the future, was the formation of the Commission of National Salvation under Vice-president Godoy, grouping the far-right sectors of UNO who claim that the president and her advisors have been too tolerant of the Sandinistas. Armed groups called "Brigades of National Salvation" have also come on the scene, leading many to predict death-squad activity in the future especially against Sandinista leaders. It is also expected that the brigades, which will consist of ex-National Guardsmen and ex-contras, will break strikes, and heads.

Late on July 11 government officials met with top Sandinistas and labor leaders and worked out the basis for a settlement. Wages would be increased by 43 percent in July (not keeping up with inflation); the government would stop renting out state lands to those who claimed ownership; and, among other points agreed upon, a national dialogue would ensue. The strike was over, for now; the barricades were taken down and streets began to be repaired; and the contras who had held parts of Ciudad Jardín were given asylum in the major seminary of the archdiocese.

In the weeks that followed, firings for political reasons continued, and tension in the rural areas grew as former owners, with the support of UNO forces, invaded and took over cooperatives. Most people felt that Nicaragua was in a kind of intermission between rounds, with hostility rising on both sides.

On July 4, in an act which *Barricada* claimed was to honor the U.S. holiday, the director of the public library in León held a public book-burning, saying that it was necessary "to cleanse the library of communism."[15] Reportedly brandishing a crucifix, he fed the flames with fifty books, including those by Tomás Borge, Sergio Ramírez, Gioconda Belli, Omar Cabezas, and other Sandinista authors. What many found especially outrageous was that La Prensa had previously published an article telling of the librarian's pyrotechnical intentions and did not denounce the deed. The librarian said that books "considered detrimental to the national conscience would be burned" (*La Prensa*, July 3). Citing various comments comparing the act to the Inquisition and to Nazism, *Barricada* said that the librarian had been "nourished by the backward and vengeful attitude of the UNO government." Many criticized the government's cultural institute for not preventing the action. "Yesterday it was books, tomorrow it could be the authors," noted a professor.

"Without justice there is no reconciliation" was the message on one of the banners in the town plaza of Jinotepe on July 7 during the Christian celebration of the eleventh anniversary of the revolution. Four thousand people representing CBCs in most parts of Nicaragua took part in the vigil from 6 p.m. to midnight, which included a procession through the town and a Mass concelebrated by twelve priests.

The scripture readings were basic to the Church of the Poor. Exodus 3 recalled the story of the Lord's call to Moses to set the people free; the congregation in the plaza celebrated the strength they had received from the Lord in their struggle against the Somoza dictatorship. And the last

---

15. *Barricada,* July 6, 1990.

judgment in Matthew 25 focused on the social values which have motivated Christians' support for the revolutionary process. At the end of the Mass a collection was taken up to help provide food for the workers participating in the general strike.

Two days later Christian motivation for the revolutionary struggle was also evidenced when students who had taken over the government's radio station played a recording of "I Have Faith" on the airwaves. The faith being celebrated is that "everything will change" and that love will triumph.

Barricada returned to the issue of the Church-state alliance on July 10. Noting a "theocratic tendency" in the new government, the article lamented the current regression from the principle of separation of Church and state established in Nicaragua by Zelaya. "The new Church-state fusion," the author continued, "means that Catholicism is recognized as the only standard-bearer of the dominant official ideology of the new government, thus breaking down the ecumenism which has been achieved during the last ten years."

The writer described four objectives of this Church-state unity: to put the brakes to Protestantism's gains among the masses; to get away from ecumenism; to undermine the practice of theology of liberation among the poor; and to crush once and for all the growing atheism in intellectual and university circles. Thus "the hegemony of the upper echelons of the Catholic Church would be restored, with the Church controlling all of civil society." The author pointed to an anti-democratic "sacred" aura around the president, creating the danger of dissidents being seen as heretics. "Throughout history, when some fanatical prelate has been behind the throne, wanting to impose his heaven on our earth, the result has been the worst kind of hell for everyone," the author concluded.

The same day, *El Nuevo Diario* leveled its guns at the new cathedral. "The religiosity nestled in the heart of our Christian bourgeoisie is so great that a warehouse bigger than the Houston Astrodome would be needed to house it. . . . We will have the most majestic cathedral in the world to be in tune with the God of the rich."

Another article in the same edition urged Obando to heed the words of the pope concerning priests and seminarians. "They should renounce material wealth and all temptation to luxury or excessive comfort," the pope reportedly said. The newspaper said that it was not opposed in principle to the building of a cathedral. "However, to put three million dollars into a lavish building at a time when hunger is getting worse and the new government shows little human understanding is offensive to human dignity. To start that expensive project now shows not only a complete lack of human sensitivity but goes against the Christian principles promoted by Pope John Paul II."

On July 16, in his weekly column in *La Prensa*, Obando came out essentially against the strike and the barricade construction. Returning to Managua on July 13 after a meeting in Colombia, the cardinal saw the streets of Managua with their bricks torn up (the makings of the barricades) and likened what he saw to the ravages of a hurricane. "Damage to state property cannot be justified," he asserted in his article, expressing concern about the money the government would have to spend to repair the streets "in a country which is so poor."

Obando did express his understanding of the reasons for the strike. "I recognize that the economic situation is difficult," he said, "and that sometimes salaries do not provide enough to eat. I believe that there are families where father, mother, and it often seems children of five or six years of age walk around selling little things in the streets, in dangerous traffic, because they have nothing to eat." Nevertheless, he characterized the events which had taken place during his absence as "lamentable." While considering the "acts of violence" and "mob action" unjustifiable, he stopped short of explicitly condemning the strike itself.

Earlier in the article, commenting on the parable of the sower and the seed, Obando had some harsh words for those who allow the thorns to suffocate the Word of God. "They hear the Word of God but absolutize wealth, making it into an idol which demands tribute," he observed. "They are absorbed by their business dealings and by the pleasures of this world, interested only in their own things, letting themselves be carried away by selfishness and by their enterprises. To them the people are not important. The only thing they care about is that they do well in business; nothing else interests them."

Confronting such entrenched evil and greed (which many see gaining the upper hand in the new Nicaragua), were workers not justified in exercising their right to strike, and was the public going too far in putting up barricades to show support for the strike and to protest the unbearable economic conditions? But Obando opposed the obvious conclusion. "Church Condemns Mob Action" was the title of the front-page article in *La Prensa* summarizing Obando's position.

In a letter to the editor (*El Nuevo Diario*, July 17), a Catholic woman described a crisis of faith provoked by the cardinal's political activity. Identifying herself as one who sympathizes with Sandinismo but who has not been a member of any party, she wrote: "How repulsive it is to see Obando's face beaming with joy while the hateful and repugnant mayor of Managua kisses his hand in a show of servility." Having been taught that priests and bishops are "representatives of God on earth," she asked: "Is Obando not the representative of the God of the powerful, of the aristocrats, of the lying and shameless politicians who are now in abundance in Nicaragua? Does God need a $3 million cathedral?"

As represented by Obando, "God has no response for the families of those who have been kidnapped by the contras or for any mortal who smells of Sandinismo even though he may not be one. God has no future for workers who are Sandinistas. For these reasons the Catholic Church has lost so many faithful."

On July 18 the cardinal continued his practice of blessing the offices of the new government's officials, this time praying for the Ministry of Government (security forces, immigration). Appearing with Obando on the state TV news report, the head of that ministry publicly expressed his desire for divine assistance.

On July 19, in spite of a heavy downpour, the plaza of the revolution was filled with thousands of people celebrating the eleventh anniversary of the triumph over Somoza. Although President Chamorro had declared the day a holiday and said that it was significant for all Nicaraguans, the government did not join the Sandinistas in this celebration. In fact, bus service to that part of town was eliminated, and state TV featured programs which were notably better than the general fare.

The Church's decision to house the contras in the seminary was characterized by Father Xabier Gorostiaga, S.J., as "a positive contribution which avoided more bloodshed in the streets." He acknowledged that "many Christians considered it scandalous." These Christians felt that the contras could have received the protection of the UN forces who were in Nicaragua precisely for that purpose and that their request for official Church hospitality and the positive response were designed to give a political message. The Nicaraguan Human Rights Center called upon Church officials to clarify their role in harboring the contras.

Gorostiaga found other aspects of the Church's behavior more troublesome. "What does not seem justifiable," he continued, "is the role of agitator taken up by Radio Católica and by chancery spokespersons who seemed to foment confrontation by supporting the [extreme right-wing] groups which were dissenting from the government." These Catholic voices were "satanizing Sandinismo and praising the violence fomented by Radio Corporación."[16]

On July 23, with the Ministry of Education continuing to remove many pro-Sandinista principals, the Catholic pastor in La Paz Centro, Father Enrique Martínez Gamboa, was named principal of the large public high school in town. Indeed, the school itself was turned over to the Church. The majority of the teachers objected to the choice of Martínez, considering him a highly politicized anti-Sandinista pastor who had strongly supported the UNO campaign. They also said that he had no academic qualifications or experience as a school administrator and that the appointment of a priest caused anxiety among the non-Catholic students and their parents.

When Martínez was asked by the Minister of Education himself to take the position, the priest stated two conditions: that he have a free hand in enforcing discipline, and that the school's name be changed from 17th of July (the day Somoza fled from Nicaragua in 1979) to Paul VI. That was the name of a private school founded in the seventies by then-pastor Father Róger Urcuyo and several other persons. The next pastor was also principal of the school, which was turned over to the government before 1979.

In 1981 the Ministry of Education built a brand new school on a completely different site, calling it 17th of July. Martínez and his supporters claim, however, that the new site was Church ground and that a start had been made on construction before 1979.

---

16. *Barricada,* July 20, 1990.

The teachers are certain of Father Martínez's political affiliations. He is reportedly one of a number of priests in Nicaragua who refused to celebrate Mass for youngsters killed while serving in the Sandinista army. The parish facilities became a center for UNO meetings, and he has refused to recognize ANDEN, the Sandinista teachers' union.

The teachers urged me to look at a plaque in the church which, they said, was clear evidence of where the pastor stands politically. After viewing the cardboard signs on various pillars advertising Charismatic Renewal, I was struck by the large and truly elegant plaque prominently displayed on a front wall, facing the people. In gold letters on black steel, the message goes like this: "When our country walked in the shadows of sadness, hunger, war, tears, pain, and death, this people raised its eyes, tear-filled from weeping, meeting the sweet and serene gaze of our Mother of Perpetual Help (the Victorious One), and the next day in Nicaragua the radiant sun of peace shone. April 25, 1990." The pastor's name follows, in larger gold letters. The people had raised their tear-filled eyes to heaven in a prayer vigil held in the church on February 24, the day before elections. The plaque was dedicated on the day of Violeta Chamorro's inauguration.

After hearing the announcement about the new principal, which was made over a loudspeaker in town, the dissenters peacefully occupied the school in protest. After the priest was officially installed as principal (in a ceremony in the parish rectory), he and his supporters moved toward the school. A scuffle ensued when they forced their way into the building, but police restored order by getting both sides to agree to leave.

The next day someone threw a grenade at the rectory and at the UNO mayor's house. A few windows of the rectory were shattered, with no injuries to persons; the grenade at the mayor's house did not go off. A *La Prensa* headline (July 24) attributed the crimes to the Sandinistas, although no evidence could be presented. The article noted that the local delegate of the Ministry of Education, the mayor, and Father Martínez feel that the problem is basically political. In their words, "for the Sandinistas the school is a bastion controlled by the Sandinista Youth."

Two days later a *La Prensa* editorial (July 26), defending the appointment of the priest, shed light on an important aspect of what is at stake in the controversy. "What takes priority over the teachers' right to job stability is the will of the people to change systems of education based on the defense of class struggle," the lead editorial said.

With his new job, Martínez not only has additional outlets for his particular religious message but also has considerable social and economic power in the small town to give his message extra weight. Indeed, in an interview he was pleased to note that Mass attendance is already up, due to an influx of young people. He also told me that he may decide to leave his new post in a year or so, at which time "the Church would appoint another priest to be principal."

Teachers who participated in the protests and who subsequently refused to sign a loyalty oath have been fired, and eight students who took part have been expelled. In August protesters again occupied the school.

On July 27, in my first visit to La Paz Centro, I found that the pastor and many parishioners consider the Frente Sandinista a worthy target of a holy war of extermination. That evening I attended a graduation ceremony where the Jesuit-run Central American University awarded an honorary doctorate to Frente leader Daniel Ortega. Father César Jerez, S.J., president of the university, expressed the school's desire that the graduates use their knowledge in the service of others rather than in the pursuit of money and social status.

Turning to Ortega, Father Jerez said that the "university honors your personal merits and sees in you the representative of the most noble and worthy achievements of the Sandinista People's Revolution." The most significant accomplishments, Jerez said, stemmed "from direct contact with the people, from respect for the people, and from the option for the majority of the people, who are the poor. In spite of the errors committed and recognized, the government in which you served as president had a way of thinking, being, and doing which can only be explained from the point of view of that option, from the point of view of the 'logic of the majority.' That logic seeks to orient governmental action in such a way as to favor the dispossessed."

Jerez mentioned as examples the land reform and the efforts to bring education and health care within the reach of all. "And let us remember that a war imposed from outside impeded the achievement of many goals," he noted. Nevertheless, "it cannot be denied that Nicaraguans now, especially the poor, have a profound sense of dignity regained." He attributed this to the Sandinista government's continuous dialogue with the people in the "Face the People" sessions, in which Ortega himself as well as his cabinet ministers took part, and to the organizing of the people. "These have contributed to giving voice to those who previously had no voice," Jerez said, noting that this made it possible to have a "participatory democracy."

Recognizing that some violations of human rights occurred, Jerez noted that "unfortunately it is difficult to avoid them in periods of prolonged war." In many instances Ortega himself saw to it that "those violations were recognized and punished," Jerez said.

The speaker underlined the former president's untiring efforts to find a peaceful solution to the war and his contributions to the building of democracy. Jerez expressed admiration of Ortega's respect for the results of the 1990 vote. "Those who had struggled for years to gain power, suffering imprisonment and death, did not cling to that government but, in the face of an unexpected defeat, had the strength to accept the will of the people. For the first time in Nicaraguan history, a peaceful transition was possible." That was a very special contribution of the revolution to democracy, Jerez pointed out.

Jerez ended his address by commenting on the polarized political situation and calling for dialogue and moderation rather than "seeking to resolve the crisis by confrontation." It is still necessary, he said, that one side "admit without reservations that it was defeated at the polls" and that the side now in power "admit that the country is not governable without the cooperation of the losers." If that happens, he added, "Nicaragua will be the winner."

What is at stake concretely, he explained, is reconciling "a Social Democratic project with that of a Democratic Socialism," the former seeing things mainly from the point of view of the company and private capital, the latter from the point of view of the worker and "the logic of the majority."

In conclusion, Jerez said that "beyond ideologies and political analysis" the university as an institution "of Christian inspiration" has seen with joy "the achievements of these ten years of revolution in favor of the poor. It also looks with hope to the possibility of a true national reconciliation." In that lies another challenge for Daniel Ortega, Jerez said.

Over 100 representatives of CBCs from various regions of Nicaragua took part in the national assembly of the CNP (Permanent National Commission) in La Trinidad from August 1 to 4. It was clear that people had gotten over their need to grieve over the electoral defeat in February and to console one another. The sadness was still there, but no tears were shed. Nor was much time spent on analyzing why the Frente lost, why we were so surprised, etc.

The key topic for the assembly looked toward the future: "What is the Christian commitment to which God and the people are calling us? What is the challenge of the new situation in terms of defending the rights and gains of the people?"

The first session was devoted, characteristically, to small-group work in which people identified the main elements of the new regime's "project of death"—e.g., unemployment and higher taxes as deliberate elements of the new economic policy (without the "cushion" or safety net with which the Sandinista government had softened such blows); privatization of state resources and the give-back of expropriated land which had been distributed to peasants; various moves against the Constitution; the Vice-president's Committees of National Salvation, with their dangerous "brigades," challenging the relatively conciliatory approach of the Chamorro administration; diminishment of national sovereignty, especially in relation to the United States; in general, the rich getting richer and the poor poorer as the programs of the previous government are reversed.

Father Xabier Gorostiaga, S.J., presented an analysis of this data, emphasizing that this bleak picture applies to the entire Third World, not just to Nicaragua. "There is an avalanche of capital against the worker, of the North against the South," he said, noting that "democracy is falsely defined as neo-liberal capitalism." He urged the victims of this avalanche to unite in their common struggle.

Participants also identified the main characteristics of the "project of life" during the previous government. The list was long, from the right to health and education to a real sense of participation and dignity. The task ahead is to defend these social achievements and also to deepen democratic participation in the people's organizations.

Turning to Church life, Pablo Richard presented several passages from the books of Daniel and Maccabees on the struggle of the people of God against cultural imperialism, noting that today the Church of the Poor in Latin America must struggle against the false values of consumerism, individualism, and spiritualism. The lust for profit and the free-market mechanism have been absolutized into false gods which devour the poor masses.

In Nicaragua, the CBCs decided on the following priorities: to defend life against the forces of death; to announce the Good News of the Kingdom and to denounce injustice, exploitation, and imperialism; to develop a healthy sense of self-criticism with regard to political and religious organizations; to struggle to maintain a "space" for the Church of the Poor within the Church, resisting any temptation to settle for a marginal position; to be the yeast in society, especially keeping hope alive in desperate times; to be attentive to and to foster the *process* by which people become revolutionary Christians; to strengthen the participation of the laity—especially women, youth, and the indigenous peoples—in the Church of the Poor; to promote familiarity with the bible as an instrument for justice in Church and society.

The assembly, which included a one-hour period of silent prayer, ended with a Eucharist in which participants renewed their commitment to struggle, as Christians, for a more just and fraternal Nicaragua.

In their August 15 pastoral letter, the bishops of Nicaragua stated that, "in order to preserve and strengthen the incipient democracy in Nicaragua, the authorities elected by the people should govern and should carry out the program they offered." It would be a "sin against justice," they said, "to prevent those elected by the people from governing or to make arrangements or pacts which would disobey or change the popular will."

This was widely understood to refer to the power of the Sandinistas as an important opposition force, especially in its influence in unions and other mass organizations. President Chamorro and her advisors had been accused of making pacts with the Sandinistas, to which she responded that she would work with all Nicaraguans but "make pacts only with God." Many interpreted the bishops' statement in this regard as supporting the hard-line anti-Sandinista position of Vice-president Godoy.

While affirming the workers' right to unionize, the bishops limited the function of unions to strictly "labor" issues (thus echoing the standard U.S. government line as expressed throughout Latin America by the AFL-CIO's American Institute for Free Labor Development). "If the union goes beyond its limits by putting itself at the service of a political party, it deprives itself of ethical authority as a valid partner in the social dialogue," the bishops said, probably referring to the Sandinista influence in the unions which struck in July and thus echoing the government criticism of the strike as being for political purposes. They failed to note that the strikers had legitimate labor demands and that they were out in front of the Sandinista political leadership, which expressed its support after the strike had gained momentum.

While recognizing the right to strike, the bishops insisted that it must be exercised "in keeping with the just laws of the country" and that a strike is "in a certain sense an extreme measure." It should not be abused by being put at the service of "political games," they added. "Such abuse can lead to paralyzing the whole socio-economic life of society," they said, "and this is contrary to the demands of the common good." (Some pro-Sandinista economists agreed with the bishops on this, at least at this particular point in time.)

The bishops devoted a few lines to defending the interests of the poor. "Work," they said, "is the human element of the economy and that which should orient every economic policy." All Nicaraguans must strive to overcome the "deteriorated [economic] situation," they said. "The difficulties which this effort entails should be shared by all sectors in proportion to their capacities and resources: those who have more will contribute more, those who are more deprived will contribute less.

"The situation experienced by most Nicaraguans, especially the workers and peasants," the bishops continued, "obliges us once again to reiterate an option which is certainly not exclusive but which is, yes, preferential for them." (The emphasis on the non-exclusive nature of this option is, as this book has shown, characteristic of Nicaragua's bishops.) After citing Vatican II and John Paul II on this, the bishops added: "The economic problem cannot be seen just as a matter of statistics; behind every statistic on unemployment there is a human face, a human being, a family."

In November, when ex-contras and UNO mayers stopped traffic on the major highway in Region Five (Chontales), demanding land for the ex-contras and a harder government line against the Sandinistas, Bishop Vega came out clearly in support of the far-right uprising, while Cardinal Obando said their demands were just.